"Essential reading in an age of disruption."
David Reay, Senior Vice President, Sony Music Entertainment

"This is an invaluable step-by-step guide to sparking, scaling and sustaining a culture of bold innovation."
Ash Tailor, Global Brand & Marketing Director at LEGOLAND

"Packed full of practical tips to boost your company's lifespan."
Ash Schofield, CEO, giffgaff

"At a game company like Electronic Arts, we're no strangers to zombies - both in the games we produce and in our daily battles against the many disruptive forces trying to make us obsolete. It's the same everywhere. Most leaders struggle to get the innovation performance they need. This is the practical playbook they've been waiting for."
Andy Billings, Vice President Profitable Creativity, Electronic Arts

"A book of some brilliance. Everyone with an interest in pursuing sustainable, profitable relevance should read it. Compelling, fiendishly clever and full of practical ideas and tools delivered with great skill. The implications for business are vast!"
Jo Wade, Specialist Account Manager, Oncology, Pfizer UK

"In business a lot is talked about entrepreneurial spirit without giving it the oxygen to develop and thrive. Very often the difficulty is where to start. *Be Less Zombie* is an excellent and practical guide for any leaders trying to turn on higher levels of innovation in their organisation."
Denis O' Flynn, former Managing Director, Pernod Ricard UK

"This book is packed with vital knowledge and essential strategies that you can adopt and apply immediately to help create an innovation mindset within any team or organisation. Written in an engaging and impactful way it puts theories into practice, sharing new tools and insights based on a decade of innovation experiments conducted inside Fortune 500 companies of all shapes and sizes."
Chris Parles, Senior Fellow and Programme Director of Music & Branding at University for the Creative Arts Business School

"Innovation begins and ends with the right leadership and culture. It's so - fresh-ing to see more of the innovation 'how' codified ---'   and tools."
Gareth Hussey, (ile

D0814072

"The definitive leadership guide to simplifying, mobilising and humanising innovation."
Teresa Kotlicka, People & Culture, Sony Music Entertainment

"In the struggle all organisations face to drive innovation, this book defines the rallying cry you need to bring everyone together and provides an excellent handbook with the essential tools to make it happen."
Alan W. Brown, Professor in Digital Economy, University of Exeter, UK

"An indispensable read that unashamedly kicks wide-open the door to real-world innovation. Engaging, accessible and with lots of invaluable tips and insights for leaders at all levels on how to create a culture and climate in which innovation thrives. A great wake-up call for all zombies … now there are no excuses!"
David Riley, Business Psychologist

"*Be Less Zombie* is a practical guide for equipping leaders and managers trying to turn on higher levels of innovation in their business."
Samantha Seal, Talent Strategist and Director, on the wing Ltd.

"A leader's lifeline for evoking, embedding and living an innovation culture."
Laura Ellis, Head of Talent Management, EMEA, Ogilvy

"A must-read for anyone – in any business sector, at any career level – who is passionate about the serious business of innovation. A practical guide to curating a culture of innovation and navigating against the headwinds of organisational status quo."
Simon Collins, Senior Vice President, Mastercard

"At last a book that gives permission to create, collaborate and innovate. Elvin Turner intelligently challenges the status quo with a sprinkling of very good humour. Essential reading."
Lee Widdows, Associate Head of Fashion, University for the Creative Arts

"*Be Less Zombie* is more than a book, it is a toolkit for any senior executive who wants to drive positive change in their business. Turner gives you everything you need to create and deliver your own innovation agenda within the limits of your budget and ideas."
Ben Sullivan, UK/IRL Managing Director, bibliotheca

Be Less Zombie

Be Less Zombie

How Great Companies Create Dynamic Innovation, Fearless Leadership and Passionate People

Elvin Turner

Illustrated by Richard Johnston

WILEY

Registered office
John Wiley & Sons Ltd, The Atrium, Southern Gate, Chichester, West Sussex, PO19 8SQ, United Kingdom

For details of our global editorial offices, for customer services and for information about how to apply for permission to reuse the copyright material in this book please see our website at www.wiley.com.

Library of Congress Cataloging-in-Publication Data

Names: Turner, Elvin, author.
Title: Be less zombie : how great companies create dynamic innovation,
    fearless leadership and passionate people / Elvin Turner.
Description: [Hoboken, NJ] : Wiley-Capstone, 2020. | Includes index.
Identifiers: LCCN 2019057699 (print) | LCCN 2019057700 (ebook) | ISBN
    9780857088208 (paperback) | ISBN 9780857088246 (adobe pdf) | ISBN
    9780857088239 (epub)
Subjects: LCSH: Organizational change. | Leadership.
Classification: LCC HD58.8 .T876 2020 (print) | LCC HD58.8 (ebook) | DDC
    658.4/063—dc23
LC record available at https://lccn.loc.gov/2019057699
LC ebook record available at https://lccn.loc.gov/2019057700

Cover concept: Jacqueline Turner
Cover Design: Wiley
Cover Images: Zombies © Big_Ryan/Getty Images, Collection of people © Imagewell/Shutterstock, Business women © Nevena Radonja/Shutterstock, Business man © msan10/Getty Images

Set in 12/16pt AGaramondPro by SPi Global, Chennai, India

Printed in Great Britain by TJ International Ltd, Padstow, Cornwall, UK

10 9 8 7 6 5 4 3 2 1

For Jesus

CONTENTS

Innovation is an argument inside most companies –
frail, new ideas versus the overwhelming power of the
status quo. An innovation strategy helps create an
environment where new ideas can emerge and thrive.
It is the single-most important way to build and
sustain innovation performance. And it doesn't have
to be difficult.

Part Two   **Turning on a Fast-Track Innovation Process**   **59**

Great innovation rarely happens without a clear and effective process. This section shares the practical tools used by global innovation leaders that your team can begin using today.

Part Three   **Building Your People's Innovation
                  Capabilities**   **235**

Most organisations want more innovation but few
equip their people to actually deliver it. This section
provides practical strategies, roadmaps and case
studies to help your people out-innovate your
competitors.

Part Four   **Time, Money and Talent: How to Resource
                  Innovation**   **249**

Business-as-usual makes little provision for bolder
innovation. This section helps you rethink how
resources are managed and allocated so that the future
has a greater chance of showing up.

Part Five   **Innovation Culture for Realists**   **267**

Culture has been defined as 'what is ordinary'. Yet
most companies demand extraordinary innovation to
emerge from their status quo set-ups. This section
shows how to move beyond a one-size-fits-all culture
to where bigger ideas can emerge and thrive on a
repeatable basis.

Part Six **Leading an Innovation Reformation** **325**

Innovation is regularly cited as a top three priority amongst leaders, yet the vast majority of their training and experience is in business-as-usual management. This section provides practical tools for leaders who need to lead their organisations to a new level of innovation performance.

ABOUT THE AUTHOR

Elvin Turner is an award-winning leadership advisor and associate professor of innovation, entrepreneurship and marketing.

Elvin has coached hundreds of innovation and performance programmes around the world, helping leaders, managers and teams overcome the many barriers that they face when trying to develop breakthrough ideas and turn them into action.

Elvin's work spans consulting, coaching and facilitation in the areas of strategy, innovation and leadership development.

His clients include some of the world's leading organisations in the financial, technology, music, pharmaceutical, drinks and publishing industries. His experience extends from working with new and disruptive technology start-ups, through to seasoned leadership teams inside conservative, global institutions.

ACKNOWLEDGEMENTS

This book has been a collaboration with many people. I'm so thankful to everyone who has been on the ride and especially want to call out the following people:

Richard Johnston, my ever-patient and ingenious collaborator.

Jean Gomes, who set me off on the innovation track many years ago.

Simon Pratt for his continuous flow of best-selling author insight, encouragement, friendship and spiritual bulldoggedness.

Nigel Wilkinson for keeping my hands held up.

Carol Herzig for encouragement and wisdom.

Phil Tennant for helping me realise that this book was actually two books (watch this space!)

Lionel Medley for reminding me about nerds.

Tony Ryce-Kelly for talking some sense into me on many occasions.

Mark Swain, Emily Charles and Mary Cole at Henley Business School for taking the first risk with the Unicorns vs Zombies programme.

Jim Sears and Dr Ben Shenoy for insightful course corrections.

Mel Toms for being my school-run sounding board.

All who contributed to the content of the book, in order of appearance: Ben Sullivan, Managing Director, Bibliotheca UK; Andy Billings, Vice President of Profitable Creativity at Electronic Arts;

Mark Bjornsgaard of System-Two; Professor Alan Brown of Exeter University; Lee Widdows, Associate Head of School (Fashion/Fashion Business) at the University of the Creative Arts; Chris Parles, Programme Director Music and Branding at the University of Creative Arts; Ashley Schofield, CEO of giffgaff; Gemma Metheringham, Creative Director of Label/Mix; Matt Madden, author of *99 Ways to Tell a Story*; Denis O'Flynn, former Managing Director of Pernod Ricard UK; Bridget Gardner, Head of Employee Capability, Pernod Ricard UK; Patrick Venning of Breakwater Marketing; Rafael Orta, Chief Product Officer at moneysupermarket.com; Harvey Wade, Managing Director of Innovate 21; Alex Osterwalder, Co-founder of Strategyzer; David Reay, Senior Vice President at Sony Music Entertainment; Teresa Kotlicka, talent and culture advisor at Sony Music Entertainment; Emily Bollon, Founder of Motivation by Music; Jo Twistleton; Becky Allen, President of Decca Records; Dr Alice Cook; Simon Walsh; Bob Dickman; Malcolm Hassan; David Riley; Jennifer Robison of Gallup; and Fiona Conway, Director of Retail Customer Operations at Santander Bank.

The many experts and pioneers who have directly and indirectly influenced the content of this book and direction of my thinking, including Alan Klement, Arthur Burk, Eric Ries, Professor Clay Christensen, Bill Johnson, Steve Blank, Kathy Sierra, Professor Rita McGrath, Doug Sundheim and Robert Quinn.

The continual cry of members of Guildford Community Church: 'There's more!'

The editorial and production teams at Wiley.

And my incredible family: Jackie, for your endless sparkle; Daisy, for your inspirational cake fuel; Luke for your chirpy banter; and Leilani for your 'home-from-school' hugs.

Thank you all, so much.

Elvin Turner

INTRODUCTION:
UNICORNS VS ZOMBIES

© Richard Johnston.

It was a perfect day to meet zombies.

Inside the idyllic rural campus of England's prestigious Henley Business School, 40 executives were jostling for position along a line that I had marked out on the floor:

'More unicorn' at one end, a term that's come to mean a hot, most-wanted, $1bn innovation powerhouse.

'More zombie' at the other, meaning a decaying monolith staggering into the future.

The task: Stand in the place on that spectrum that best describes your organisation.

There were a lot of self-declared zombies out that day.

But the truth is there are a lot of zombies out *every* day. Research shows that company lifespans are shrinking fast.[1] But it's not just companies. The experience of working inside an off-kilter company can be deadly for the people inside, too. Simply being at work is now the fifth biggest killer in the United States because of the illnesses that stem from rising workplace stress.[2]

So what's driving this zombie advance?

Clinging to What Kills Us

Imagine standing on the edge of a chasm that is widening before your eyes. Your side of the chasm is crumbling fast. Getting to the other side is your only chance of survival. There is a rope in your hand that you could use to swing across. But fear stops you from jumping and keeps you rooted to the spot, gripping on to that rope for dear life. Meanwhile, the ground crumbles beneath your feet. The wider the

---

[1] https://www.cnbc.com/2017/08/24/technology-killing-off-corporations-average-lifespan-of-company-under-20-years.html
[2] "Dying for a Pay Check", Jeffrey Pfeffer, Harper Business, p38

chasm yawns, the riskier the swing, the greater the fear, the less likely that you'll leap.

A little Indiana Jones, maybe. But that 'holding on' instinct, that false sense of security of hanging on to what we know, sets off a chain reaction of subtle and painful demise inside many organisations: declining margins; efficiency initiatives that mean more work for fewer people; an exhausted and disengaged workforce that is continually putting out fires; sales teams who would rather lead with discounts than push the new, longer lead-time solutions; and less appetite and resourcing for innovation which is ultimately what gets us across the chasm.

Over the last 25 years I've seen variations of this scenario play out inside companies of all shapes and sizes. But I've also observed two factors that can make a huge difference to the inevitability of innovation and high performance showing up:

1. Move Some Different Needles

We get what we measure, and we measure what we value. So what are we overvaluing that opens the doors to zombieism?

In most companies, a minor business model tremor creates a standard, anxiety-driven knee-jerk response: 'Grab the cash while you can.'

'The prevailing mindset inside most boardrooms is "We love money,"' says Ben Sullivan, Managing Director of bibliotheca UK, a library technology company. 'It's too easy to say "yes" to this quarter's numbers at the expense of developing the ideas that the future needs. No-one ever frames it in such black-and-white terms, but deep down, the dopamine hit of a short-term cash injection usually feels too good to resist.'

Yet the twenty-first-century rate of change means that business model tremors are now an everyday occurrence. The short-term, cash-grabbing response is often triggered by the anxiety of having nothing in the new product pipeline. And it is anxiety's sibling, fear, that stops companies from backing the more risky ideas that the future pipelines need. It's a circular paradox resulting in companies that are literally scaring themselves to death.

Organisations need to put in place counterbalances to resist the short-term, control freakism that shuts down any appetite for innovation that ventures beyond the status quo.

'Incremental improvement guarantees obsolescence over time, especially in fast changing industries,' says Joi Ito, the former Director of the MIT Media Lab.

We need some new dials and needles in our corporate dashboards. Ones that compel us to make the decisions that our future needs us to make today; those specifically relating to better performance around innovation and change.

2. Demystify the 'How' of Innovation

'Don't tell me why, don't tell me what, just tell me *how* to get innovation moving in this place,' is how I was once greeted by a frustrated CEO who was smarting from a recent, failed innovation initiative.

It's the underlying narrative inside most organisations that I meet. More specifically, whilst organisations tend to want more overall innovation, their greatest need is a bigger bag of bolder ideas that could become tomorrow's cash cows. So where are they hiding?

Well, if we define culture as 'what is ordinary', we can't realistically expect many 'extraordinary' ideas to emerge and thrive from business-as-usual operations. 'Extraordinary' creates an understandably allergic reaction from the status quo. It's a life form likely to mess with our repeatable, predictable ways of working.

(An interesting anagram of Be Less Zombie is 'blob seizes me'. It's how I imagine a bold idea feels when it encounters corporate bureaucracy.)

It's not surprising that the bold ideas cupboard is pretty empty in most organisations.

Hmmm … Looks like we'll need to discount our way out of this one again, Winston.

Innovation has a reputation for being a black art, but it's really not. Yet because so few companies have designed a deliberate system for repeatable innovation, its ad hoc nature causes it to fail, or at best deliver more of the same.

After coaching hundreds of innovation projects around the world and mixed with my own research and that of other experts, I've discovered that bolder innovation becomes a more inevitable and repeatable outcome when teams and organisations focus on six areas, each of which has a simple 'turn-on' path.

'TURN IT ON'
INNOVATION STRATEGY FRAMEWORK

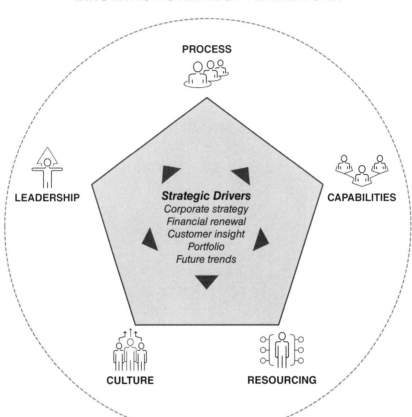

Turn It On framework © *Elvin Turner*

Innovation Strategy   Ad hoc innovators tend to be continually frustrated. A clear innovation strategy, on the other hand, galvanises the whole business behind it.

Process   A clear, efficient and effective innovation process that everyone understands. Give everyone a roadmap for their ideas.

Capabilities   Deliberately acquiring and developing the capabilities needed to deliver today whilst discovering and designing tomorrow.

Resourcing   Dynamically allocating sufficient and appropriate resources to incremental and disruptive growth initiatives. With the right process in place, this often results in significantly reduced resource wastage in innovation.

Culture   Calibrating the culture and climate to the innovation outcome, rather than one-blob-fits-all. Incremental ideas are generally tweaks, working with relatively well-known cause and effect dynamics. It's predictable and feels safe, so metrics around certainty of outcome are appropriate. Bold ideas, on the other hand, have high failure rates, so they need a context which gives them a higher chance of making it out of the building alive than status quo operations usually afford.

Leadership   Equipping and incentivising senior managers to orchestrate appropriate levels of innovation and entrepreneurship.

When these six elements combine to become a deliberate innovation system, companies give themselves the greatest possible chance of thriving today and showing up in the future.

Turn it on, then *turn it up*   My aim with this book is to help you succeed where most companies fail: to turn on innovation and to keep it turned on with proven tools that you can tailor for your context. Establish foundations, get some quick wins, build confidence … and *then* turn up the scale and sophistication as and when you need them.

What's more, every organisation is unique. Whilst the tools I'm sharing are universally applicable, beyond a certain point in your journey towards greater innovation performance, only you can know what's right for your specific context. This book helps you *turn on* innovation, but beyond a certain point only you can *turn it up*.

What works for Apple is unlikely to work in exactly the same way for you. Discovering and developing your unique innovation DNA is a pathway towards competitive advantage that few companies deliberately pursue.

Not for Geeks   Finally, this is not a book for innovation geeks. It's for everyday business people who need practical tools, ideas, workshop formats and coaching tips to turn on innovation. So I've deliberately written this in short, sharp chapters with practical advice that you can try out immediately. (Sorry fellow geeks, not much innovation jargon in here – I hope.)

This book is based on what I've learned from companies that are recalibrating themselves to pursue sustainable, profitable relevance.

They are creating healthier organisations, happier people and more hopeful futures.

They are being less zombie.

Be Less Zombie

Part One
Innovation Strategy For Pragmatists

Innovation is an argument inside most companies – frail, new ideas versus the overwhelming power of the status quo. An innovation strategy helps create an environment where new ideas can emerge and thrive. It is the single-most important way to build and sustain innovation performance. And it doesn't have to be difficult.

1 The Power of Strategic Intentionality

Why innovation doesn't happen without a deliberate leadership choice.

Innovation is an argument that most companies lose.

Why? Because usually they are far too casual about it.

Innovation demands change in the status quo. And typically, the greater the change, the bigger the argument.

So, when companies aren't deliberate enough about innovation, efforts evaporate quickly: business-as-usual is too busy and too powerful to make room for upstart, inconvenient, unproven, resource-hungry ideas. It's a fight that is always rigged.

The transition from a casual 'dating' mentality with innovation to a *strategic always-on commitment* is what sets apart the innovation powerhouses that we read about: Amazon, Google, Pixar, Netflix, Corning, Tesla and the like.

In these companies, innovation is a deliberate, never-ending pursuit. It is strategically aligned, deeply embedded, appropriately resourced, and meaningfully rewarded across the organisation. And anyone can do it.

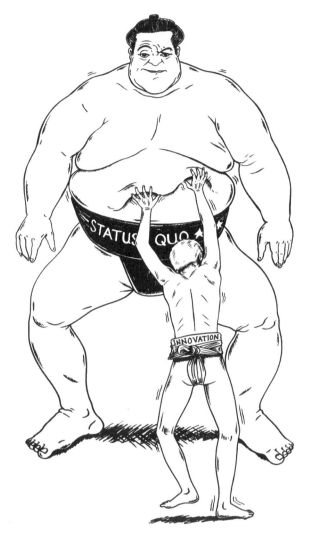

© *Richard Johnston.*

Innovation has to be as intentional as any other function in the business. A company will usually have a sales strategy, finance strategy, marketing strategy, IT strategy and HR strategy … but rarely a meaningful innovation strategy. Of course, each function is supposed to layer on some innovation as part of its own strategy; but the truth is that it's rarely enough. At best, it delivers incremental levels of innovation across the organisation.

The bottom line is inescapable. If you need more innovation (especially more disruptive innovation) you must have a dedicated innovation strategy. But it doesn't need to be complex.

Starting an Innovation Strategy

How do you create an innovation strategy that galvanises a sustainable higher performance state?

Whilst every innovation strategy will be subtly different, all will benefit from a focus on two foundational elements:

1. Strategic Drivers

This the 'why' of innovation and covers the strategic 'needles' that innovation needs to move. It also includes understanding our preparedness for the changes that are approaching from the future:

- **Alignment with corporate strategy** – What is the overall direction that innovation needs to support?
- **Financial renewal** – What levels of growth and renewal do we need to deliver now and in the future?
- **Customer insight** – What matters most to our customers, today and in the future?
- **Portfolio** – Do we have the right balance and flow of new products and services coming down the pipeline?
- **Future trends** – How could our fortunes be impacted by emerging trends?

2. Innovation Framework

This is the 'what' and the 'how' of innovation: With the strategic drivers in mind, how should we organise and mobilise innovation to turn the right ideas into new value? This falls into five broad categories:

- Process (how we develop new ideas and turn them into value)
- Capabilities (the skills, experience and partnerships required)
- Resources (the level, flow and management of resources)
- Culture (the beliefs and behaviours that support innovation)
- Leadership (who makes decisions, and how)

Aligning these areas allows a company to answer the question that an innovation strategy is designed to answer: 'To what extent are we creating the conditions where bold ideas can emerge and develop?'

'TURN IT ON'
INNOVATION STRATEGY FRAMEWORK

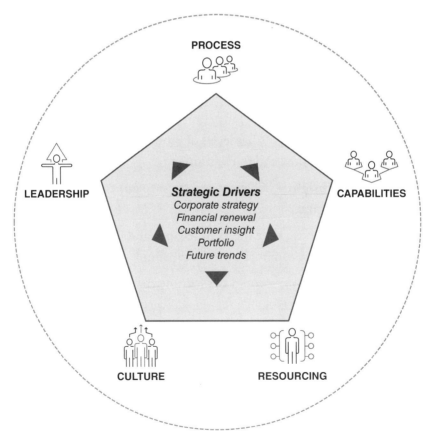

Turn It On framework © Elvin Turner

Throughout the book, we'll be looking at how to practically 'turn on' each of these areas. We'll also be looking at approaches to governance that keep innovation moving on an even keel.

Whilst every innovation strategy will benefit from a focus on these areas, bear in mind that every company's approach will be subtly different. The 'perfect' innovation strategy is the one that most powerfully supports your unique culture, direction and context.

So let's get started with a brief look at what is often the sink-or-swim issue for sustainable innovation: alignment to corporate strategy.

2 The Do-Or-Die Issue of Innovation Performance

How alignment with strategy creates powerful and sustainable innovation momentum.

According to research,[1] 54% of companies struggle to align their business and innovation strategies. That's a lot of ideas potentially 'flying blind', and my experience is that when they do, most crash and burn.

When an idea can't point to a meaningful strategic landing strip, turbulence is inevitable.

Alignment with strategic goals makes innovation sustainable. It simultaneously connects innovation with hard commercial outcomes and provides the motivation for a crucial chain reaction to take place behind it. If innovation becomes the means by which we will meet our numbers, suddenly the resources, processes, culture required rise up the list of leadership priorities.

Alignment with strategy pulls the whole innovation system forward. And this is especially important when allocating and defending

---

[1] www.pwc.com/us/en/services/consulting/innovation-benchmark-findings.html?WT. mc_id=CT2-PL200-DM2-TR1-LS2-ND30-BPA10-CN_InnovationBenchmark20172-PRandmedia

the resources required for strategic creativity which often get cut during leaner times.

Stuck at First Base?

But first, a reality check. Many executives that I meet coyly admit that their company doesn't actually have a strategy. Instead they have a revenue objective and a 12-month plan that serves as the strategy. This makes alignment with impactful, sustainable innovation strategy tricky.

But no strategy doesn't mean you can't make progress with innovation. In fact, often, a corporate strategy is inadvertently born during the process of developing an innovation strategy. The conversations force a point of view about the most important factors that define a company's future.

So, if you're light on strategy, jump to Chapter 13, 'Quick-Start Innovation Strategy Workshop', for a pragmatic starting point.

Connecting Strategy and Innovation

If your company does have a strategy, hopefully it will include some clear points of view on:

- The intended overall impact of the organisation (in multiple dimensions).
- Some intended commercial/financial destinations.
- Markets in which to operate.
- Differentiation in business and operating models.

In most contexts, the strategy demands growth in scale and impact. Often that growth exceeds what can be achieved by the status quo business and operating models.

But it's not always a growth issue. Often strategy requires operational change provoked by shifts in underlying industry dynamics that have varying degrees of do-or-die significance.

The reality for most companies is a combination of both – growth amidst change.

Either way, when the status quo model won't quite cut it, success becomes impossible without innovation. The greater the stretch, or the more turbulent the market, the greater the requirement for more transformational levels of innovation.

That gap between the destination that the strategy demands, and the status quo future trajectory, is essentially what informs the innovation strategy.

Inside the gap will be a mixed economy of needs, ranging from incremental, continuous improvements through to transformational shifts that deliver exponential impact.

The role of the innovation strategy is to assess the strategy gap and co-ordinate an appropriate portfolio of programmes, projects and experiments that will close that gap.

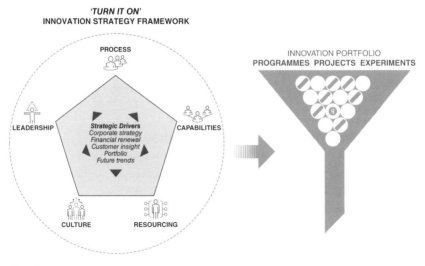

© *Elvin Turner*

There are no right answers on how to approach this; every company will develop their own process that is aligned to their individual strategy-setting cycle. Throughout this book I'll be suggesting approaches that can help, but the most important thing is establishing the connection: making it explicitly clear how all innovation activity directly contributes to delivering the strategy.

That makes good financial sense (so that we're not allocating scarce resources to too many 'moonshots') but it also makes good strategic sense: innovation is too easy to sideline in both good times (through complacency) and bad (through cost-cutting). When that happens, we become strategically vulnerable.

One of the most effective ways of maintaining the connection between strategy and innovation is to create a financial dependency, which is the focus of the next chapter.

3 Money Talks

Metrics that make innovation a commercial inevitability.

Many innovation strategies are dead within 12 months. The reason? 'Show me the money.'

Rule 101: Innovation strategy ultimately must deliver more money somehow, somewhere, sometime soon. If it doesn't, the status quo will quickly discredit and overrun it.

Genial innovation strategies often stumble because they spark too many initiatives that have slow-burn fuses or are commercially naive. We'll look a little later at how to strike the right balance.

But whatever your balance, executive patience will wear thin if financial returns aren't appearing on the horizon before long. Smart executives use this to their advantage. They design financial targets that make innovation an inevitable outcome.

3M uses a method that fits handily onto a Post-it® note, one of its 55,000 products: '30% of each division's sales must come from products less than four years old.' Sales targets affect bonuses and so everyone pays attention.

What if the museum's challenge was something like— 50% of exhibits must be less than 10 years old?

Money Talks   13

> "30% of each division's sales must come from products less than four years old."

It's a rough gauge but useful because it marries financial growth with customer-focused innovation. If new products don't create meaningful customer progress, they won't deliver sustainable revenue. That helps avoid the temptation to do innovation for innovation's sake too, a common problem in many companies.

The right ratio of sales from new initiatives also helps mitigate against a dangerous overemphasis on incremental innovation.

I once knew of a company that pitched too low. It demanded that 10% of revenues came from products that didn't exist 12 months ago. If you are an unstoppable disruptive innovation machine with a product range that is simple to reinvent rapidly, awesome. Go for it.

But the reality is that this kind of focus will mostly lead to a lot of thin repackaging of existing products that are called 'new'.

In a mature industry where you're continually looking for new forms of growth, that kind of innovation is likely to be an important part of the marketing innovation mix. And in the short term it can work. But beware of the giddy feeling of succeeding in the area of low-hanging fruit at the expense of investing in long-term growth.

So, over to you. Looking forward, what renewal rate would ensure that innovation is focused on delivering the right kinds of growth? Only you can decide and it may vary according to business unit. A range of factors can influence this, including:

• Speed of industry change
• Oncoming industry inflection points

- Depth of competitive advantage
- Strength of current innovation capabilities vs competition.

Depending on your company's circumstances, I would suggest beginning with a moderate degree of stretch. Establish the cause-and-effect principle across the company, experiment with different ratios in different areas, and work towards something that is most likely to deliver ongoing profitable relevance.

It's a great question for an executive off-site. What cause-and-effect relationship between revenue and innovation would deliver the healthiest future for us?

It's one of the most important conversations an executive team can have. And, perhaps most practically, it's a financial metric that directly correlates to bonuses. A strong motivator for keeping innovation front-of-mind in the boardroom.

4 The Innovation that Customers Buy

Creating a laser focus on the innovation that matters most.

Creating a cause-and-effect relationship between revenues and innovation is a powerful galvanising force.

But there is a lesser-known relationship that has equal potency. It de-risks innovation, creates a focus on what matters most, and reveals the most profitable areas of creative pursuit.

It is the specific amount of *progress* that customers make in their lives *because of you*.

What does that mean? I'll be covering this in much more detail in Part Two: Turning on a Fast-Track Innovation Process. But for now, think about these questions:

- Given the current speed of change, in five years' time, why will today's customers still actively choose your products and services, rather than switch to a competitor's?

- On what basis? In which specific dimensions?

Five years?! Who can predict customer churn, retention and growth levels across that time frame?

'We're doing well, but our whole company could unwind within three years,' a senior executive of a 30,000-employee company once told me. This was a hot, born-digital brand, well-versed in agile transformation principles.

But what if you *could* predict what will matter most to customers? You'd be looking into the future and investing in innovation with greater certainty and at lower risk.

Using techniques that I'll describe later, it is possible to decode the 'units of progress' that are likely to matter most to your customers, and that actually change very slowly – often only incrementally nudging over decades.

'Computer games are largely similar to what they were 30 years ago,' says Andy Billings, Vice President of Profitable Creativity at Electronic Arts, the world's largest video game company. Quite a statement in an industry with a reputation for fast and furious innovation.

Looking at the historical rates of customer progress, this information can help leaders predict the approximate rates of increased progress that they will need to match in the future to stay relevant.

Aligning innovation investments to a likely trajectory of customer progress gives leaders some choices to make around competitive advantage. Rather than pitching for the minimum rate of progress with incremental innovation, they can choose to aim higher and beat the progress curve that the industry will likely trend towards.

Rate of customer progress is an approximate and subtle metric. It's not a magic formula, nor will it deliver 100% certainty. But it's another important tool to keep innovation aligned with what matters most to customers, and to avoid the temptation to pursue ideas that are born fizzy but quickly go flat.

After reading the chapters in Part Two, be intentional about developing specific progress metrics to guide your innovation strategy.

5 How Much Innovation Is Enough?

How to plan innovation resources that deliver a big enough tomorrow.

'How do I get my people to make innovation the first thing they think about in the morning?' a frustrated senior executive once asked me.

There are many answers to that question. But ask 'those people' and their loudest and most consistent answer will be, 'Give me time!' A 60–70-hour week leaves little space, energy and motivation for meaningful innovation.

Despite what we'd like to believe, you can't squeeze innovation around the edges and hope that it works, any more than you can with other business-critical functions in the organisation.

Imagine the bleary-eyed finance director only dedicating a few spare minutes to the end-of-quarter reports once he's put the kids to bed. Yet that's how innovation plays out in many organisations.

Successful innovators are deliberate about strategically resourcing their future. To meet their financial renewal target (e.g. 30% of revenues from products that didn't exist three years ago), they realise

that resources need to be adequately deployed against three broad
categories of innovation: *→ these could be*
our objectives

Enhancing

- **Product:** Incrementally improving core products and services.

- **Market:** Serving and growing the core customer base.

- **Organisation:** Improving the day-to-day efficiency and effectiveness of the organisation.

Extending

- **Product:** Piloting promising new products with existing customers.

- **Market:** Extending into adjacent markets with core and emerging products and services.

- **Organisation:** Developing the organisational capabilities, systems and structures needed to support new growth.

Exploring

- **Product:** Experimenting with emerging technologies.

- **Market:** Exploring less obvious customer segments with core and emerging products and services.

- **Organisation:** Experimenting with new organisational capabilities, systems and structures needed to support transformation.

Every organisation needs an ongoing balance of innovation
investment across each of these areas. This ensures a three-way
focus on optimising the performance of today's business model,
building a pipeline of new growth opportunities for the future, and
ensuring that the organisation is sufficiently agile and equipped to
self-transform in line with market developments.

Risk vs Reward

Inevitably, the further we venture from the core business, the greater the number of unknowns, and the higher the risk of failure. Yet the greater the potential rewards.

Risk understandably tends to provoke an overemphasis on incrementalism which typically accounts for 85–90% of a company's innovation efforts.[1] And as we learned earlier, incremental innovation is important but not sufficient in most settings.

What's more, those incremental product enhancements are often feature requests from large customers, many of which aren't relevant to the broader market. Unfortunately, this kind of 'customer-driven' innovation can become an investment in the gradual demise and irrelevance of the products that it is designed to sustain.

Yet one study[2] showed that even though only 14% of product launches could be described as 'substantial' (more disruptive), they delivered 61% of all profit from the companies that were surveyed. He who dares, wins, it seems.

Striking the Right Balance

The challenge is to optimise investment across the three categories of innovation, which is broadly connected to the speed of disruptive change in a given industry.

A rule of thumb is to start with a 10/20/70 allocation to innovation investment:

- 10% Exploring new markets and experimenting with new technology.

---

[1] https://hbr.org/2007/12/is-it-real-can-we-win-is-it-worth-doing-managing-risk-and-reward-in-an-innovation-portfolio

[2] W. Chan Kim and Renée Mauborgne, 'Strategy, Value Innovation, and the Knowledge Economy,' *Sloan Management Review*, Spring 1999.

- 20% Extending into adjacent markets and investing in promising new technology.
- 70% Enhancing the core of the business.

Inevitably, the further we move away from the core, the greater the number of unknowns, the higher the risk, and the increased chances of failure. That reality causes most organisations to underinvest in Extend and Explore innovation, with serious consequences on future sustainable growth, and organisational agility.

That's because most organisations have a one-size-fits-all approach to managing innovation, which is a car crash waiting to happen: high-risk projects that receive too much funding too soon, and which create a huge pain when they fail.

We'll look at this in more detail later, but a useful metaphor to consider alongside the 10/20/70 split is 'Tank, Pond, Ocean'.

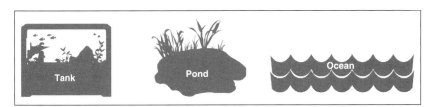

© Mark Bjornsgaard

Coined by Mark Bjornsgaard of System-Two, the term describes three broad stages of an idea:

- **Tank (10):** This is the Explore zone. We run lots of experiments but spend very little as the majority of them will fail. A handful show promise and graduate to the …
- **Pond (20):** This is where ideas are incubated and developed to a point where they show real potential for future growth.
- **Ocean (70):** Those ideas that demonstrate sufficient market traction become part of the core business.

This deliberate and ongoing three-way focus ensures a sustainable pipeline of risk-managed growth and organisational calibration.

But 10/20/70 may not be right for you. It's a useful starting point to begin a conversation but every company needs to understand what is appropriate for their unique circumstances – which will inevitably change over time.

With that in mind, here is an exercise that I strongly recommend that leaders run with their teams to start identifying the right balance of innovation:

1. **What's the balance?** Ask leaders to individually write down approximate percentages of how much resource is allocated to Enhance, Extend and Explore innovation right now.

   The leaders take turns to share their thoughts and then discuss the assumptions behind any significant discrepancies. Based on those discussions, agree what you believe to be a broad three-way split of how innovation is resourced today.

2. **What does it mean?** Discuss the implications of this investment split on delivering the corporate strategy. If you don't have a strategy, what implications might the percentages have on your organisational health three years from now?

3. **What should we change?** Based on what your strategy/future needs, create a revised percentage breakdown of innovation resources.

Almost every organisation that I've worked with finds that the majority of their investment is tied up with short-term, incremental product enhancements. That's a vulnerable place to camp.

There are no hard and fast rules about what the right allocation of resources should be as it really depends on the speed of change in your industry. More speed generally needs more exploration.

It also depends on your corporate growth targets. The higher the ambition, the greater the level of Explore innovation required. Higher rewards tend to hang out in unexplored spaces.

Reality Check about Explore Innovation

Explore innovation generally needs dedicated resources and capabilities to succeed. Much better to have two people dedicated to a project full-time than six people fitting it around other things.

That statement provokes a hard swallow or a shrug of impossibility amongst many executives. The choice to reallocate resources to the future with no immediate return rarely feels easy.

The solution often lies in defining reality: taking a hard look at how the organisation is currently structured and resourced (e.g. towards growth vs maintenance), the rate of change in the industry, and asking the question, 'Who do we need to become?'

And yet whilst allocating more resources away from the core feels like risk, it is actually prudence.

It's an inevitability that the future comes knocking sooner or later. Deliberately investing in a balanced innovation portfolio means that we are taking strategic initiative rather than busying ourselves with denial.

But you have to *choose*. The power of the status quo won't allow it to happen on its own.

Halfway House?

Despite what I said above about the need for dedicated resources for Extend and Explore innovation, under some circumstances it can work with full-time employees having a proportion of their hours dedicated to new projects.

In my experience, it's a hit-and-miss approach though, most likely to end up with employees doing the innovation project as an evening job (which burns their energy and motivation for the day job).

But it *can* work, especially if people are being asked to dedicate specialist resources to an Extend project that is already gaining traction with customers – which is easier to blend into daily resources, systems and skill sets.

However, for Explore innovation, real success tends only to happen (at least at pace) with full-time dedicated resources.

Being deliberate about striking the right balance between Enhance, Extend and Explore innovation is one of the characteristics of high performing innovators.

So, if you don't already have an approach to deliberately allocating and tracking innovation portfolio resources, start with a 10/20/70 split and learn your way forward.

Performance through the Portfolio

As well as intentionally allocating resources *across* the portfolio, it's important to manage the volume, potential value and speed of ideas *through* the portfolio.

If organisational friction damages the flow of ideas in these dimensions, it'll interrupt the financial renewal rates that your innovation strategy is aiming for. You can't expect 30% of revenues to come from products that didn't exist four years ago if gatekeepers and processes that control the idea traffic flow are based on status quo metrics. It'll be red lights all the way.

We'll look at how to manage idea flow in more detail in Part Two (Process) and Part Five (Culture). But here's the leadership principle to hold on to: based on the strategic outcomes that your innovation needs to deliver, be deliberate about setting balanced investment ratios *across* the portfolio and idea flow rates *through* the portfolio.

Pipeline Metrics

With innovation resources aligned with progress and financial targets, now you're in a good place to define metrics that will suck the right quality and quantity of products through the pipeline.

Within each category of innovation, a number of projects will be cooking. They will all be at different stages in the development process, with different risk profiles and resource allocations.

Understanding what's in the pipeline is important, yet vague in many companies. When we have a good understanding of what's going through the pipeline and at what speed, we can make the best possible investment decisions for the present and the future.

Not enough Explore ideas moving into Extend? Look at the decision criteria, resourcing or handovers. Too many incremental ideas clogging up resources in the next three months? Re-prioritise. Not enough ideas making the leap from Extend into the core? Check for the business model assumptions and customer insights further up the chain.

Start Simple

Sometimes leaders can be put off by the apparent complexity of this. Sure, you can have highly sophisticated stage-gate tracking tools with return-on-investment predictors, and they can be excellent. But if you're starting out, my advice is to begin simple.

The CFO of a large UK leisure company began with a simple Excel spreadsheet, a few categories, and a handful of questions:

Alignment: 'Which part of the strategy does this project support?'

Value: 'What specific value is this project aiming to deliver, and by when?'

Resources: 'What is the resource allocation to this project?'

Status: 'What is the status and next step?'

When you're starting out, these are enough to start a useful conversation. Dial-up the sophistication as you need to.

Pipeline Metrics that Can Stifle Innovation

A quick word of warning. This CFO had good instincts but his questions about the level and timing of returns backfired slightly.

These figures drove people towards more predictable innovation projects that could have revenue or efficiency numbers attributed to them quickly. Because Explore projects have learning as their main outcomes, they became a tricky fit in the spreadsheet and attracted a degree of suspicion.

No prizes for guessing what happened to the number of Explore projects that were proposed.

So, tread carefully and measure for the appropriate outcome.

Pipeline Resource Renewal

Tracking the short, medium and long term also allows for more informed strategic resource planning discussions that will affect the pipeline productivity in the future.

Knowing that a particular technology trend is likely to land five years from now allows us to plan new capability and partnership strategies that will be essential for us to develop the products that customers will demand in the future.

In turn, that will also inform capability development discussions. Which capabilities and roles will matter most in five years and how do we get a head-start on finding the best talent now?

ludes leaders. None should take it for granted that
nost qualified people to steer the company into its
)wth.

This kind of integrated innovation pipeline analysis is crucial
because it connects strategy, customer progress, trend scanning,
scenario development, experiments, pilots and ongoing product
enhancements. When the numbers are aligned, the flow of innovation
is much healthier.

6 The Future Is Coming Ready or Not

Three questions to continually ask about the future.

An innovation strategy needs to be rooted in reality – what's happening now and what's coming from the future. Unfortunately, this isn't always the case.

When strategy and decisions are based on assumptions whose salience has inconspicuously shifted, a company is heading for rocky waters.

Successful innovators build a radar that helps them pre-empt the future and make two kinds of choice: how to *instigate* change and how to *respond* to change.

Their radar is continually asking three questions:

- What's happening?
- What does it mean?
- What should we do?

When everyone in the organisation is asking these questions in all directions all of the time, a level of strategic curiosity develops that is absent inside most organisations.

It's a superpower for profitable relevance.

It also leads to what the MIT Sloan Business School calls 'sense-making'. According to their research, it is the most reliable indicator of having better vision, better innovation and better execution.

Next, we'll look at how to work with the first two questions. The rest of the book addresses the third.

7 Detecting Weak Signals from the Future

Finding the saboteurs and saviours of tomorrow's growth.

© *Richard Johnston.*

Your business model is under continual attack from the future.

What made you red-hot relevant yesterday has already cooled imperceptibly overnight. Someone somewhere figured out a better way to do some part of what you do, or how you do it.

'If you don't burn down your own business every year, a competitor will supply the match,' says Andy Billings, Vice President of Profitable Creativity at Electronic Arts, the world's largest video games company.

Failing to spot this gradual fade to grey turns out to be the single-largest cause of stalled growth, according to Matthew Olson and Derek van Bever, authors of the book *Stall Points*. Every company has deeply held assumptions about the ingredients and recipes of its success. Over time, market dynamics subtly shift and the failure to recalibrate leads to eventual demise.

The better we can sense and respond to the future, the greater our chances of showing up there.

Unfortunately, many companies are in a continual state of shock. For them, the future always seems to appear suddenly, like a Star Wars space cruiser arriving from hyperspace.

I guess this shouldn't be a surprise. We saw earlier that companies don't naturally allocate sufficient resources to the future. Neither do they pay close enough attention to the oncoming forces that will ultimately disrupt the way they successfully create progress today.

But getting the basics in place doesn't have to be an onerous and expensive task. Like anything, there are levels of sophistication, but here are two fundamental starting points to consider:

- Executives spending more time in the future
- Creating a map of the future

Executive Time: Bend It like Bezos

How much time do the senior executives in your company spend thinking about creating a differentiated and profitable future? That's ultimately the job of strategy. Yet if we're honest, what gets called strategy in many organisations is really just a tactical action plan for the next 12 months.

Jeff Bezos, CEO of Amazon, claims to allocate around three days per week to flexible, unstructured time, typically spent thinking about future strategy.

If his board of directors are working on anything that relates to today, he tells them they are not doing their job. After all, today is relatively well understood, so if those smart, well-paid direct reports aren't managing the show, something is out of whack, surely?

A good gauge of how much emphasis the future gets from its leaders is the monthly board meeting. Most tend to be dominated by updates on status quo issues and sharing information that could have been consumed in advance. It's more of a status report than a strategic gathering.

That emphasis gets reflected in daily life too, with leaders far more involved in the operational aspects of their teams than their job titles justify.

I was recently in a workshop where a rising star bemoaned the lack of time he had to devote to innovation. The global CEO flashed back at him, 'How do you think *I* feel? I'm the CEO and *even I* don't have any time for that stuff.'

I bit my fist. Ironically, in that context we didn't have time to open that particular can of worms. But if *anyone* has a choice about how they spend their time, it's the CEO. This one's sense of priorities was clearly having an impact further down the organisation.

But even if you find yourself in an organisation where your nose is pressed firmly to today's grindstone, there are ways of creating space for the future. We'll come to that later.

Ask the Question, Pick a Number

Quite often, leaders aren't focusing enough on the future because no one specifically owns it. The same could be said about entrepreneurship in general inside most companies.

But all leaders need a stake in the future if we're going to rebalance the scales away from an unhealthy compulsion for today.

Asking these three questions in a board meeting is often all it takes to start:

1. 'How much time do we spend thinking about and discussing future strategy (beyond 12 months from now)?'
2. 'As the team that's responsible for future strategy, how much *should* we spend on it?'
3. 'What would need to be true for that to happen sustainably?'

If the word 'future' is too fuzzy for your team, use the word 'strategy' or 'innovation' instead. Whatever works, just get the conversation moving. Then agree a realistic number that you can start from.

Doing a Jeff Bezos might be a stretch for most executives to begin with. But agreeing to a 10% time allocation is a good starting point to build from. Spending 4–5 hours a week drawing down and processing the future would be a game changer in many organisations.

That requires letting go of some work, usually things your team has been longing for you to delegate to them for ages anyway.

So, ask the questions. Get the future on the agenda for the next meeting. At the end of the discussion, those leaders that your future needs will all agree that the conversation was a very good use of their time. They always do. Those who don't? Maybe your future needs to show up without them.

Create a Future Map

But then comes the tough bit.

What would we actually *do* with that time?

I mean, how do you think about the future for 4–5 hours every week? How far out do you go? What are we looking for? What do we do with it?

I recommend keeping it simple to begin with. You can build sophistication later, but for now you need to build confidence and interest amongst the team that this is a good use of time and effort.

Start with two tried-and-tested strategy tools:

First, the Business Model Canvas. Developed by Alex Osterwalder, CEO of innovation firm, Strategyzer, it has quickly become the go-to tool for rapidly assessing and innovating business models. You can either download it for free from www.strategyzer.com or jump to pro-status and spontaneously sketch it on a piece of flipchart paper. Always raises an eyebrow or two.

*Illustration designed by Strategyzer; Creative Commons
Attribution – Share Alike 3.0 Unported Licence.*

Next, select a part of your business and using no more than
2–3 Post-it® notes per box, complete the canvas for it.
This is a 30,000 feet view of the business model so keep
it to headlines at this stage. I like to start with the Value
Proposition box (this is where you describe the progress
you create for customers) and then jump to the Customer
Segment box. I like to start with the Customer Segment
box which describes a specific customer profile and
then jump to the Value Proposition box to describe
the progress that you create for customers. After that, it's
up to you.

I recommend watching the 6 x 3-minute video series that Strategyzer has developed for a more comprehensive overview of
how to use the Business Model Canvas. Search for the Strategyzer channel on www.youtube.com.

You've just identified the essential factors that make your current business model work. Now it's time to shift the focus to the factors coming from the future that could impact your success, positively or adversely.

Again, I suggest keeping it simple and using something like the strategy tool PESTEL, which stands for Political, Economic, Social, Technological, Environmental and Legal. Add other categories if you need to.

With your business model in mind, identify PESTEL factors that are emerging on the horizon. It can be helpful to plot them in three time zones, according to your estimated moment of significant impact: within 1 year, 1–3 years, 3–5 years. There are no hard and fast rules so pick the time frames that work for you.

Will, Won't, May, Must

Now, with each PESTEL factor in mind, ask the following questions:

- What *will* change for us and our key stakeholders, and why?
- What *won't* change for us and our key stakeholders, and why?
- What *may* change for us and our key stakeholders, and why?
- What *must* change for us and our key stakeholders, and why?

This is a good way to start building a picture of your collective assumptions about the future.

In 2019, Decca, the record label with a strong reputation for innovation took this in an imaginative direction. When the leadership team began developing a new innovation strategy for its 90th anniversary, each member was given a 'journal from the future'.

Over 2–3 weeks, the leaders individually spent a few minutes a day researching future trends, noting down insights, ideas, daydreams, questions, and anxieties that were provoked by their findings.

The team then convened to discuss what they had discovered and created an innovation 'manifesto' and roadmap to direct the development of their innovation strategy.

Broaden the Conversation, Focus the Ownership

Mostly likely you'll only get so far based on your current levels of knowledge. So, open up the conversation and bring in some expertise to help. If you try and limit this to a boardroom-only discussion, the depth and variety of the insights will inevitably be constrained, which has a knock-on effect on your decision-making.

If one area has a particularly significant impact on your business, drill deeper and further into that area. New technology tends to be the driving factor in most industry transitions, so all other things being equal, consider giving that more focus as a default setting.

Also, consider creating a team per PESTEL element, perhaps comprised of employees and outsiders. Do whatever is needed to bring this piece of strategy work to life.

Visualise the Future

Another useful tip is to visualise what you find. This helps to keep the conversation current, accessible to everyone, and more engaging than a 100-slide PowerPoint deck (keep that for in-depth meetings).

For example, producing a quarterly 'insights radar' that shows the current flow from the future is a great way to give people an instant snapshot of what's coming from the future and when we can expect to start feeling the impact.

Get Out of the Building

With this future framework in place, go and start talking to customers about what you're seeing and how it might affect the way they make progress in the future. Go to conferences, have lunch with geeks, visit the fringes of your solar system and the ones that look as if they could collide with yours. Hear me well: THIS IS A GOOD USE OF YOUR TIME! Much more valuable to the company than stealing growth and experience opportunities from your succession plan.

Future Now

How deliberately are you doing this? If you *are* doing it, are you satisfied with the quality of the incoming data? If not, what could you do about that?

If you don't have anything in place, find one of your high potential people who is looking for a challenge and give them 90 days to create a prototype 'insights lab'. No budget and nothing fancy to start with, just something that creates a radar and a regular flow of insight that the board (and others) can explore. See what you learn in those 90 days and gradually increase the sophistication as needed.

Go and visit companies in other sectors and see how they do this. Look especially for those who are far down the track in data analytics and save yourself falling into the same holes that they did.

Daylight Robbery

The future comes faster and more unpredictably every year.

One of the biggest thefts that I see in business is when leaders are stuck in the operational weeds of today instead of the tracking the information feeds from the future. When that happens, the organisation is robbed of the strategic thinking that the executives are uniquely employed to provide.

8 Blurred Vision

Three voices that want to distort reality.

'The first responsibility of a leader is to define reality,' said Max De Pree, author of *Leadership is an Art*.

The trouble with reality is that it is a drink that can be served in different strengths and measures. A diluted version is often more palatable than neat. A sip more so than a quaff. And without being made to down a flagon of full-strength brew, how would you know anything other than a milder version?

Yet whilst reality can't be escaped, as the declining lifespan of companies testifies, it *can* be distorted or denied.

Before we look at how to deal in reality, here are three counterfeits to beware of: thin, kin and spin.

'Thin Reality'

This is about breadth and depth. We build our picture of reality based largely on instincts, standard reports, customer anecdotes and media headlines. These are all useful but not a strong or reliable enough signal to inform strategic decision-making that builds long-term relevance.

The impact of new technology often falls into this category. Buzzwords abound with knowing nods, but few actually understand the true applications of the technology and the implications on the business model. We know enough to pretend.

'Kin Reality'

Reality tends to serve up awkward, big questions that rarely have quick answers. Next quarter's numbers typically won't bear the wait.

'Let's bring that back at the next meeting when we've had a chance to think about it,' we fudge.

A 'more pressing' tactical agenda item takes the stage. A collective denial prevails, the ducked reality creeps closer.

Any zombie worth its salt will ensure that elephants always out-number executives in the board room. It's a kin thing.

'Spin Reality'

Here's a scene that you've undoubtedly experienced a version of in your career:

Five tired managers stare bewildered into the distance of a cramped meeting room. Fraud incidence reports are scattered across the desk.

One leans forward, rubs his face and offers, 'Look, why don't we just tell them the truth?'

'Ha!' barks another. 'You can't tell the board the truth! They can't handle it.'

The version of reality that we work with is usually the one that we attract. Do people bring you tarnish or varnish?

Navigating and responding to today's complex environment is an almost impossible task for leaders. There are no silver bullets.

But to endure, we have to embrace the uncomfortable necessity of facing reality. *Real* reality. Internal *and* external realities. Past, present and future realities. And that means making our ability to define and respond to reality a source of genuine competitive advantage.

So if Thin, Kin or Spin hang out inside your organisation, choose today to grab them by the neck, chase them out of the building and set the dogs after them.

What version of reality do you attract?

9 What Does the Future Actually *Mean*?

How to make sense of what's coming and its likely impact on your future prosperity.

Anyone can gather data from the future. It's just a choice to mobilise good fact finding.

Turning that data into valuable, actionable insights is where the magic begins.

There are three important approaches to interpreting this data that your future will thank you for taking seriously. Few companies do them all well, so a pigeon-step in this direction is a leap of potential competitive advantage.

Data Analytics

This is big data. It's crunching numbers, spotting patterns and suggesting potential scenarios. 'Data scientist' is one of the fastest-growing jobs for good reason – these people can help you predict the future, to some degree.

Those crunched numbers need to come from somewhere and part of the skill here is designing a strategy that aligns the right mix of inputs, analysis and outputs. The Internet of Things is a driving force in Big Data, as Professor Alan Brown of Exeter University explains.

> *'Imagine you make coffee cups. What happens if you embed a sensor inside them? Now they can tell you where they are, what's inside them, the temperature of the liquid, the speed of consumption, the way they are held and tilted, how long they get put down between sips, the heart rate of the holders, their distance from one another, and so on. Suddenly your coffee cups become thousands of instant feedback loops giving you data that can become the lifeblood of your innovation.'*

Data science isn't the whole answer, but the depth and breadth of insight that it can provide means you can't afford not to be making this a priority.

Extrapolation

At its simplest level, this is taking an existing issue and pushing it out into the future in logical progressions and asking, 'So what?'

Moore's Law is a useful example. It states that the overall power of computers doubles every two years, which it has done since 1965. With that in mind, a 1985 computer chip manufacturer could look at that data and roughly extrapolate the rate of progress and plan future innovation ambitions and resource requirements accordingly.

But the greater value comes with higher levels of sophistication – seeing how multiple factors may collide and result in futures that aren't immediately obvious. Or 'seeing around corners', as Professor Rita McGrath calls it.

What will happen when the coming biotech, immigration, capital flow, farming, and media consumption trends collide and land on your business model canvas? That's tougher to figure out, but a treasure map worth designing.

It can provide crucial information for decision-making in four areas:

- What is the overall *likelihood* of impact?
- What is the likely *moment* of impact?
- The likely *nature* of impact?
- What is the likely *scale* of impact?

This is the stuff of scenario planning, made famous by Arie de Geus and his team at Royal Dutch Shell in the 1970s and 80s. Now common practice in many organisations, scenario planning requires a cocktail of good data, sustained effort and strategic imagination.

IKEA's Life at Home project is a good example of sustained, strategic scenario planning. Every couple of years the company publishes its vision of the future, most recently sharing six of its future home scenarios after synthesising research that included 22,000 interviews with citizens of 22 countries.

Science Friction

Fortune 50 hardware store, Lowes, has put an interesting twist on developing future scenarios. Its strategists have developed an approach called Narrative Driven Innovation. Here's how it works.

Lowes passes data to experienced science fiction writers. Their job is to imagine plausible future storylines where trends collide and where friction could show up in customers' lives.

Those scenarios are then handed to cartoonists who visualise them into comic strip stories. These cartoons become the basis of innovation development discussions, both internally and with customers.

It's an excellent way to bring abstract concepts to life, something that is notoriously difficult when trying to get a firm grip on something as slippery as the future.

Anyone could do this. What stops you from piloting an approach like this to identify how it might boost the overall quality of insight and subsequent innovation in your organisation? Start simple and decide to make it a superpower over the next 1–2 years. Speed of high-quality learning is one of the few remaining sources of competitive advantage and it isn't going away.

As you develop this muscle, your ability to identify 'predictable surprises' will improve, and your chances of thriving in the future will increase.

Seeing What's Missing

The third element of interpretation is the rarest and possibly the most valuable.

It is the ability to look at the world and to see what's missing. It is noticing something people haven't yet realised they want. It is articulating a cry or a longing that people are feeling but can't yet express well.

'It's Stormzy wearing Banksy's Union Jack stab-proof vest at the Glastonbury festival,' says trend expert Lee Widdows. She's describing the UK grime artist's headline set which went viral as it creatively drew attention to London's knife crime problems.

'The most important cultural insights aren't spotted by algorithms,' she says. 'They're identified by people whose instincts have been developed to spot meaning.'

Whilst Widdows recognises the value of data analytics, for her, the human factor is where the magic of interpretation still happens.

'Synthesising data, spotting an original insight, and then creating a resonant expression of that insight, is the heart of creativity and breakthrough product innovation,' says Widdows. 'It comes from a keenly developed set of instincts that is lacking inside many organisations, and yet it can be taught.'

I meet Widdows at the UK's University of Creative Arts (UCA) where she is currently the associate head of fashion. 'So how does a company develop these instincts?' I ask.

'It's what art schools used to teach,' she says. 'It really comes down to creating a safe space where people can learn to detect signal amidst noise, to experiment, to observe what works, and to learn what fails. Over time, with good coaching, the instinct to see what's missing begins to develop.'

At another level, this art school thinking is the ability to spot what someone else has already done, recognise the value in it, but take it in a slightly different direction and surpass the originator.

Apple is well known for this. Most of its products were better versions of what someone else imagined.

Be More Banksy

Every company needs a version of art school. I'm serious. What if every year you put a cohort of people through your own bespoke art school programme, tailored for your industry? Teach them how to see what's missing and plug them into innovation projects. Then create your own internal, TED-style conference to share and explore what's bubbled up. I guarantee you'll be the only ones in your industry doing it.

As I leave the UCA I find out that Widdows predicted beards. Well, beards as 'a thing', that is. A few years ago, she advised a global beauty brand that beards were about to be big (literally), but they passed on it.

Within a couple of years, that company was overtaken by much smaller competitors who'd jumped on the hipster grooming products bandwagon.

Seeing isn't always believing.

If you want to build your knowledge in this area, some useful resources include:

Predictable Surprises: The disasters you should have seen coming and how to prevent them by Max H. Bazerman and Michael D. Watkins (Harvard Business School Press).

Peripheral Vision: Detecting the weak signals that will make or break your company, by George S. Day and Paul J. H. Schoemaker (Harvard Business School Press).

Flash Foresight: How to see the invisible and do the impossible by Daniel Burrus and John David Mann (Harper Collins).

10 The Future and Its Naysayers

Three more voices that try to fudge the future.

Standing in the pathway of turning data into meaningful, actionable insights, lurk three zombie forces. Their names? Bias, ignorance and complacency.

Even the best-resourced organisations in the world are susceptible to their powers. In fact, in many cases, the larger the resources, the more powerful the forces.

Bias

Bias, whether conscious or unconscious, triumphs over logic on a regular basis. If our underlying beliefs about ourselves, our teams and the world are wonky, we're likely to make decisions that aren't in our collective future's interests.

One important source of conscious, yet unspoken, bias that I encounter frequently is fear. A manager sees a situation appearing on the horizon that provokes fear inside of him. That leads to denial or crazy-making control and micromanagement, neither of which lead to good decision-making about the future.

A lot has been written about the range and power of biases inside organisations. If you haven't done any analysis on the prevailing biases in your team or organisation, start now. *The Choice Factory* by Richard Shotton is a good place to begin.

Ignorance

Ignorance looks at the data and shrugs its shoulders. Either it's too complex or too technical to understand. But instead of inviting in an interpreter, pride will often kick-in at a senior level and the issue is dismissed as unimportant or 'parked for review' later in the year.

Complacency

Complacency looks at the data and genuinely believes it presents neither significant threat nor opportunity (with bias and ignorance often joining the party).

It is easy to underestimate the impact of future trends. History shows that this is especially true if you are a large organisation witnessing a cloud forming in the distance composed of start-up companies. It's the theme of one of the most influential innovation books ever written: *The Innovator's Dilemma* by Professor Clay Christensen. If you've never read it, get a copy now.

'Just a blip', is how organisations such as Airbnb, Uber, Netflix and many other industry earthquakers were described by now creaking (or decomposing) industry titans.

I once worked with one of the world's largest telecoms infrastructure providers. At the time, Chinese firm Huawei was trying to get in on its act and grow its international market share. One of the jokes I would often hear during client meetings was, 'Huawei … Who are we?! Who are we?!'

Within two years Huawei was market leader.

Which 'blips' are you currently overlooking?

11 Leading from the Future

Questions that your future needs you to answer today.

Ultimately, an organisation's leaders choose its future. But the status quo can be a formidable foe that too easily distracts executive attention from what's coming.

At the very least, leaders should build in a rhythm of meaningful review of the following areas:

Resourcing the future

- Whose primary responsibility is it to think about the future?
- Is the quality and quantity of their 'future time' sufficient?
- What additional resources do we need to more accurately detect 'weak signals from the future'?
- Are we investing in oracles or expecting miracles?

Trend-spotting

- Which trends are we tracking right now and why?
- Which trends have the greatest potential impact on our business model?
- How regularly are we tracking trends?
- What is the quality of our sources?

Interpretation

- How often are we renewing our market scenarios?
- How effectively do we turn trend data into actionable insights?
- What is our track record in designing accurate scenarios, e.g. accuracy of a 1-year, 2-year, 5-year, 7-year scenario?
- How regularly is the board engaging deeply in scenario discussions and their strategic implications?
- How are product development team decision-making processes demonstrably responding to emerging market insights?

You would be surprised how many companies don't track the future meaningfully. Measure for a gradually improving ability to do this and you'll be investing in zombie kryptonite.

12 Innovation Strategy: Turn It On

A checklist, action plan and resources to turn on your innovation strategy.

Innovation delivers when it's deliberate. Only then can it resist the overwhelming power of status quo business dynamics.

Whilst there is a wide range of potential 'most important' factors in an innovation strategy, my experience is that when you are starting out, these steps will help you make most progress most rapidly:

1. **Work back from the future:** Define a picture of the future and work backwards to define what needs to be true to attain it.

2. **Define money metrics:** Agree a non-negotiable financial metric that makes innovation an inevitability (e.g. 30% of revenues from products that didn't exist three years ago).

3. **Chart customer destinations:** Create an approximate customer progress trajectory and make some choices about where you want to play in relation to the average. (If this feels too new or too hard for now, skip it, read the relevant chapters, work on it in the background, and bring it in back later.)

4. **Allocate resources:** Define some innovation portfolio resourcing targets that make the financial and progress targets achievable: Bake in sufficient levels of more disruptive exploration that, left to its own devices, the organisation would otherwise avoid. Start with a 10/20/70 split of investment and then learn your way towards a more accurate allocation based on your unique context.

5. **Appoint owners and funders:** Define who is going to own and fund the innovation (central vs distributed). For example, Enhance innovation projects may be resourced locally, Explore innovation may be funded centrally, and Extend projects may be a hybrid model.

6. **Create an innovation pathway:** Appoint a 90-day team to define the necessary pathway (and dependencies) for Explore ideas to progress all the way through to Enhance status. Create target average journey times for ideas to travel across the portfolio with metrics designed to minimise friction.

7. **Create accountability:** Define how you will hold yourselves to account for what you've agreed.

A dedicated innovation strategy gives you the greatest chance of increasing and sustaining your innovation performance. We do it for every other part of our business, so why should we expect innovation to be any different?

As you work through these areas you will inevitably have to make some assumptions and, on occasion, simply start with a guess. But just as any strategy is a form of hypothesis, determine to quickly learn your way forward to a position of greater certainty.

Those who wait for certainty never get started.

13 Quick-Start Innovation Strategy Workshop

A step-by-step, pragmatic workshop to help your team create an innovation strategy.

This is a broad outline of a workshop that I use to help companies get started when a clear strategy isn't always available. Feel free to adapt it to suit your own purposes.

Preparation

- Schedule a meeting for the senior team in a month's time (ideally no more than 12 people, fewer is preferable). In my experience you'll need the best part of a day to do this justice. Don't be tempted to shortcut it – you will *definitely* regret it on the day.

- As part of the invitation provide each person with three blank postcards. On each postcard participants must write one critical milestone that the company needs to have achieved in three years' time. This is a milestone for the *whole company*, not just their function. Keep it deliberately vague at this stage (you'll see why in a moment). Also ask them to consider emerging trends and their potential impact on these milestones, too.

- Book a meeting room (ideally offsite) with a large wall that everyone can comfortably stand in front of, and that you are allowed to write on or cover with flipchart paper. (Nothing worse than the first step of your innovation strategy failing because the venue doesn't allow Blu Tac!)

The Meeting

- Copy the chart provided onto the meeting room wall.

Year 1	Year 2	Year 3

- On a separate piece of flipchart paper, write the title 'Dependencies' followed by these headings (which will act as prompts):
  - Insights
  - Products/services
  - Revenues/savings (or other value)
  - Resources
  - Relationships
  - Capabilities
  - Collaboration
  - Partnerships

- Leadership
- Decision-making
- Put the flipchart paper somewhere visible nearby.
- Invite each team member to briefly share their top three priority postcards with the group (the leader goes last). Either stick the postcards on a wall or lay them on the floor and gather around them.

A quick aside: This is a great way to reveal the true alignment of your collective assumptions and priorities, something that often remains hidden and can be a cause of team conflict. It's actually based on a technique that music industry expert Chris Parles uses to help rock bands develop business strategies.

'When people are forced to reveal what matters most, it subtly points to their values, beliefs and expectations – which are often hidden,' he says. 'That's not only a great way to create strategic alignment but also helpful in considering the cultural journey that a rock band, or any team, will need to go on together.'

Keeping the original question about milestones vague forces everyone to volunteer what matters most to them, rather than leading the conversation with revenue targets or market share. It's a useful technique in lots of settings.

Back to the workshop …

- When everyone has shared, discuss what has emerged. What stood out for people? Which factors were most common? What does that potentially reveal about you as a group? What's missing? If everyone brought financial metrics, what does that say about our true value for people and culture? If it's overly competitor-focused are we lacking in true customer focus?
- Collectively agree the top three milestones for three years' time.

- With this in mind, turn to the three-year timeline on the wall and, using the list of prompts to help, ask yourselves: 'What would need to be true for us to deliver these milestones?' Start by writing down some specific dependencies in the right-hand box and work backwards chronologically, i.e. in the example above, complete the Year 3 box first, then move to the Year 2 box, etc. (Note: you don't need to use all of the dependency prompts, only those that make sense.)

This process will help you lay the foundations of an innovation strategy in broad terms. Inevitably, you'll be making a lot of assumptions at this stage, but you've started! You've overcome the biggest barrier stopping most companies from becoming more strategic about innovation.

By the end of your session you'll have a three-year prototype innovation strategy to begin working with. Of course, you'll need to take it to the next level of detail to be actionable, but you will have made a good start.

You'll also have started building some powerful storytelling collateral that will be invaluable when you engage the rest of the business with the journey. The UK board of drinks giant Pernod Ricard framed an exercise like this as a '1,000 day journey'. It became a very useful communications hook to hang initiatives, progress and plans on to – helping employees to see how the bigger picture was continually unfolding beyond the cut-and-thrust of everyday busyness.

Typically, most leaders say that a workshop of this kind this is the best and most valuable conversation that they have had in a very long time. 'We should do this more often!' is a common refrain.

The next task is to start validating those assumptions and identifying trends coming from the future that could prevent you achieving your success outcomes. But also look out for those which could work to your advantage. Use the two resources suggested earlier to help – the business model canvas and PESTEL.

Appoint owners for the different areas that you've discussed. Agree another meeting date in 30 days' time.

The aim of that meeting will be to assess your learning and narrow your conversations to a more refined version of the strategy. At that point you're ready to start communicating with the wider company and developing action plans.

No One Leaves the Room Yet …

But here's what typically happens next.

You leave the meeting feeling energised, only to be sucked into your inbox's zombie tractor beam, and 28 days later you all find yourselves looking for excuses to postpone the meeting. Which you do. But when the momentum is lost, it rarely recovers.

Before you leave the room, devote the last 30 minutes to answering this question: 'What would need to be true for us arrive back in 30 days ready for a productive discussion?' Be deliberate, be realistic, and be accountable to one another. Design the journey that you need to succeed. (This alone is a good reason to invite a facilitator to lead the session.)

And if you're tempted to tag the discussion onto the end of your next board meeting, don't. Believe me you *won't* get to it. And even if you do, it'll only receive the dregs of your energy and the conversation will fizzle. This conversation needs its own space.

This is a good enough way to get started. It's a way into a conversation that can otherwise feel too tenuous to begin. It also helps to ground people in the reality of what it will *really* take to innovate and what people's respective leadership roles will need to be.

However, because innovation is an argument, the senior team must make this a new top three priority for themselves and design accountability measures to keep it there. I've worked with so many companies who leave the first meeting feeling invincible, only to find it was largely forgotten six months later.

Peter Drucker famously said, 'Culture eats strategy for breakfast.'

Zombies are more subtle. They quietly gnaw away at innovation strategy until you don't realise that it's missing.

If you decide to run this workshop, a template for you to modify is available here: http://www.belesszombie.com/turniton.

One last thought before we move on.

Making Innovation a 'Performance State'

'There's a 95% chance that your company will fail because of a lack of innovation and creativity,' says Andy Billings, Vice President of Profitable Creativity at EA Games. 'You *have* to be deliberate to be in the 5% and recognise that it doesn't happen overnight. It's a multi-year strategy.'

A deliberate, executive-sponsored, self-renewing innovation strategy is the single-most important factor in keeping you in that 5%.

But the great innovators take it even further.

Sure, they have a bespoke innovation strategy but that's just a focus and co-ordination necessity that serves something greater: innovation as a corporate state of mind, as an organisational performance state.

That performance state is urgent about today and hungry for tomorrow. Rather than innovation showing up as an inconvenience (as it does in most status quo-driven companies), the model is flipped. When innovation is under threat or absent, there's a healthy revolt.

Part Two
Turning on a Fast-Track Innovation Process

G reat innovation rarely happens without a clear and effective process. This section shares the practical tools used by global innovation leaders that your team can begin using today.

14 Why Zombies Hate Innovation Process

How a simple innovation process increases your competitive advantage.

One of the most important levers of influence over innovation performance is reassuringly dull. Process.

Dull, because, well, that's what process is, in contrast to innovation's reputation for spark, colour, risk and creative genius. Reassuring, because process is predictable, can be managed and measured, and consistently delivers good outcomes in every other area of organisational life.

Process makes innovation safer. Not risk free, but much more likely to deliver what you need it to.

And zombies hate a good process.

Yet in my own work only 10% of managers say that their company has a clear innovation process. Which means 90% are either winging it or doing a terrible job of communicating it.

That's bad news for organisations that are serious about their future relevance and profitability. Not only does a lack of process encourage mediocre idea generation and execution, but it makes innovation management, measurement and planning tough as there is little insight into the following:

- The ideas that people are working on across the company.
- The value that those projects are intended to create.
- Their alignment with strategy.
- Duplication of effort across the company.
- What stage ideas are at.
- What resources are allocated to which projects.
- How effective the innovation journey is (speed, quality, scope).
- What happens to 'orphan ideas' i.e. those that fall outside of their team's remit.
- And many more …

The bottom line is that without some kind of basic innovation process your company will always struggle to deliver the results that it needs.

Where to Start

It needn't be complex, but it does need to be clear. That's especially true when working with ideas that are outside the core of what we do today. Incremental ideas tend to need less process because ordinarily they form part of business-as-usual and can be delivered with existing teams and resources.

But the more disruptive the idea, the greater the chance of gear crunching, resource wasting, and executive nerve-jangling.

And given that most leaders tell me that disruptive innovation is what they want more of, a process of some kind is essential.

So what kind of process do you need for ideas outside the core?

Inside the world's most innovative companies you'll find a very similar, lightweight process that follows three essential and sequential steps:

Step 1: Finding Opportunities (Customer/Opportunity Fit)

- Identifying the right problems and opportunities
- Designing innovation questions

Step 2: Finding Solutions (Opportunity/Solution Fit)

- Generating ideas
- Assessing and selecting ideas
- Testing assumptions with experiments
- Scaling and integrating experiments

Step 3: Finding Business Models (Solution/Market Fit)

- Identifying viable business model(s)

Ideas only progress between steps when there is sufficient data to warrant it.

The best innovators balance focus and flexibility. They have a clear process that guides their innovation but they understand that, for optimum results, that process needs to have flexibility.

This section of the book will give you a behind-the-scenes look at these stages and share practical tools for quickly turning on a similar process inside your own team or organisation.

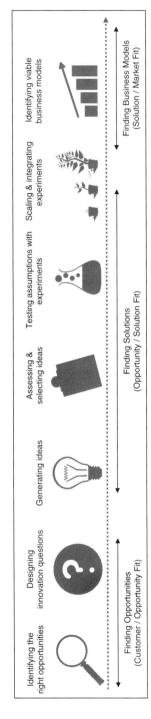

© *Elvin Turner.*

15 Starting with Insight: The Innovation Particle

De-risking innovation by focusing on what most companies miss.

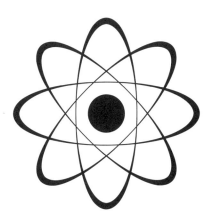

You are here

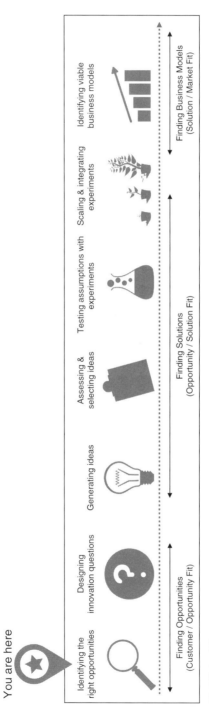

© *Elvin Turner.*

O n a scale of 1–10, how much would your customers miss your company if it disappeared tomorrow?

Aside from the headache of moving to another supplier (the thought of which often holds unhappy customers captive), would anyone *really* miss you?

You should check. Most companies overestimate the answer. According to growth expert, Sean Ellis, less than 40% means you're on shaky ground.

Why does it matter? Because even though it's a very rough test, it indicates whether a crucial element is present in your company. And that element has the power to de-risk your innovation.

The Innovation Particle

Risk aversion is the chief stifler of innovation and change inside most organisations.

Risk is the prospect of what might not happen. A picture of the future with something or someone missing.

Ironically, what's missing inside many organisations is the very thing that can reduce the paralysing power of risk aversion. I call it the 'innovation particle'.

It determines whether customers will keep buying from you, and the speed and quality of the work your employees can do for you.

In short it determines your sustainable relevance.

So what is *it*?

What They Really, Really Want

Let's take things right back to basics.

Customers buy things to *achieve outcomes*.

Sure, they are buying a product, but what the product enables is *progress – specific progress* in a *specific context.*

And progress is what the customer is *really* buying. When companies re-orient their thinking around progress rather than products, everything changes.

Why? Because unlike the fast rate of technology change in and around your products, the progress that customers crave actually *moves very slowly.* That means progress-driven innovation offers greater predictability and lower risk innovation.

The best companies have one eye bigger than the other. The lesser eyeball guides the hunt and development of great *products.* The larger obsesses over seeking better customer *progress.* They look at a customer context, understand the progress she is trying to make, identify the friction points to that progress, and set about removing them.

When progress is the centre of gravity, market vulnerability is abated. That's because a progress mindset is technology agnostic. It understands our greatest threat to tomorrow is our passion for today's technology. We cling to *our* past instead of *our customer's* future.

Progress-first confers greater predictability. Product-first courts greater vulnerability.

We'll explore this idea more in the next chapter.

Corporate Quicksand

Whilst customers buy things to make progress in a specific context, employees are tasked with making and delivering products in specific contexts. They are trying to make progress, too.

When employees' ability to deliver progress is inhibited, it shrinks company performance *and* saps their motivation. And the correlation between employee motivation and customer satisfaction is well established. A Glassdoor survey[1] showed that in a 5-star survey, every 1-star improvement in employee satisfaction predicted an increase in customer satisfaction of up to 3.2%.

Customer progress is a function of employee progress.

Company relevance is a function of both.

© *Elvin Turner.*

giffgaff, the disruptive UK mobile network operator, bases its whole strategy around the idea of 'mutuality' which draws out a progress mindset in its people.

'We didn't start with a product, we started with a community and a question,' says Ash Schofield, CEO of giffgaff. 'Our question was, How can we do mobile in a way that people would love us?'

Love is a bold ambition in an industry only narrowly ahead of banking in terms of customer trust. And it challenges one of the biggest elephants in the industry's boardrooms.

'People hate the feeling of being locked into their mobile supplier – it's like being held captive,' explains Schofield. 'If we wanted people to really love us, we had to deal with that issue head-on.'

So giffgaff has no contracts. Any one of its 3,000,000 members is free to come and go as they please. True love sets people free.

---

[1] https://www.glassdoor.com/research/studies/employee-customer-satisfaction/

Feels like a risky strategy. 'Only if you don't believe you can give members something worth sticking around for,' counters Schofield.

That baldly honest approach to strategy demands a progress-first mindset amongst its people. They are in continuous pursuit of helping their members make more progress than any other mobile provider. They have to be: no contracts means customer advocacy has to be off the charts. And it is, with three times the industry average levels of customer satisfaction.

The philosophy has led to some counter-intuitive innovations.

One was the decision to have no customer service department – which resulted in giffgaff winning industry awards for the highest levels of customer service (yes, you read that right).

'We learned that people much prefer self-service when it comes to solving their problems,' says Schofield. 'We also realized that every question imaginable has already been asked through decades of mobile phone customer service call centres. So why not turn that knowledge loose to the members themselves and help them make maximum progress in solving their problems?'

So while giffgaff provides a large amount of support advice on its website, it also facilitates member-to-member problem solving. The vast majority of problems get solved quickly and easily.

This mutuality, progress-first mindset builds deep brand advocacy amongst members in some unlikely ways.

'We once we had a major network outage,' remembers Schofield. 'One of our members turned up at our offices – not to complain but with freshly baked cakes because she thought the team might be having a bad day.' How many of your customers bake for you when your product fails?

So here's the question: To what extent are you aligning strategy, innovation and performance metrics with dimensions of meaningful customer and employee progress?

How clear are we on what progress matters most for which customers and which employees in their respective contexts?

Or as William Taylor, co-founder of *Fast Company* magazine says, 'What do we need to be the "most" of?'

The clearer we are, the more confident we can be in our innovation choices. If risk aversion is an issue in your company, the likelihood is you're not quite clear enough.

So how do we find and orientate around the *real* progress that our customers are trying to make?

16 'Why' Matters More Than 'What' with Customer Insight

Great innovation orients around specific 'units of progress' that customers want to make.

If you've ever rented a holiday property on Airbnb.com, the chances are you've shown up on a poster inside their San Francisco offices.

Don't worry, this isn't another story about hidden cameras inside apartment bedrooms. The reason you're on the wall is because Airbnb has designed its environment to help today, tomorrow and the future show up simultaneously on an innovation continuum.

It works, and anyone can do it.

That poster that you show up on is one of over 40 that distil insights that are the foundations of Airbnb's strategy. Each of these codified crown jewels captures what Airbnb calls an 'emotional moment'. These are the most critical aspects of a host's or guest's experience that can make or break their relationship with Airbnb.

You are here

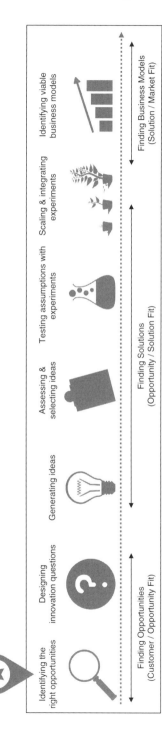

| Identifying the right opportunities | Designing innovation questions | Generating ideas | Assessing & selecting ideas | Testing assumptions with experiments | Scaling & integrating experiments | Identifying viable business models |

Finding Opportunities (Customer / Opportunity Fit)

Finding Solutions (Opportunity / Solution Fit)

Finding Business Models (Solution / Market Fit)

© *Elvin Turner.*

In other words, these emotional moments are the *units of customer progress* that matter most and that the company must deliver in order to grow. The company's ruthless focus is to eradicate any friction that shows up in any of these moments. Less friction, more progress, more customer satisfaction, more recurring revenue.

More Progress, Lower Risks

But there's more. Orientating around these units of progress also lowers the risks associated with innovation.

According to research by innovation consultancy, Strategyn, only 17% of products succeed when they follow a typical product innovation pathway. However, Strategyn claims an 86% success rate for its clients who adopt its Outcome Driven Innovation approach, which emphasises progress orientation.

Why? Because while technology and delivery mechanisms inevitably change in every industry over time, the units of customer progress don't. Or if they do, they move much more slowly and by smaller increments. The music industry is a good example.

For decades people have wanted to access and manage the music that they buy. In the early 1900s that was pretty tough. Songs were only available on awkward cylinders that were not very portable.

But over the next 100 years or so, the ability of consumers to make better progress in their ability to access and manage music radically improved; Vinyl, 8-tracks, cassettes, CDs, MP3s and then streaming technology each allowed consumers to make more progress in the dimensions of accessing and managing music.

| 1877 Phonograph cylinder | 1902 Vinyl record | 1960 Eight-track | 1963 Cassette tape | 1980 CD | 1991 MP3 | 1999 Napster | 2008 Spotify | 2011 iCloud |

© Elvin Turner.

So what? Whilst the technology changed, the desired consumer progress essentially *stayed the same*. Unfortunately, the same can't be said for the suppliers to the industry. Each technology shift created an upheaval inside every supplier, and few companies survived the transitions intact.

When those transitions occurred, customers weren't buying new products, they were buying *better progress*.

The cry of every customer, whether they articulate it verbally or not, is 'Help me make more progress in this specific context!' When another company helps them make better progress, customers vote with their wallets.

Profit Follows Progress

Another benefit of being progress-minded is profit.

In 2018, Apple's iPhone commanded just a 13% share of the smart phone market and yet captured 85% of the profit. Dyson, the company famed for its powerful vacuum cleaners and hand dryers, makes similarly impressive claims.

Break down what they are doing and you'll see that they have deeply understood the functional and emotional progress that customers are trying to make in specific contexts. Then they have identified the roadblocks to progress and focused their innovation on removing them better than anyone else. The outcome is an unmatched customer experience, deep customer loyalty and exceptionally high margins.

And Apple is well aware of inevitable sell-by dates of current technology. That's why the company wasn't afraid of the iPhone eating into the iPod's market share, or the iPad Pro eating into MacBook Air's market share. If *they* didn't do it someone else would. Might as well be Apple that builds the product, that pushes the customer progress forward, that delivers the profit, that no other company can match.

Thom Yorke, front man of the rock group Radiohead, recently summed it up well: 'You have to be prepared to torch (the business) at any moment.'

Netflix: Innovation Agnostics

One core reason for Netflix's meteoric success is its ambivalence over technology but fanaticism for customer progress.

' … one of the biggest challenges that we had, which I think is also one of the things we did very well, is recognize very early on that if we were going to be successful, we had to come up with a premise for the company that was delivery agnostic,' said Netflix co-founder Mark Randolf in 2014.[1]

'And in this case, we very, very early came up with the idea that Netflix would be about finding movies you love, which in fact has nothing to do with how you choose to receive them.'

Remember the music industry example? The jump from CD to downloads and streaming caused huge financial pain to the major record companies. I watched executive hair get greyer first-hand.

But Netflix's DNA came pre-programmed with the expectation that DVDs *would eventually fade*, and the company aligned itself accordingly. Sure, it wasn't all plain sailing, but when is the last time you rented a movie from Blockbuster?

What Kinds of Progress Are We Talking About?

Progress-thinking draws from a broad range of backgrounds but ties most neatly back to an innovation methodology called 'jobs-to-be-done'. In any context we hire products to do jobs for us, goes the theory. Those jobs are units of progress.

---

[1] https://www.bizjournals.com/sanjose/news/2014/01/08/netflixs-first-ceo-on-reed-hastings.html

There are different schools of thought on how to define and categorise progress, but at its simplest in can be thought of as 'something I want to do or feel in a given context'. But the key is less about the 'what' and more about the 'why'.

At their simplest, the most common units of progress boil down to faster, better and cheaper. Most people want more of these dimensions in most contexts, even if they aren't articulating it. But orienting around progress becomes much more powerful when we look beyond the obvious.

Consultancy Bain & Co. has created a useful graphic called 'The Elements of Value.'[2] It maps 30 elements that a customer may want more of less of in any given context. Google it, it's nicely designed and a great way to fast-track learning around the idea.

The potential list of elements is very long. In my own work I've identified some additional units of progress that build on the Bain framework. They include:

Speed – Control – Simplicity – Intimacy – Trust – Customisation – Productivity – Novelty – Status – Cost – Efficiency – Scale – Risk – Access – Convenience – Usability – Capability – Excitement – Fear – Anxiety – Joy – Empathy – Closure – Confidence – Integration – Organisation – Connection – Hassle – Quality – Choice – Information – Wellness – Hope – Self-actualisation – Nostalgia – Belonging – Credibility – Self-esteem – Fun – Wealth – Reward – Therapeutic value – Achievement – Sensory appeal – Freedom – Recognition.

Progress in Practice

So let's put this into practice with a simple example. Why does a teenage boy buy a skateboard? To learn how to skate? Partly. To be part of a tribe? Partly. To earn the right to ask out that cool girl who hangs out at the skate park? Partly. To be like my big brother whom I secretly admire? Partly.

---

[2] http://www2.bain.com/bainweb/media/interactive/elements-of-value/#

Why we buy is a science that enduring businesses have no choice but to grapple with. But it begins with motivation. What's *really* going on in that context for that teenager? What units of progress is he really trying to make – functional and emotional? What constrains that progress? What makes him anxious and stops him from clicking 'Buy'. It's less likely to be the price and more likely to be the doubt over whether he'll really be able to skate … and get the girl.

© *Richard Johnston.*

Progress-thinking applies in any context where someone is trying to achieve something. Often, it's a combination of subtle factors that may feel too vague to measure (e.g. hope, connection, fear). But consider it an innovation challenge to identify specific progress and a specific way of measuring improvements in that progress. It's a powerful asset to own in a world of shrinking sources of competitive advantage.

In 2018, IKEA published its 'Life at Home' report.[3] Its global research programme identified five common elements that constitute a sense of 'home' for people: belonging, privacy, security, comfort and ownership.

Each of these are area of progress that matter deeply to IKEA's customer base and therefore become platform of innovation in their own right. Each can be explored in more subtle shades, but knowing that these elements matter more than anything to customers is a firm foundation for innovation.

The better we understand the 'why' the deeper and more valuable our insight becomes, and the more likely we'll develop more magnetic customer experiences than the competition. And those experiences extend well beyond the product: advertising, sales, purchase, installation, support and beyond all benefit when designed from the perspective of progress.

So how do we find the progress?

---

[3]https://lifeathome.ikea.com/about-life-at-home/our-research/

17 Working with Customer 'Progress' Insights

Do you make awesome products or awesome users? Your answer changes everything.

Careful customer observation and interviewing can reveal the underlying units of progress that matter most to customers. Then it's possible to create a linear narrative that shows two things: the overall progress a customer is trying to make in a specific context, and the individual steps of progress he/she is trying to make along the way.

Here's a real-life example that formed part of a TEDx talk that I gave in the UK called, 'The Secret Life of Great Ideas.'[1]

When I was 15 years old, I stabbed the palm of my left hand trying to separate two frozen burgers. Home alone, I dropped the burgers and three simultaneous thoughts went through my mind: Ouch! That's a lot of blood! Have I just given myself mad cow disease? (This was the height of the Creutzfeldt-Jakob disease crisis in the UK.)

---

[1] http://bit.ly/BLZTED (The first 30 seconds has an audio glitch, but it's fine after that.)

You are here

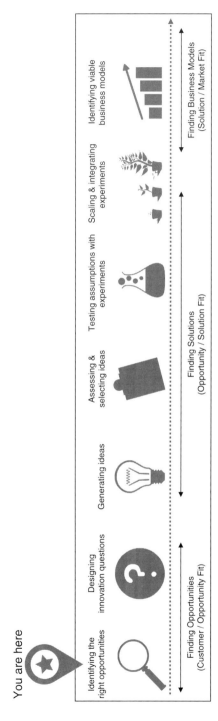

© *Elvin Turner.*

So we have a specific context: a teenager at home alone with a bleeding, possibly fatally infected hand. Perfect. Kind of.

What progress do I want to make in that context? Stop the bleeding, stop the pain, and understand my chances of dying from CJD (come on, I'm a teenager, we gotta have *some* dramatics in here!).

What solutions are available to me in that kitchen context? Paper towels? Dish cloth? Band Aids (or plasters as we call them in the UK)? Band Aids will help me make maximum progress in that context. Great, let's find them.

Over the next two minutes I create a marvellous set for TV murder show: blood trails criss-crossing the kitchen floor and crimson handprints on every cupboard and work surface. My frantic hunt for plasters finally ends with an old box stuffed in a drawer.

It takes another two minutes to one-handedly fumble through the box, find the right size, open the plaster and stick it over the wound.

Progress made, panic over.

Aren't plasters wonderful?

Well, maybe. How was my experience through the progress journey? Could I have made more progress, faster and with less pain and anxiety at any stage? Or every stage?

Typically, if we were to present this scenario to a plaster manufacturer, the progress improvements would have been looked at through the lens of the existing product: 'Customer insight reveals that we need to make the plasters easier to open. Let's get to work.'

Nothing wrong with that. Incremental improvements to today's products are important.

And it stands to reason: we are a plaster manufacturer. The system is designed and incentivised to make plasters efficiently. It's our core capability so we need to innovate in that space. I agree. Mostly.

But if we look back across the journey, the plaster stopped the bleeding, but it didn't help me make progress with my pain, help me understand whether I actually needed stitches (or have actually done more harm than good with a plaster), or relieved my anxiety about mad cow disease. All important dimensions of progress for me in that home-alone context. The reality is, the plaster-only journey is still fraught with friction that fights against me making the holistic progress that I want to make.

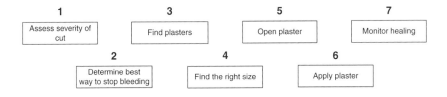

Let's present the same scenario to a tech healthcare start-up. They aren't thinking about plasters. They are thinking about the question, 'How can we stop this boy's bleeding as fast as possible, reduce the pain, help him understand whether he needs to visit a doctor, and reduce his anxiety about contracting mad cow disease?'

If they can help make me progress in *all* of those dimensions (not just stop the bleeding), the overall outcome for me is significantly better than a plaster. And if my experience of having the bleeding stopped exceeds that of the plaster ... remind me again why we need plasters?

The start-up guys have a different starting point: progress before product. Having deeply understood the progress they start to explore solutions with no affiliation to any specific technology. They are agnostic, free to imagine and explore the best possible solution, unlike the plaster innovation team which is somewhat stuck to plasters.

They start to wonder … What if there was a box that you could put your hand into, that:

- Scans your injury and immediately sends a copy to your doctor.
- Administers an antiseptic and anaesthetic spray while assessing the image, and makes a recommendation about the need for a hospital visit.
- Plays soothing music accompanied by the fragrance of lavender and a voice encouraging you to slow your breathing.
- Sprays a quick-setting gel accurately to cover the wound and stop the bleeding.
- Assesses the wound for potential sources of infection by way of a sensor in the gel, and monitors the healing progress.

All within 30 seconds.

That messy, painful seven-step journey just became a one-step process with a lot more progress in all dimensions.

Should they build it? Most of the technology already exists, so it's likely to be feasible. But viable? Who knows? Desirable? Well, if we find a context where people cut their hands a lot and need rapid healing (working inside a 2-star Michelin restaurant kitchen?), there might be a market.

But that all comes later. At this stage, we're just trying to find the progress that matters without the constraints of any specific product needing to be the answer. Like plasters.

Inside many organisations, what we do today blinds us from what the customer wants tomorrow.

It's not a case of either/or. Progress *and* product innovation matter.

But when we understand the desired customer progress, the specific context of where and when that progress takes place, and the barriers to that context, we're in a strong position to focus innovation activity accurately. Then we can ask, 'What combination of technologies, business models, partnerships, etc. would deliver most progress?'

Your Customers' Progress

So what about your customers' progress journeys? How do you uncover them? I propose a quick-start approach at the end of this chapter, but if you're interested in specific interviewing techniques, I recommend that you take a look at www.jobstobedone.org where you'll find a useful online course called 'Mastering Jobs-to-be-done', developed by experts Chris Spiek and Bob Moesta.

These units of progress can then be mapped, prioritised and turned into progress-driven innovation questions that help align strategy with resources.

If, like Airbnb, all of your employees deeply understand the underlying progress customers are trying to make in specific contexts, you stand a greater chance of developing products and services that keep you relevant both now and in the future.

Awesome Products vs Awesome Users

Here's where it starts to get interesting.

'Ultimately, people are interested in being a better version of themselves,' says Alan Klement, jobs-to-be-done expert and author of *When Coffee and Kale Compete*.

This can crunch against the way product development happens inside many organisations, where innovation is focused on *feature* upgrades, more than *user* upgrades.

Think about our girlfriend-hunting pre-skater boy. Is he more interested in a skateboard with faster trucks or a skateboard that comes with free lessons that help him do three tricks inside 10 days?

Speed of travel might matter to him later; but in his specific context, it's the *speed of progress* towards his ultimate goal that matters most. In his mind, it's a better version of himself that gets the girl. The skateboard is secondary in many ways.

In that case, *user* innovation should always precede *product* innovation.

'Don't make a better (X), make a better *user* of (X),' says Kathy Sierra in her excellent book *Badass: Making Users Awesome*.

So ask yourself: 'To what extent are your users *better* than the competition's users? Do your products help them make more, better progress than the competition?' When we see others doing great things, we want to know how. *Your brand* needs to be the how. Your products are often just a means to that end.

Predicting Potential Progress

With a progress mindset, companies can allocate resources against an innovation portfolio that is in pursuit of ever-greater progress. It's important to start with a picture of reality.

How much important progress are your customers currently experiencing from you, versus your competition?

Is it rising, static or falling relative to the competition?

And how much more progress will you need to deliver in the future to remain relevant, and by when?

All tricky questions, but tracking against these indicators pulls innovation forward in a healthy, customer-focused pursuit.

Pick a customer and ask, 'Over a three-year period, what increase in important customer progress should we be aiming to deliver to maintain our relevance?'

In other words, what should customers be able to achieve in three years that they can't achieve today?

Working back from that outcome, what would the rate of improvement need to be and how could we turn that into measurable milestones?

Let's go back to our romance-hunting pre-skater. Why is he considering buying a skateboard? To make progress in multiple dimensions, but most importantly to get the attention of a particular girl at the skate park. Achieving a level of competence on a skateboard is the pathway to that progress.

So how could a skateboard manufacturer help him achieve a 'Nollie Shove It' trick (I'm so down with the kids) in an average of two hours rather than the usual four hours? Speed-to-girlfriend is the ultimate metric he is tracking, but speed-to-Nollie-Shove-It is an important interim measure. How could the skateboard company increase his velocity in both dimensions?

What about you? Make it standard practice for teams to identify an important customer progress metric and design an innovation question that focuses their attention on the improved customer experience.

How do you know which metric to pick? This is likely to be a process of trial and error as this is an inexact science. But starting retrospectively can be helpful.

With your team, draw a historical timeline of your market and plot the major transitions in progress performance and technology. What underlying patterns can you spot? What has been the average rate of increasing customer progress in the most important dimensions?

Draw that average as an approximate curve and extend it five years from today. Are your products currently on track to deliver that progress? What about your competition?

Think back to our music industry example.

1877	1902	1960	1963	1980	1991	1999	2008	2011
Phonograph cylinder	Vinyl record	Eight-track	Cassette tape	CD	MP3	Napster	Spotify	iCloud

© *Elvin Turner.*

The progress that customers want is to access and manage their music any time, any place. Pick a task that involves making progress in those dimensions, say, arranging the music for a wedding party. Then dial back along the timeline and walk through the process of achieving that task.

How long would it take? What are the major difficulties of music access and management? Then, walk forward through the transitions and see what improvements there would have been in speed and ease. Can you spot patterns, cycles, progressions, rates of change, consistent precursors to change?

As we said earlier, customer progress can take many forms and it is likely that some of them have never been meaningfully tracked in your industry. So, design bespoke metrics to make this work for you. How valuable would that be, both as a means of directing your innovation and as a source of industry competitive advantage?

It's hard to predict the future of product development, but we can often predict the *direction* of progress.

In a standard corporate context, this process will often feel uncomfortable. It's an inexact science using lots of fingers in the wind. Sometimes you just have to guess and see where it takes you, and learn your way forward.

But start with what you can and learn your way towards metrics that have most meaning for you. It's going to take some work and patience, but your future will thank you for it.

Wait a Minute

'Isn't this just customer insight dressed in a different costume?' you may be wondering. I had the same suspicion when I first encountered this thinking. But then I realised that for many of my clients who spend a lot of money on customer research, innovation was flat and risk aversion was high.

The reality that I encounter is that product development is rarely well aligned with genuine customer progress. Customer insight often gets watered down or adjusted to better align with an internally driven political need. Or just sloppy process. Then developers end up building products that miss the mark with customers.

I recently encountered this firsthand. A division of a global technology company was struggling to maintain market share. The company's recent products had flopped due to some fairly fundamental flaws. The customer insight reports showed what was needed, but by the time a sanitised version of the insight reached the engineers, they were asked to develop something slightly off-base. There's nothing more deflating for an engineering team than building something no one ever wanted.

'Why not just let the engineers meet the customers?' I suggested to the vexed leader. He looked at me incredulously. 'Every hour away from their desks is an hour of wasted productivity,' he replied. 'And besides, you can't put engineers in front of customers. They have no idea how to communicate.'

Better to let them keep building that stuff no one wants, I guess.

Flexible Progress

Finally, be flexible with this approach. Some categories of progress are easier to measure than others, but the effort required doesn't mean that they should be overlooked. If fact one might argue these are areas that have the *strongest* case for establishing progress data benchmarks as a basis of deep competitive advantage.

For example, consider a company that sells wedding photo albums. Nostalgia will be one of the key units of customer progress that drives sales. With that in mind, how might that company measure the increasing ability of customers to feel nostalgic towards weddings that they have attended, say over the last 20–30 years? And how about other contexts? What approaches are other industries using to increase feelings of nostalgia and what could we learn?

We may need to devise our own metrics to track something like this with a combination of subjective and objective measures. And just like scenario planning, it'll be an approximation. But it's worth it. If you own proprietary data that reveals likely future trajectories you can make some powerful choices about where to play and how to win.

So before starting any innovation project, use these principles to design a question most likely to deliver the level of progress you need now.

Then design some future-focused sibling questions that allow you to build a greater level of predictability into more ambitious innovation projects.

Castles Made of Sand?

So, is your organisation more interested in making *awesome users* or making and selling *products*?

Are you trying to create a generation of Jimi Hendrixes or persuade more people to buy your guitars?

Of course, both matter, but which is the dog and which is the tail?

If you care most about the former, the latter is more likely to be an inevitability. It's not so certain the other way around.

18 Framing Great Opportunities

How to identify the right problems and opportunities.

Ideas give innovation a bad name.

Depending on whose research you believe, somewhere between 60–90% of new products fail.

A study[1] by innovation guru Alberto Savoia found that new ideas tend to fail for one of three main reasons:

1. Building the right thing, in the right way, but with the **wrong** launch.

2. Building the right thing, in the **wrong** way, with the right launch.

3. Building the **wrong** thing from the start.

The latter is well known to be the biggest reason for start-up failures. My experience is the majority of more disruptive corporate ideas fall into the same category. Or were in the right ballpark, but missed the subtleties of the problem that *really* needed solving.

---

[1] www.jamasoftware.com/blog/f-l-o-p-analysis-new-products-fail-market/

You are here

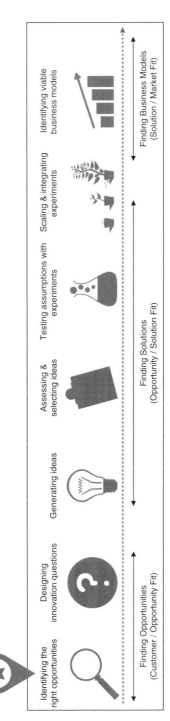

© *Elvin Turner.*

One of a zombie's favourite innovation trapdoors is rushing people into brainstorms prematurely. So many ideas fail because a team was answering the wrong question from the start. And the further we move from the core business, the truer this becomes. 'To assume makes an ass out of u and me', as the saying goes.

Start a Charter

So how do you ensure that you're working on a great laser-focused problem or opportunity? One technique used by many organisations, including Cisco, is to start with a 'project charter' that clearly articulates the 'why' of the problem or opportunity.

This allows a team to define reality as they see it today: to declare all of the assumptions that they are making about the problem. This provides a powerful touchstone of clarity to return to throughout the project. This is *really* useful for two reasons:

1. **Rabbit-hole avoidance:** Before any course of action, we can come back to the charter to check that we are actually answering the question. It's really easy to chase 'good ideas' on the spur of the moment that take you one degree off course from the problem you're trying to solve.

   When you're clear on the 'why' of a project, you can be clearer on the 'why not' of ideas that try to take you off-piste.

2. **Revising the question:** As you start to test ideas later, you'll usually learn that you're not actually answering the right question after all. Taking that learning and adjusting the charter is a really healthy process. It allows you to readjust your focus, determine whether the project still makes strategic sense (i.e. Has the potential return for this project now become too low?), and reshape the question as appropriate to guide future development.

   This is one of the characteristics of high-performing innovation teams: the charter gives them clear but flexible boundaries to work within which can provide an ongoing reality check about whether a project should persist or end. Otherwise it can be too easy to keep finding justifications for ideas that feel exciting but should really be killed off so that resources can be reallocated to something more valuable.

So how do you create a charter? I've created a template that you can amend at www.belesszombie.com/turniton.

But before we look at some principles to apply, an important sanity check. Very often when I help coach innovation programmes, a team will report back that they've found another team elsewhere in the organisation working on the same thing. This is 3–4 months into the project. Save everyone a lot of wasted effort and motivation by checking first!

Charter Principles

Start with Strategy

If we're not working on something that contributes to strategy in some way, why are we doing it? It's usually easy to justify any idea in some roundabout way. But the more disruptive your focus, having a clear line back to strategy is really important for two reasons:

1. Usually companies have limited innovation resources so aligning them with what matters most is a smart future investment.
2. Later down the line, if your idea needs investment, you're much more likely to get it if you can demonstrate a clear alignment with strategic objectives.

For every problem or opportunity that presents itself, clarify its strategic alignment. If you have several simultaneous issues, rank them in your team according to their strategic alignment and priority.

Why This, Why Us, Why Now?

Many teams that I meet are often unclear as to why they are working on a particular problem. 'Just following orders' is a common refrain amongst product engineers. Not great for engagement.

When you begin an innovation project, give your team as much context as possible:

- Why does this problem/opportunity matter?
- To whom?
- What factors have led to the current problem/opportunity
- Which outcome 'needle' are we trying to move and by how much?
- Why does it need addressing now vs in six months' time?
- Why are we being asked to work on it?
- Who else is involved?
- What timescales are we working to?

This will help the team connect with the purpose and value of the project from the start and improve their chances of deeper engagement throughout.

Going further, state how much you understand about the problem/opportunity space that you will be exploring:

- What are the root causes of the issue? (Using the '5 Whys' or Fishbone questioning techniques can be useful starting points to identify root causes. There are more sophisticated tools, but start here if this is new to you.)
- What important cause-and-effect dynamics do we know about in this issue?
- What ripple effects or unintended consequences could occur from a change in this issue?

- What don't we know? Whose input do we need?
- Is there a better problem to solve? Is this question a subset of a bigger/better one?

As we saw earlier with the plaster example, one useful approach to exploring these issues is to map out the stages of any existing process that occurs in your problem/opportunity context.

Articulating what happens at each stage and why, and then identifying 'friction' in the process helps to flush out more specific problems to solve.

As you go, ask the question: 'What progress is the user trying to make in this context?' Often the process impedes progress – perhaps it needs to be two steps, not five, for example.

The more forensic you can be, the more likely you'll zone in on the best possible framing for the innovation project. But put a time-frame around this piece of work according to the potential complexity and familiarity of the issues that you are working with.

Basic Instincts

Great products aren't just functional. They are deliberately emotional, too. They plumb depths of customer connection that pure logic can rarely reach. And yet logic often wears the trousers in product development.

To balance the logical and emotional needs of the entire customer experience, it can be very useful to have an agreed marker at the start of the project that unites them. It also helps put a name to the gut feeling we have about whether an idea is on track.

'The better you know your customer, the more accurate your guiding instincts can be during development,' says Gemma Metheringham, former creative director for women's fashion brand Karen Millen.

'A simple question guided all of our creative reviews at Karen Millen: "Is it remarkable?"' says Metheringham. 'Because we deeply understood the overall brand experience that our customers wanted, we knew that was a key question. "Does it look remarkable?" "Does it feel remarkable?" "Will it make me *feel* remarkable?"'

Often, a product idea can make sense logically, but somehow we know there's something not quite right about it. Defining a guiding instinct for a project that encapsulates the functional and emotional experience that customers will want, is a powerful guiding light.

Of course, you still need to test ideas with customers to avoid building from a wonky instinct. But when you are pursuing an outcome that demands something deeply original, and you don't know what the final product needs to be, a guiding instinct can be very helpful along the way.

So, as a team, consider the customer progress – functionally and emotionally, and create a guiding instinct question that aligns your development journey with the required customer brand experience.

When you feel that you've adequately framed the opportunity on your charter, it's time to design a question to focus and catalyse what happens next . . . .

19 Catalytic Questions

Designing questions that provoke focused, creative eruptions.

Most brainstorms leave participants underwhelmed and frustrated. Bold ideas are shut down. Small ideas aren't edgy enough. Variations on old ideas come out yet again. And the 'cool' ideas don't actually solve the problem.

We'll talk more about developing better creative dynamics later. But one of the main causes of a low-voltage brainstorm is a dimly lit starting point.

The saying 'we get what we ask for' was never truer for innovation. One of the most powerful tools for predictably increasing creativity is designing great questions.

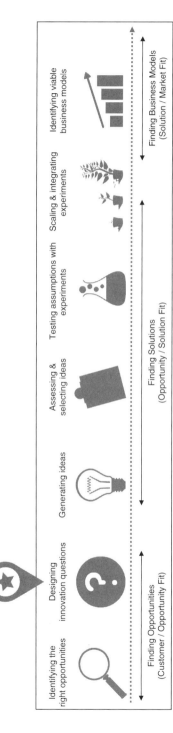

© *Elvin Turner.*

In fact, I believe that great question design is a genuine source of competitive advantage. Here's why.

When 'catalytic questions' emerge, a sequence of five important innovation outcomes is activated:

1. **Increased strategic alignment** – We provoke ideas whose intended outcomes clearly tie back to strategy.

2. **More effective outcomes for managers** – We calibrate idea generation to deliver the most appropriate kinds of ideas.

3. **Less frustrating brainstorms for participants** – Everyone is clear on the kind of ideas that we are pitching for, yet we have creative freedom to imagine wide-ranging solutions.

4. **More creative ideas** – We break the stupefying power of the status quo over our imaginations.

5. **Short-term and long-term alignment** – We can define some commercial parameters of innovation both now and in the future.

Designing 'Catalytic Questions'

There are three main steps to designing a catalytic question: defining the outcome, identifying assumptions and flipping reality.

STEP 1. Define the Outcome

Creativity is the design of cause and effect.

The clearer we are on the effect we need to create, the more likely we'll generate the ideas to cause it.

One of the world's biggest video games companies, Electronic Arts, has a great way of approaching this.

'If creating a game is like keeping an elastic band stretched, you need to know the optimum stretch between crazy, creative, imaginative inspiration on the one hand and predictable, profitable, sane development on the other,' says Andy Billings, Vice President of Profitable Creativity at Electronic Arts.

'One of the tools that we use to help us consistently deliver profitable, creative work is to help the development team understand what we call "Creative X" of the game – the centre of the experience that we're trying to create for customers. This provides a high level of shared strategic clarity and ensures that we're as efficient as possible in our common pursuit of creative problem solving.'

So, to start the process of designing a catalytic question, begin at the end and start to define your Creative X:

- What actually needs to happen because of our idea?
- What specific progress do we need to create?
- For whom?
- In what context?
- In what manner?
- With what constraints?

For example, 'Customers bail out of the buying process when they wait too long. They need to complete the checkout process much faster but not too fast otherwise they will worry that security is being compromised.'

Metrics Matter Framing the progress with a number or metric can be really helpful here for three reasons.

First, it forces you to think clearly about the real business outcome that's needed, rather than simply 'be better'. If the strategy requires a 25% increase in performance in a specific area within 12 months, the ambition of the question needs to align accordingly. This leads to sharper innovation all round.

Second, it helps managers deal in reality *personally*. A broad question can tempt a sponsor to pick low-hanging ideas that generally tick the box. A specific question with a number sharpens our focus on what would need to be true to achieve it, including the personal risk associated with pursuing an idea beyond the brainstorm. Better to enter the brainstorm with a prepared mindset than let it creep up on you during the session.

So when considering the design of the catalytic question, consider issues such as:

- What degree of disruption and potential risk is the right question likely to require?
- How comfortable are you with that level of disruption?
- To what extent is your comfort level going to constrain the brainstorm's outcomes?
- If there's a mismatch, what would need to be true for you to sponsor more disruptive ideas in the session?
- What resources are you prepared to commit or fight for (amount and type) for ideas that emerge?
- What level of confidence do you have in your team to develop and deploy bigger ideas (current capacity, energy, team dynamics, capabilities, etc.)?
- What potential organisational and political issues may constrain your ability to execute?

Thirdly, having clarity on these issues is also likely to reduce frustration for brainstorm participants. When outcomes and risk levels aren't declared, we assume that anything goes. That leads to 'wrong' ideas being shut down without justification. When everyone understands the boundaries, the process is more enjoyable and productive.

Defining reality early always leads to a smoother journey later.

For example, a 5% increase in checkout speed might set the expectation amongst participants for incremental ideas that are unlikely to require significant risk or resources.

A 100% increase, on the other hand, would signal a desire for ideas that significantly challenge the current way of doing things.

Customer Progress	Enhance	Extend	Explore
Reduce checkout time	How could customers checkout 50% faster?	How could customers checkout 100% faster?	How could we remove the checkout stage?

Every situation is different, but choose the metric that makes most sense for you. It'll make a huge difference to the overall performance and outcome of the creative session.

Even if it's somewhat made up, just start with something realistic. You can always adjust it later. Better still, ask the team what level of progress you collectively believe is required and start from there.

Sometimes Simple Is Enough   If you're looking for quick and simple incremental ideas, turning your Creative X into a question might be sufficient: *'How could we increase the customer checkout speed by 5% without damaging confidence about security?'*

However, if you need something more disruptive, keep moving…

STEP 2: Identify Assumptions

When we deliberately begin to mess with the 'rules of the game' – those things that hold the status quo in position – we start to uncover some more provocative questions that spawn even sparkier ideas.

So think about the way that the problem is currently solved. What factors must be in place in order for the solution to work effectively e.g. pricing, resources, capabilities, legislation, technology, traditions, habits, expectations, distribution, relationships, etc.?

Which factors have the greatest influence? Which ones would it feel impossible to tamper with? Make a list.

STEP 3: Flip Reality

Now turn your list into deliberately provocative questions.

You're trying to hot-wire your creativity by disrupting the status quo conventions that constrain our thinking without us realising. The more we shake them, the more we can question their validity with greater objectivity.

Here are some examples of variables that can be helpful to include when designing questions:

- **Scale:** Less, more, none, heavier, lighter / x10 / x100 / x10%
- **Speed:** faster, slower, static, reverse
- **Control:** more, less, total, none, shared
- **Simplicity:** harder, easier, fewer, impossible
- **Relationship:** more virtual/more intimate, more emotion/more logic/more 'magic'
- **Format:** Digital/analogue/hybrid

I've worked with a number of organisations in the music industry in recent few years. Using this approach some great catalytic questions emerged, some of which provoked ideas that are currently being explored:

- How could music make you healthier?
- How could our profitability increase by 100% if people paid less for streaming services?
- How could deaf people listen to music?
- How could we predict 50% of our hits without listening to music?
- How could people listen to less music but feel like they've listened to more?
- How could robots consume music?
- What would edible music be?

This approach can make some people uncomfortable. It can feel as if we're not dealing in reality; it potentially challenges the future value of the core capabilities of people in the room; it might provoke ideas in the brainstorm that seem … plain stupid.

But hold your nerve. Great ideas often emerge when we engineer the deliberate collision of elements that have never previously met.

Beyond the Obvious

Following these steps will definitely improve your innovation performance. But sometimes the most logically extrapolated question isn't always the best route.

A company based in a high-rise tower block was receiving increasing numbers of complaints from its staff. The wait for the elevator was far too long first thing in the morning and people were complaining that it was impacting productivity.

The company looked into the price of a new elevator. Out of the question.

But then someone took another look at the problem. Was the speed of the elevator the real problem? He wasn't so sure, so asked for permission to run an experiment.

The following Monday morning, employees arrived at the elevators to find full-length mirrors installed throughout the lobby. The number of complaints evaporated overnight.

So, what was the real question to answer? 'How can we increase the speed of the elevators?' or 'How can we reduce people's boredom while they wait for the elevator?'

Both are right but digging a little deeper can often root out a better question to answer.

As advertising legend Rory Sutherland said, sometimes it's important to interpret what customers said *laterally* rather than *literally*.[1]

So choose to become designers of great catalytic questions. Reward the best questions of the year. Make sure that everyone in your team is clear on the specific questions that matter most.

I once read that 80% of ideas emerge outside the context of a meeting. If people are always clear on the biggest questions that the company needs to answer, the greater the chances of creative lightning bolts striking more frequently, wherever they are.

---

[1] https://www.entrepreneur.com/article/331260

20 Hot Love

Creating fertile ground for ideas to breed.

Whilst idea development is a journey of continuous iteration and evolution, ideas have to be conceived and born somewhere.

The majority of ideas don't happen in the context of meetings. But sooner or later it's helpful to have some kind of gathering to either catalyse ideas or take them to the next stage.

For me, brainstorms are a form of speed dating: insights, facts, feelings, questions, dreams all colliding and looking for a spark of life.

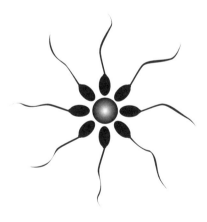

Yet brainstorms, like speed dating events, are loved and loathed in equal measure: personality preferences, process quality, environment, timing, participants, and politics all play their part in the success of a brainstorm.

The next few chapters include a collection of tips that I've accrued in a wide range of environments covering the before, during and after of a great creative session.

21 Preparing for Greatness

How to supercharge your team's creative prowess before anyone walks into the room.

G reat creative sessions are often a function of what happened before anyone walked into the meeting room.

Sure, the process and mechanics of the brainstorm have a big impact on the quality of ideas that will emerge. But if your brainstorms need to pack a bigger creative punch, there's a little bit of groundwork that it's worth considering in advance.

There are some key ingredients that you can adjust according to the outcome though, many of which relate to the kind of question that you're aiming to answer. The more complex or ambiguous the question, the more likely you'll need to mix up the approach.

1. Social Dynamics

I regularly ask people who have attended brainstorms what they feel distinguishes the great from the gruesome. There's a long list of answers but at the heart of them all is one single problem: people.

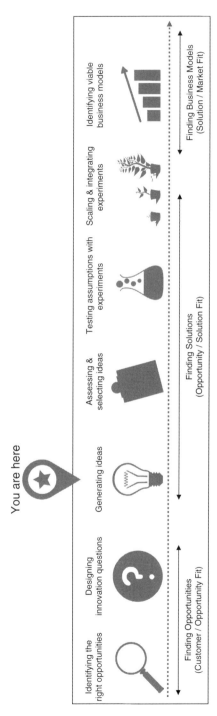

© *Elvin Turner.*

Loudmouths, naysayers, the shame of suggesting something 'stupid', speed of the brainstorm process regardless of thinking style, social pressure to spontaneously give birth to genius ... These are just a few of the creative constipators that fight against great ideas in most brainstorms.

So how do we re-engineer the process so that we don't get in the way of ourselves?

Separated at Birth   There's one simple thing that you can do to radically increase the chances of great ideas emerging from everyone in the group: separate the creative thinking part.

Share the question that you're trying to solve several days in advance of the session and ask people to arrive with their best 2–5 ideas.

Deceptively simple, but creatively a game changer. Why?

Giving people the opportunity to develop ideas in their own time and at their own speed (with no fear of judgement), does several things:

- It overcomes almost all of the social barriers that prevent people from sharing ideas in group settings (you're on your own, after all).

- It reduces social anxiety, which increases the likelihood of better creativity.

- It gives time for people with more reflective thinking styles to develop ideas at their own pace, rather than having a blank mind when forced to magic-up ideas in the moment.

- It empowers the introverts. Rather than hiding from the cut-and-thrust of a typical brainstorm, introverts arrive at the session on a level playing field with the extroverts: everyone brings their best ideas.

- It allows time for incremental idea development, meaning people have more time to mull on and refine the ideas before the brainstorm. That said, counsel people not to develop things too far or it can be hard for them to break their emotional attachment to off-base ideas later.

- It stops us being overwhelmed with the tidal wave of Post-it® notes that often breaks across a brainstorm, making it hard to prioritise which ideas matter most.

So, in advance of any creative session, get clarity on the kind of outcomes that you really want, and genuinely give people time to develop ideas in advance.

Your charter is a great tool at this stage. It defines reality and provides a narrow question for everyone to answer.

Intuit, the renowned innovator and maker of Quick Books software, uses a similar tool called '7-to-1'. Team members are each tasked with bringing seven ideas to a creative session. That creates a level of stretch for most people who can usually come up with a handful of ideas quite easily. But seven forces you to think beyond the obvious.

99 Ways to Tell a Story If you've never seen Matt Madden's book *99 Ways to Tell a Story: Exercises in Style* you must. It is a brilliant resource for seeing how a single idea can be spun in 99 different directions. Buy your team a copy and encourage them to spend five minutes flicking through it before a creative session. I guarantee that it'll hotwire their imaginations.

2. Who to Invite

Who is in the room has a huge impact on the creative output of a brainstorm. Having perfect harmony is rare, but where it is in your power, be selective about who takes part.

So, who should get an invitation?

First, we need to take a step back. I often get asked whether *anyone* can be creative. My answer is unequivocally yes. However, we each have strengths that lend themselves better to different parts of the innovation process, and we need all of them.

Some people are great at dreaming up outlandish ideas; others spot connections between ideas and improve them; others ask brilliant questions that can take an idea off into an even better direction; others incisively point out why an idea can't work.

The starting point to forming healthy creative teams is helping people see two things:

First, that innovation has discreet stages – identifying an insight, framing a question, generating ideas, choosing ideas, testing ideas, and then scaling ideas.

Second, help them see which stages their individual strength will add most value.

As well as affirming everyone that they can be a valuable part of the creative process, it helps to take the politics and emotion out of who shows up at different stages. We can objectively agree that in the very early stages of idea generation we need divergent thinkers, and as we start to interrogate and select ideas, we need those whose strength is seeing the potential roadblocks.

But what unites people is an ability to see what's missing. In the early stages it's seeing an idea to fill an opportunity space; in the latter stages it's seeing a hurdle that's in the way of making it happen.

There are many profiling tools that can help you here, including Team Dimensions, the GC Index, and the Nine Innovation Roles.

Avoiding Creative Elitism   That said, I would treat this as a rule of thumb. Shutting critical people out of early brainstorms forever, for example, doesn't send an especially collaborative message and can lead to a feeling of creative elitism.

Simply helping people understand their strengths and being clear about the kind of input we are looking for at different stages can be enough to allow more people can take part. We just ask everyone to play by the rules of the stage and reserve the right to gently help one another recognise when we are moving beyond them.

So, back to the original question: Who should get an invite? It depends on the stage of the process, the outcomes the stage needs, and the mix of capabilities and experience that are most likely to provide that outcome. Be deliberate, be objective and help your team recognise their respective creative strengths.

Finally, think beyond your team. The best ideas tend to emerge at the intersection of disciplines. So be creative with who you invite from outside of your team. Experiment with different combinations of people and see what emerges.

But also invite those who will have a role in delivering the idea later in the journey. Their engagement and support will be higher if they are part of the idea's genesis, and they will also be able to identify blockers and opportunities that your team is unaware of.

Inviting outsiders also has an important side benefit. It helps us to overcome the bias that we can have towards our own ideas. Someone who has nothing to lose is more likely to question a leader's idea than a direct report. And research shows that the more senior you are, the more likely you are to overestimate the value of your ideas.[1]

3. Brainstorm Length: Sprints and Marathons

How long should a brainstorm be? Ideally, we should always be munching on progress-driven questions in the background, so in a

---

[1] https://journals.aom.org/doi/abs/10.5465/amj.2017.0438

sense, collective, passive brainstorming should be continuous. But what about dedicated time to work on a specific question?

A simple question looking for an incremental improvement to a well-understood issue may only need a 30-minute creative sprint to arrive at some suitable ideas to explore. A deeply complex scientific problem may need a 30-year of evolution of "slow hunches" to incubate and iterate forward, to borrow Stephen Johnson's term.

Above my desk I have an ancient, scrunched Post-it® that reads, "Solve hard problems". These tend to be the ones that create most value and often need more time. They are creative marathons, not inspiration sprints. And it's this order of problems that deliver the disruptive innovation that companies crave more of.

Two-Brainstorms Rule These days, as a minimum I recommend that teams don't have one brainstorm but two, creating space for ideas to brew into something more interesting in the interim period. Great creativity needs incubation time. It's how our brains are wired so we might as well agree with our biology instead of fighting against it. The chapter called 'The Five-Day Brainstorm' describes a process that's worth experimenting with in this area.

4. Timing and Energy

Better ideas tend to show up when people are engaged.

Unfortunately, creativity isn't something most people can just switch on. If you're tired, stressed, on a deadline, or worried about your job, your personal chemistry makes it less likely that great ideas are going to show up.

Your ability to schedule brainstorms with team dynamics and commitments in mind (inside and outside of work) will pay dividends in the quality of creative outputs you generate.

Most teams treat this as a nice-to-have. 'Just get a date in the diary and we'll crank something out.' I understand the diary pressure that most people are under. Yet with some intentional focus, teams can help one another understand the optimum timing and rhythm of team creative sessions.

Also, the more fun people have, the better your outcomes will be. Some people hate being told this as it makes creativity seem frivolous, fluffy, cheesy and slightly awkward. This is *business* after all! You can disagree with the decades of scientific proof if you wish, but side-stepping fun as another ingredient to help discover big ideas is a lost opportunity.

Be more human.

Host your brainstorm at a time when most people are most likely to show up with maximum energy levels. This needs some deliberate advance planning but can make a huge difference to outcomes, especially when working on higher-order questions.

5. Location

Your office environment subtly reinforces the status quo: the 'rules of the game' that silently convince us that new ideas will never work.

As far as possible, leave your building for idea generation. A lot of research has been done on environmental factors that can boost creativity, especially being in nature. It's worth a web search. My experience is that better ideas emerge when you simply leave the mothership. The status quo tractor beam has less influence even if you go to the coffee shop next door.

6. Stimulus

Inviting outsiders to your session will boost your discovery capability. But to multiply creativity it can be useful to encourage people to think like a stranger during the session, too.

Create some questions that force participants to think about situations from the perspective of someone else or that deliberately disrupt the status quo dynamics. Here are some examples to try out:

- How would Batman solve this problem?
- If the customer was Lady Gaga, how would we solve this problem?
- What if we couldn't use electricity?
- How could we give it away for free, yet create more value?
- How would we triple the price and grow market share at the same time?
- What would our competitors hate us to do?
- What would cause all of our customers to fire us tomorrow? What does the opposite look like?

I've posted a longer list on http://www.belesszombie.com/turniton.

The answers that emerge won't always make sense but be OK with that. Great ideas often emerge as an offshoot of another, less feasible idea.

As Astro Teller, head of Google's X programme says, 'A terrible idea is often the cousin of a good idea, and a great one is the neighbor of that.'[2]

Roger Hargreaves' 90-million selling *Mr Men* book series emerged this way. One day, his six-year-old son asked, 'What does a tickle look like?' His father sketched what became the character 'Mr Tickle' and the rest is history.

Other stimulus techniques include creating dedicated spaces that are covered in market insights, questions, images and provocations.

---

[2] www.wired.com/2016/04/the-head-of-x-explains-how-to-make-audacity-the-path-of-least-resistance/

This needn't be expensive – keep it simple and ask the team to bring 10 A4 pages each, to stick on the walls. That said, you can go to town with this (as many large consumer brand companies do) and set up permanent customer environment installations.

Whilst stimulus is an important way to break out of the status quo mindset, don't allow it to distract you from the question that you're trying to solve. The 'Batman questions' are simply ways to break up people's fixed ideas on how the problem should be solved. It's fun in the bat cave but don't overstay your welcome. Stay focused on the progress that your solution needs to deliver.

7. Leader Preparedness

Just as we tend to hire people who are like us, we tend to back ideas that mirror our personality. And that can be a problem.

If you lead a team charged with finding more disruptive ideas, yet your preference is for low-risk ideas, first acknowledge the potential performance constraint. Your comfort level is in direct competition with strategy, and also the ideas that your people are itching to suggest.

Then pursue a coaching conversation to identify what drives your risk aversion. Your ability to improve your relationship with risk will only improve your leadership ability, commercial value, and (I believe) the overall stress levels in your life.

If you leave this issue unaddressed, people will be entering brainstorms under false pretences. The project charter calls for one thing, but your comfort level pursues another.

We'll be looking at some specific techniques for de-risking innovation later.

Build the Muscle   I mentioned earlier that creativity is the most prized capability by CEOs. Yet how many teams, divisions and companies are deliberately and measurably trying to build their overall creative performance, year-on-year?

The bigger your collective creative muscles, the more likely you'll leave brainstorms with more original ideas than the competition.

I strongly advise leaders to initiate and pursue a team conversation about this issue. What would the destination be? What would it take? What would we need to do more of and less of before creative sessions?

Ultimately, leaders hold the keys to the creative performance of great brainstorms. Like many things that I'm recommending in this book, the more principles that you can weave together, the greater your chances of increased creativity.

In what dimensions will your team's brainstorming performance have increased this time next year, specifically because of what happens *before* the brainstorm? How could you systematise some of these principles so that they show up automatically?

22 Running a Creative Session

A simple process that just works.

Regardless of the outcome that your brainstorm is pursuing, it needs to follow a basic flow of divergent and convergent thinking:

Generating Ideas

Categorising Ideas

Choosing Ideas

This chapter will focus on generating ideas; the next chapter will look at categorising and choosing ideas.

Whilst no process is perfect, one broad approach has emerged in recent years that is a good default setting to work from.

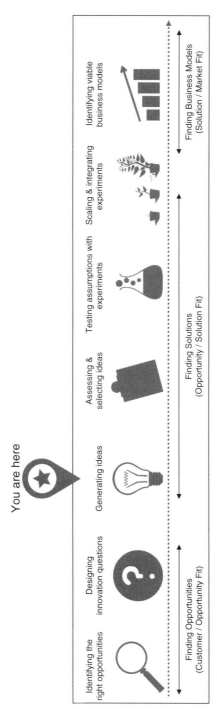

© *Elvin Turner.*

Generating Ideas

1. **Set-up**
   - Write the question that you need to answer on a flipchart or whiteboard.
   - Introduce the session, reminding people of the objective of the project and the specific question that you are answering and the outcome it needs to achieve.
   - If you haven't circulated your charter in advance, now is a good time to remind everyone of the key elements.

2. **Warm-up**

   When people arrive they are usually still preoccupied with the issue they were dealing with back at their desk, or already starting to think about what they need to do after the session.

   For maximum creativity you need everyone to be fully present and to be as relaxed as possible. That means you need to deliberately interrupt people's mental and emotional state and help them tune into a state of mind conducive to creativity.

   I'm not going to prescribe anything here as everyone's culture and context is unique – you will know what will work best for your people. Look around online, there are plenty of icebreaker ideas out there that you can adapt.

   For some it's watching five minutes of a comedy show. For others it's focused breathing. Others like to visualise leaving the mental and emotional baggage they are carrying at the door of the room. Still others like to get people doing something physical like juggling.

   You choose, but don't just 'launch it' onto people. Give it some context and explain the importance of being deliberate about being more playful and relaxed in pursuit of higher levels of creativity. And that it works.

Brainstorm

The brainstorm element of your session has four parts to it: Spark, Sift, Share and Sort.

1. **Spark:** With the question that you're answering written on a flipchart, give everyone a pad of Post-it® notes. Set a stopwatch for five minutes and ask people to generate as many ideas as possible – on their own, in silence, uncensored. At this stage it's all about the number of ideas. (If you have already asked people to bring their ideas to the session, jump to step 3.)

2. **Sift:** Next, ask everyone to look over the ideas that they have individually generated. Tell them to pick out the 2–5 ideas that they are most excited about.

3. **Share:** Then, everyone gathers around a blank wall or flip chart and takes it in turns to share their 2–5 ideas. No long explanations, just a 10–20 second overview for each idea. Remember it's sharing, not selling.

   Give everyone the chance to clarify that they've understood the idea before moving on to the next. No debates or long conversations. Just checking that everyone gets each idea. You're going to vote on them in a moment and you can't vote for an idea that you don't understand.

4. **Sort:** Now you're facing a mosaic of Post-it® notes and have most likely realised that there are some duplicate ideas. If not duplicates, then ideas that could easily be combined because they're occupying very similar territory. If that's the case, group those Post-it® notes together.

23 How to Choose the Right Ideas

A fast way to shortlist and select the best ideas to take forward.

Categorising Ideas

At this stage, people have already started making up their minds about which ideas they prefer. And that's not usually a good thing, especially if you're looking for disruptive ideas.

Even though one disruptive idea can deliver higher returns than a string of incremental ideas,[1] they usually get filtered out at this stage. And two overlapping perceptions are to blame: 'It's too risky,' and, 'It's too difficult.'

---

[1] **Source:** W. Chan Kim and Renée Mauborgne, 'Strategy, Value Innovation, and the Knowledge Economy,' *Sloan Management Review*, Spring 1999.

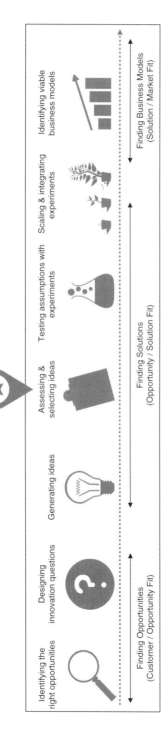

© *Elvin Turner.*

Both may be true, but it's too early to make those assumptions. So, to help keep the 'crazy' ideas alive a little longer, start to categorise them according to their potential impact and ease of implementation:

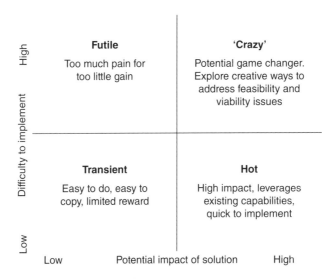

How to Use It

1. Sketch the above diagram on a flipchart.
2. Take each idea and ask the group in which area it should sit.
3. Now take a step back and see what you're left with. Ideally you'll have some Hot ideas that you can take to the next stage of development – ideas with a lot of potential impact and that are reasonably easy to implement. But don't wrap things up here.

Create a Monster ... On Purpose

Sometimes, great ideas emerge by accident. Serial innovators like Amazon, Google and Pixar know this and design their buildings to encourage serendipitous, creative collisions between employees – for example, in the lunch queue or on the way to the bathroom.

Unexpected epiphanies sometimes emerge when we thrust ideas together. And it's free, so why not just try it once in a while? Better still make it a part of your organisation's strategy for increasing creativity.

In the context of this creative session, look at the ideas that have landed on the grid and push them together. You might end up with some 'What if …' statements like:

- What if we made raspberry ripple ice cream for cats?
- What if our board games reversed dementia?
- What if all meetings were silent?
- What if our advertising only featured our new internal expenses policy?
- What if our delivery van drivers could only drive in reverse?
- What if our new gearbox system was manufactured in the staff canteen?

It's five minutes of your life. Nothing may emerge. Or an ugly spine-tingler might be born that sparks a more realistic idea. Don't get too straitjacketed by the approach – just see if anything interesting pops out. Teams that are serious about finding breakthrough ideas will believe it's worth it.

Saving Crazy Ideas

It's likely that your most disruptive ideas will have been put in the Crazy quadrant. In many circles, that's shorthand for 'cute, but too risky or too hard' and they are destined for the shredder, with a sigh of relief.

Don't fall into this trap. So many potential game-changing ideas are shut down unnecessarily at this stage.

The truth is that disruptive ideas are often vague, have lots of fear-provoking unknowns, are likely to challenge current capabilities, and generally very likely to crunch the gears of the status quo.

Research Sprints: Slaying Fantasy and Nightmares

The challenge is keeping these ugly babies alive long enough to test people's underlying assumptions.

Most likely, the people in the room are on a Fantasy vs Nightmare spectrum. At one end of the spectrum people (usually including the proposer of the idea) are probably living in a fantasy world. They can see customers frothing at the mouth over the product trailers, causing server meltdowns as billions of them share the YouTube ad, and then queuing for a week outside stores, desperate to be the first customers.

At the other end of the room, nightmares are playing out in people's minds. They are dreaming about the tripwires and trapdoors that will cause them to be fired as the idea pulls everyone down into the abyss of eternal unemployment, specifically because they worked on this idea.

The reality is somewhere in the middle, and the task is to get out of dreamland and move into the realm of facts. Specifically:

- What is the *real* potential value that this idea could create (testing real customer desire and market size)?
- Is this idea really as difficult to implement as we think? (Testing the feasibility of implementing the idea. Often, we just haven't imagined a viable or feasible solution yet.)

One of the fastest ways to kill a Crazy idea is for an executive to ask, 'So how much money will this idea make, and by when?' It's too early to ask that question, but in many cases if the idea proposer can't answer it, the idea is assassinated on the spot. I've seen it happen many times.

Instead of killing a Crazy idea, flip it in a different direction and assign it a 'research sprint'. If you spend a few weeks in focused pursuit of validating those assumptions that make the idea *feel* crazy, you could have a game changer on your hands. Or not. But if you don't look, you'll never know.

So, before moving on, take the Crazy idea that the team is most engaged around and ask two questions:

- Why did we put this in the Crazy box and not the Hot box?
- What would need to be true for it to move to the Hot box?

Now, task the person who came up with the idea to spend 30 days testing the assumptions that emerge. Then review the findings and see whether you've moved it any closer to the Hot box. If not, put the idea on ice, put a reminder in your diary and pull it out again in a few months.

Breakthroughs are rarely flashes of insight but instead deliberate, cross-discipline pursuits, usually over time.

Some of Einstein's theories took 20 years to brew. Some of that was raw cerebral processing going on in the background; some of it was related to other discoveries and ideas that were happening in parallel. Eventually, that combination of processing and new stimulus gave birth to something groundbreaking.

Hear me well. Spending money on that Crazy idea right now probably *would* be crazy. But if it's true that the idea has the potential to create incredible progress for a customer, it shouldn't be written off yet.

Choosing Ideas

It's likely that you haven't yet zoomed in on one idea that you want to progress. If that's the case, you need to narrow the field.

Whose idea gets picked, and why, is a source of frustration, confusion, and disengagement for many, especially when ideas are chosen for political reasons.

One way to address this is to introduce an element of democracy. Here's how it works.

1. Everyone gets 2–6 votes. There are no fixed rules on how many, and it depends to some extent on how many ideas are in front of you, and how many people are in the room.
2. With a pen, each person puts one or more dots next to the ideas that they believe answer the question most effectively. It's OK to vote for your own ideas. Some teams like to use small dot stickers which are easier to move if you change your mind.
3. Once everyone has voted, count the dots and find your winner.

Now you're getting *closer* to identifying the idea(s) that you want to develop, you have an important choice to make: What do you do with the ideas that didn't make it? We've already talked about the Crazy category, but what about the other surplus ideas that are actually very good, but not quite good enough to get shortlisted.

Most teams simply throw them in the bin, sometimes with a twinge of regret because it feels like a waste. And it is! You can choose to be smarter about how you curate your team's creativity.

I'd recommend appointing someone whose informal role on the team is to curate ideas that don't quite make the cut ... this time, at least. Every so often, that person should put them out on the table and remind the team that they exist.

A Swedish telecommunications company does this on a regular basis. Occasionally good product ideas from a couple of years ago are suddenly red-hot-relevant and go on to become important revenue streams.

Timing is often everything with new ideas, so don't let potentially great ideas-for-the-future slip through your fingers because they died on the flipchart.

Also, share these ideas. What if 10 internal teams all had informal creative curators who met up once a quarter to compare surplus ideas? A lot of serendipitous value would be created for free. Have a go – find some friends and try it for a few months. You've nothing to lose.

Longer, Deeper, Wider

I've used this idea generation and selection process successfully many times. It's a useful way to create structure, ensure momentum, overcome difficult social dynamics, and get to a result within a given timeframe.

That said, I wouldn't use it for everything. Bigger, more complex ideas don't always show themselves right at the start of the discovery journey. The more disruptive the question, the longer, deeper and wider you need to dream, think, debate and incubate.

24 The 'Five-Day Brainstorm'

Want better ideas? Stop rushing.

T oo often we limit the creative process to the length of a one-off brainstorm. But our brains like to keep munching on problems and processing ideas in the background.

If we're smart about synchronising our creativity with the idea incubation process, we can develop better ideas, simply by returning to them a few days or even hours later.

Think of it as a continuous improvement approach to brainstorming.

So next time you need ideas, instead of stopping the creative process at the end of the brainstorm, try the 'Five-Day Brainstorm' approach:

1. Write a short description of the five most promising ideas that emerged during the brainstorm session.

2. Take a picture of each idea description.

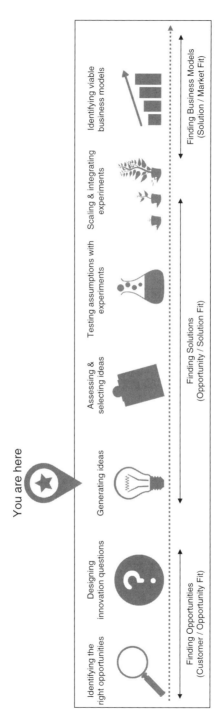

© *Elvin Turner.*

3. Schedule a follow-up meeting in five days.

4. At the start of each of those days, email your team one of the five ideas. Encourage them to munch on that idea during the day: poke it, daydream about it, talk about it, break off parts of it, and add new ones. At 5 p.m., everyone shares by email any thoughts that have emerged for them.

5. Reconvene in five days and take turns to share what emerged and reconfigure ideas accordingly.

Try it out and tweak the process to make it work better for your team in your context.

Great ideas tend to emerge over time. This is especially true when working on more complex problems. So don't stop at the brainstorm – make a habit of scheduling in time for the incremental incubation of ideas.

However, it's a balance. Don't get too carried away with new ideas too quickly. Overdevelopment leads to love affairs that can be painful to end if an idea turns out to be less valuable than we had originally thought.

25 Tracking Idea Progress

How to monitor idea status across an organisation.

W hat is the total potential worth of the ideas inside your company right now?

What stage of development are they at?

What resources are dedicated to them?

How many of them have patent potential?

Where are your best ideas coming from?

Many companies have no way of answering these questions, which makes the management and development of strategic creativity very difficult.

The good news is that over the last few years some great software solutions have emerged that can give leaders insight into all of these areas.

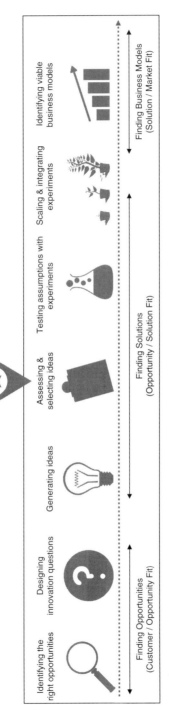

© *Elvin Turner.*

Democratising Innovation

These idea management platforms allow managers to run idea campaigns across a team, division or company. Questions are posted and then employees propose solutions. Many platforms also allow employees to vote on the ideas.

This is a great way to open up innovation to people outside of your team. It's also helpful for 'discovering' people from different parts of the organisation who have a knack for dreaming up good ideas consistently.

Like most software the solution is only as good as the data coming in. These platforms also need a commitment to good campaign design and management support at key stages if they are to prove their worth. Beware the vendors who make 'simple plug-and-play' claims. Ease of installation is one thing. Pulling out the potential value from the system is quite another.

That said, managed well, they do offer tremendous potential value. If you don't currently have an idea management system in place, I strongly suggest running team-level trials with 2–3 different platforms and finding one that could work well for you.

26 Overcoming the Execution Problem

Most ideas fail during the execution phase. It doesn't have to be that way.

'Ideas aren't our problem. Turning them into action is.'

There are a few statements that I can usually predict that leaders will say when I first meet them, and this is one of them.

That's not me being smug; it's just a factor of how common the problem is.

It's shocking how few ideas survive beyond the brainstorm. It wastes resources, drains people engagement, and shrinks the future.

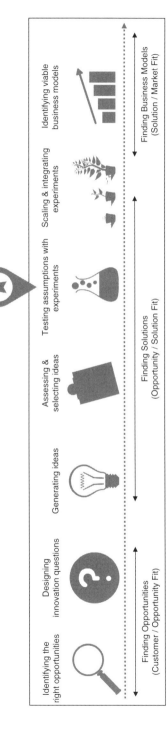

© *Elvin Turner.*

What's going on here? In my own research, a few consistent culprits cop the blame:

- Projects frequently de-prioritised because of more urgent demands.
- Risk averse managers.
- Lack of resources.
- Lack of the right capabilities.
- Bureaucracy blocks progress.
- No clear innovation process.
- Ideas not having a strong business case, making it difficult to justify resources.

Many of these factors are a function of having a one-size-fits-all approach to innovation that really only suits incremental ideas.

As we've already seen, there are things that leaders can do to overcome some of these barriers: encouraging people to start with well-thought-through charters; giving teams autonomy to design the required innovation space; having a joined up innovation strategy, to name a few. And your innovation performance will definitely increase if you do these things.

Yet if I could only make one recommendation in this book that would have an immediate impact on your innovation performance, it wouldn't be any of them.

It would be an action-oriented, intuitive, low-risk, low stakes, high-speed, game-changing innovation technique. It would overcome almost all of the enemies of innovation listed above. And you could start tomorrow.

I've seen it work all over the world and heard CEOs call it the most important innovation tool they've ever encountered.

Welcome to the world of experiments.

© *Richard Johnston.*

27 Innovation Rocket Fuel

The single greatest innovation accelerator that you can turn on today.

'**E**xperiments changed everything,' says Denis O'Flynn, former UK managing director of global drinks giant Pernod Ricard.

He is reflecting on 'Project Ingenuity', the 1000-day journey that O' Flynn led the company through from 2013. Its aim was to inject fizz into the company's flattening revenues, a tough ask in the UK's mature drinks industry.

At the heart of the journey was a philosophy: *Dream big, start small.* Come up with big ideas, but don't bet the farm on them. Yet.

Bridget Gardner, Pernod's head of employee capability, was charged with developing a fast-track training programme for all of its UK employees, starting with the board.

The programme centred around a handful of key tools that would help individuals generate and implement new ideas that could fuel growth and profitability.

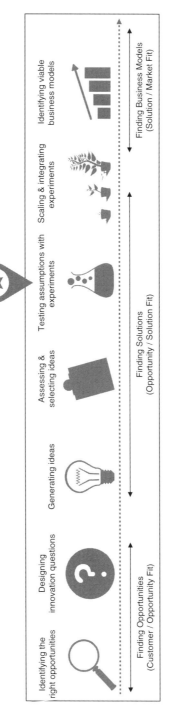

© *Elvin Turner.*

Denis O' Flynn, former Managing Director, Pernod Ricard UK
© Richard Johnston.

But the tool that got everyone's attention was the experiment.
Here is the key concept:

Most new ideas are a mix of right and wrong. Right instincts and
assumptions, and wrong instincts and assumptions. And
everything in between.

A major main reason that ideas fail is that we discover those
wrong instincts and assumptions too late. We built the thing
only to find out that no one *really* wanted it (even though
they said they did). We implemented a change programme
that underestimated the deep-rooted employee antipathy.

But what if you could discover whether people *really* wanted your
product *before* you built it?

That question sparked one of the century's most important business books, *The Lean Startup* by Eric Ries. After being part of several failed start-ups, Ries studied the principles of lean manufacturing, looking for potential lessons for founders.

His conclusions sparked global movement that has not only torn through the global start-up community but has slowly begun to embed itself in pockets of the corporate world.

Here's how it goes: When you develop an idea, first identify all of your assumptions. Then rank them according to importance and certainty. The assumptions that could have the biggest impact on your idea's success, and which you are least certain are 100% true, are called 'leap of faith assumptions'. If those are wrong, the whole idea has a strong chance of going nowhere.

So, before investing resources in your idea, test those assumptions. How do you do that? Create what Ries calls a Minimum Viable Product (MVP): The smallest, cheapest, fastest possible experiment that would validate your assumption (or otherwise). It's a low-risk, low-stakes, high-speed, test-and-learn way to work.

If the experiment comes back with data that's contrary to what you expected, you have a strong reason to question whether you should proceed. If your assumption is validated, then you have confidence to increase the scope of the experiment. If it's somewhere in between, you may run a new, 'pivoted' experiment based on what you learned.

This sense-and-respond approach to innovation is a game-changer in most corporate contexts. Suddenly, the risk of innovation is radically reduced, it's safer to allow many more ideas loose across the organisation, and when management is asked for more resources, decisions are based on real data, not gut feel or employee enthusiasm.

It's pay-as-you-go idea development. It's innovation rocket fuel.

I vividly remember the moment I introduced experiments to Pernod Ricard during an executive development programme. I had a graveyard session after lunch. Eyelids were drooping and I suspected few people were listening.

Suddenly, Patrick Venning, then marketing director, sat bolt upright and said, 'So what you're really saying is that we should stop asking, "What can I *build* for £50K?" and start asking "What can I *learn* for £50?"' That remains my favourite explanation of the idea to this day.

Within a few weeks, experiments were buzzing around Pernod Ricard's West London HQ. 'It became infectious,' says O' Flynn. 'We had instituted educated risk taking. There was this sense amongst people that "If I come up with an idea they might actually *do* something with it."'

A year down the line and employee engagement, revenues and profitability were moving in a very healthy and sustainable direction.

Whilst Project Ingenuity was a multifaceted change programme, I have no doubt that experiments were what made the ultimate difference. And I see the same everywhere. Give people the tools to make low-risk progress with their ideas and the whole innovation tide rises.

In the technology sector, where MVPs first flourished, experimentation has become standard operating procedure. 'eBay's strategy is based on winning through a portfolio of experiments,' says Rafael Orta, a former eBay and Tesco executive, now chief product officer at moneysupermarket.com. 'Experimentation is deeply embedded in the company culture, and it's a safe place to take smart risks.'

So let's look a little closer to see how companies work practically with experiments, starting with finding your 'leap of faith' assumptions.

28 Innovation Trapdoors

How to quickly find any fatal flaws hidden inside your idea.

Done well, innovation is the pursuit of truth.

It's the search for an elegant solution to an accurately understood problem in context. And that search is trying to correctly answer two questions about an idea: *Should we build it? Could we build it?*

Invariably, we're so wired to *do* stuff, that 'could' is off and running before 'should' gets a look-in.

The familiar endgame is investment decisions based on subjective half-truths that lead to expensive abject failures.

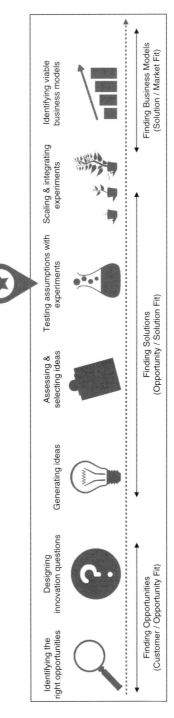

© *Elvin Turner.*

The more truth we trade in, the greater our chances of success, and the lower the potential pain of failure. But when political agendas, biases, blind spots and sloppy work get involved, the purity of the truth is compromised.

One of the biggest truth-benders in innovation is the untested assumption. It's the main reason that up to 90% of new products fail. It's innovation's nemesis.

But what do we expect? Emotional, irrational, political, overcommitted human beings are at the wheel. Truth can have shades of grey, be difficult to uncover, or be plain inconvenient when we're running at the speed of twenty-first-century business.

But speed and convenience aren't always the issues. Often, it's pure infatuation. We form an emotional bond with our idea that blurs reality. We convince ourselves that our idea is so hot that it will melt any problems that dare to stand in its way.

Yet, reality bites hard. 'No business plan survives first contact with the customer,' says Stanford University professor, Steve Blank. The most potent reality definer is experiencing no customers showing up to a product launch that you're convinced they asked for.

Two other truth-fudgers are experience and expertise, which can be simultaneously a help and a hindrance to innovation. The rate of change in the world means that the half-life of any skill is shrinking, and the way something played out previously is less likely to repeat itself. It's difficult to predict the future success of an idea using backward-facing information.

Seeing the Unseen

If you were creating a list of innovation superpowers, 'seeing what's missing' would be near the top. This particularly applies to finding and testing the assumptions that could sink or supercharge an idea.

Thankfully, there are some simple but powerful tools available to help flush out assumptions and define reality. Here are four that I regularly use to help teams integrate into their innovation work.

1. Desirable, Feasible, Viable

According to design consultancy, IDEO, a successful innovation lives at the intersection of three neighbourhoods:

Desirability: The extent to which anyone wants your solution.

Feasibility: How difficult it would it be to make the solution.

Viability: Whether the solution can become financially sustainable.

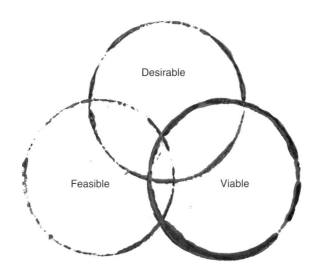

Coffee stain image design © Leilani Turner.

As you interrogate the assumptions behind your ideas, this is an excellent framework to orient your team around.

Some common examples of assumptions that seem obvious, yet are often overlooked, include:

- Is the user and customer the same person?
- Do they have the specific problem that we assumed?

- Which parts of that problem matter most?
- How urgently do they want a solution to those parts?
- How much will they pay to solve the problem?
- What capabilities would we need to build the solution?
- What resources would we need?
- What internal collaboration would we need, and how likely is it?
- How long would it take to build?
- What would the decision-making process be?
- What kind of customer relationship would be needed?
- How will we acquire customers most effectively?
- How many customers would we need to break even?
- What business model would make this profitable?

Having a project charter can be useful here. Use it to help you identify and capture your assumptions as you'll need to refer back to them frequently.

2. 'What Would Need to Be True … ?'

One of the most powerful tools for keeping us reality-minded is a simple question: 'What would need to be true for … X?'

It forces us to confront reality, simultaneously putting the brakes on runaway ideas, but also rescuing those that are flailing in quicksand.

It is especially useful when you sense that someone is trying to railroad an idea through because it 'obviously makes sense'. At this point I might say, 'You're probably right, so let's create a quick list of dependencies so that we can accurately plan the resources we'll need.'

Then we walk through the end-to-end customer journey and create a longlist of 'need to be trues'. Usually a wider reality begins to dawn across the room as unforeseen issues emerge. It's not about being a smart alec. It's making sure that we don't allocate scarce resources too quickly to ideas that are still on unsure foundations.

'What would need to be true...?' Ever since I heard Professor Rita McGrath challenge a group with this question, it has become one of the most helpful tools that I use to help people identify assumptions. Use the question in conjunction with the other tools here and it'll help you identify a lot of hidden trapdoors.

3. Dream-Storming vs Mare-Storming

Sometimes, simply asking the question isn't enough to flush out some of the more subtle hidden assumptions.

This is where the third technique can help. It's actually asking the same question in a different way that forces more assumptions to the surface.

It involves going to the future twice: once to predict a mind-blowing, five-star experience, and a second time to envision utter failure.

It turns out that when we imagine that an event has already happened, our ability to correctly identify reasons for future outcomes increases by 30%.[1] So it's worth the effort. Let's start on the sunny side.

Dream-Storming   Imagine that your product has launched, and customers have begun to review it.

With your specific customer and solution in mind, consider what the perfect reviews would contain, drawing attention to the most important aspects of the overall experience and benefits.

Now craft 5–10 detailed, five-star reviews as if they had been written by customers. Make sure the reviews only focus on what you

---

[1] https://onlinelibrary.wiley.com/doi/abs/10.1002/bdm.3960020103

believe to be the most important areas of progress that customers want to make with your product.

Working backwards from those reviews, ask what would need to be true to create that five-star experience in the following areas:

- The context(s) in which customers used the product.
- The specific progress the product helped them make.
- The specific behaviours needed and the beliefs/attitudes that led to those behaviours.
- Why the product is better than alternatives.
- The customer relationship with the brand.
- The buying experience.
- The end-to-end user experience (including when things go wrong).
- The business model needed to bring it to market.
- The capabilities, resources and partnerships needed to create the product.

Amazon uses a similar process. If you propose a new idea you have to do it in the form of a launch press release for the product: what is the product, who is the first customer, what did the customer say, how much did they pay, which distributor signed first …

Forcing yourself to confront the reality of what would need to be true for those elements to happen is a great way to find the assumptions that you would need to test early on.

Mare-Storming Talking about success is easy, though. What if your idea was dead-on-arrival and completely flopped? What could have caused that?

Dealing in reality means embracing the beautiful and the beastly with equal enthusiasm. It's innovation due diligence.

But hidden assumptions aren't the only threat at this stage. A more powerful innovation enemy often slithers under the table unchecked. And that's fear of speaking up.

When we have to imagine points of potential failure, usually we have to point to weaknesses somewhere in the chain. And those weaknesses can often be the people in the room with you. Awkward.

When it's not safe to speak up, our chances of success go down.

Enter the 'pre-mortem', a term coined by psychologist Gary Klein. Whereas a post-mortem identifies the cause-of-death after the event, a pre-mortem seeks to do so beforehand.

This approach significantly disempowers the fear of speaking up, because the whole point of the exercise is to imagine points of failure. We're not talking about what *will* happen, which creates defensiveness, discomfort, blame and shame. We're looking for what *could* happen if we *weren't* diligent. Which, of course, we are. It's leaving no stone unturned. It's logical, responsible, due diligence.

So after your dream-storm, run a mare-storm:

First, spend one-hour imagining and writing one-star reviews from fuming customers. What perceived promises did we break? What would have led to those customer experiences occurring? Be sure to include a couple from people who completely misunderstood what the product was in the first place, and those who obviously disregarded the operating instructions and can't make the thing work. Stupid product. (We're dealing in reality here.)

It can be helpful to have some set pre-mortem categories to work back from, for example, product quality issues, delivery and installation problems, product understanding, availability, support, awareness, returns, guarantee issues, customer injuries, lawsuits, etc. This way, everyone knows that all business functions will be 'under investigation' so no one feels the pressure of having to call out other parts of the business.

But also have an 'other' category for issues that fall outside the responsibility of everyone. Doing an internet search for some terrible customer reviews can help warm people up for the exercise, and also unearth some potential 'others' that may not have otherwise occurred to anyone.

Finally, rank the issues according to impact and likelihood. These can feed into the final stage of assessing all of the assumptions that you have begun to identify using these tools.

There are a couple of useful side benefits to this approach. Often everyone takes away a list of things that weren't openly discussed but they now realise they need to work on. Gulp. Shhh. Also, it helps to remove bias in the group, especially optimism bias and confirmation bias.

4. Only … If …

In most cases, successful innovation requires a behaviour change for someone, somewhere. Underestimating this is the downfall of many innovation projects, and often is overlooked during the early stages.

So, understanding how deeply engraved current behaviour patterns are in users' minds, for example, and what it might take to change them, are crucial pieces of data.

Understanding human behaviour is a science in its own right. But a useful shorthand is to look at the context of your idea in four dimensions:

1. **Motivation: 'They would only want this if … '**
   - What motivations hold the user's current behaviour in place (familiarity, comfort, habit, the fear, perceived pain or hassle of changing etc.)?

- What drives these motivations?
- What different motivations would they need to switch to our solution?
- What would create these new motivations?
- What would need to be true to weaken or cut the ties with today's motivations?

2. **Resources: 'They could only have this if … '**
   - What resources would users need in order to adopt and use our product (e.g. necessary equipment, finance, time, space)?

3. **Opportunity: 'They could only access this if … '**
   - How would users gain access this solution (distribution, connectivity, relationships)?

4. **Capability: 'They could only use this if … '**
   - What skills, abilities or experience would the user need to adopt and use our product?
   - How accurately do users currently perceive their skill, abilities and experience levels?
   - What would need to be true for users to attain the required skill, abilities and experience?

Innovation is as much about behaviour design as it is about product design.

The better your understanding of what needs to be true in each of these areas, the more likely you'll create solutions that are adopted.

However, be mindful of blind spots. Here are some common ones to look out for.

Overestimating Motivations

Surveys are notorious for returning false positive responses. That is, people say they would do something or buy something, but when it comes to it, they don't. (Believe me, I've learned the hard way on this one). Presenting people with a call-to-action and observing their real response is a good way to sniff out true motivation levels. We'll look at that more later.

Competing Commitments

This is where customers genuinely *do* want your solution (and may even buy it for a while), but a stronger, opposing force is in operation.

Products that aim to support New Years' resolutions are a good example. The bedroom mirror sparks the determined resolution to un-flab. January sees peak usage of gyms, but regulars know that the traffic tails off by the end of February. Competing commitments kicked in.

There are three varieties that show up often:

1. **Practical competitors:** We underestimate the true cost of using the product (often time and energy). When reality kicks in, our motivation backs off.

2. **Habitual competitors:** Existing habits and rituals that continue to compete with your new behaviour (e.g. watching TV from 8 p.m. every evening. 'Oh come on! It's *that* episode of *Friends* tonight, you *can't* possibly go out to the gym! What if they never repeat it!')

3. **Inner competitors:** Our inner critic and neuroses that want to avoid pain of a new behaviour (e.g. the self-consciousness of EVERYONE in the gym obviously holding in a snigger as you wobble past them. Never coming back.)

I have a friend who develops resources for therapists working in niches within niches. He calls his customer base 'wounded healers' – the joy they receive from helping others masks the pain of avoiding their own problems.

Be deliberate about hunting down these competing commitments in the early stages of solution development.

Ranking Assumptions

Whichever approach you use to identifying assumptions, it's now time to prioritise them. Put the list of assumptions before your team and score them according to importance to the idea's success, and certainty of assumption.

What you're trying to identify is assumptions that the group believes would have a high impact on the idea's success but have a low sense of certainty about cause and effect.

For example, let's assume you are making packaging for ultra-luxury yoghurts that can tell customers when the product is about to pass its use-by date.

You've figured out that it's possible to embed a sensor into a yoghurt pot, and in theory it should be able to communicate with the user's phone from inside the refrigerator. But you're not sure about the impact of the thickness of the fridge on transmission performance, the temperature of the fridge on sensor accuracy, the impact of a price increase on consumption, and actually whether anyone really cares enough about their yoghurts going out of date in the first place.

Assumption	Importance	Certainty
Transmission will reach phone	10	7
Temperature won't adversely impact sensor accuracy	8	3
Solution solves important customer problem	10	4
Customers won't mind a price increase to cover costs	2	9

In this example, whilst it's important to test the feasibility of the solution, a bigger priority is establishing whether it actually solves an important enough problem for any customer group in the first place. If not, the whole idea is academic.

Ideally, you've already established this in your research phase. But that isn't always the case: we often overestimate the extent to which customers want our products. It's the biggest reason that start-up companies fail.

The assumptions that are most important but that you are least certain about are called your 'leap of faith assumptions'. Before you take your idea any further forward, your number one priority is to validate these assumptions with experiments. That's the focus of the next chapter.

In innovation projects that contain a reasonable level of uncertainty, expect to keep discovering new assumptions for some time. It's a fact of life on the journey to discovering 'solution/market-fit' – the perfect solution to a customer's problem with a business model that can scale it to viability.

Pro Tips

Before we move on to look at designing experiments to test your assumptions, I want to share a few more tips that will help you make faster, better progress in the area of identifying assumptions:

Invite diversity: Inevitably these sessions are most valuable when all stakeholders are present. Not only does the project benefit from the widest possible range of views, but if the project does go ahead, it helps to build engagement from the start.

Assumptions[2]: It's not uncommon to find an idea that seems to make sense, but that has an intractable blocker in the way. Or so we think.

'Customers would love this feature but legal would never allow it.'

'We could increase supply chain efficiency by 15% but IT doesn't support that module.'

'We could make that kind of decision five times faster, but finance always has to sign it off.'

Sometimes we make wrong assumptions about our assumptions.

Before throwing in the towel, try these approaches:

'We Can If…': In their excellent book *A Beautiful Constraint*, Adam Morgan and Mark Barden offer a very helpful tool to help break through the power of intractable assumptions.

Instead of stating *'We can't do X because of Y…'* restate the problem: *'We can if…'*

Then spend some time thinking about what would need to be true for that constraint to be removed. Morgan and Barden suggest nine potential 'We can if…' categories:

We can if… we resource it by…

We can if… we substitute it for…

We can if… we remove… to allow us to…

We can if… we introduce a…

We can if… we fund it by…

We can if… we think of it as…

We can if… we use other people to…

We can if… we mix together…

We can if… we access the knowledge of…

Using this technique can often spark ideas that help us see past our limiting assumptions.

Hero-maker: Go and meet the particular stakeholder who you perceive to be the blocker. Better still have them take part in the sessions described above.

Explain the potential benefit of your idea, your assumption about the potential constraint, and ask for their advice on how we might find a solution together. Sometimes, the assumption turns out to be wrong, at least in part, and the blocker isn't a blocker at all.

Other times, because we are not the subject matter expert, we make even more assumptions about why something can't happen. Innovation author Eric Ries tells a story about a lawyer who was seen as an innovation blocker in his company. Yet during one session he became a project hero.

The team was making assumptions about a constraining legal process but wasn't aware of a very specific loophole that made an exception for their kind of solution. Only a specialist lawyer could have known about that. He became an instant hero.

Of course, it doesn't always work out like that. Conflicting priorities, politics, sulking, crossed wires and many other factors can cause innovation blockages throughout an organisation. We'll deal with some of these later in the book.

Pulling It Together

At this stage, it can be helpful to pull together an idea's dependencies and assumptions into one place. This is especially useful when it comes to sharing early stage ideas and seeking feedback from other teams and stakeholders.

The Assumption Tracker framework below can be a useful way to gather and structure your thinking so far. This is a living document: As you progress in your learning journey, you'll need to adapt it en route.

You can download a version from www.belesszombie.com/turniton. For illustration purposes it appears as one page in this chapter but has one page per element in the download for ease of use.

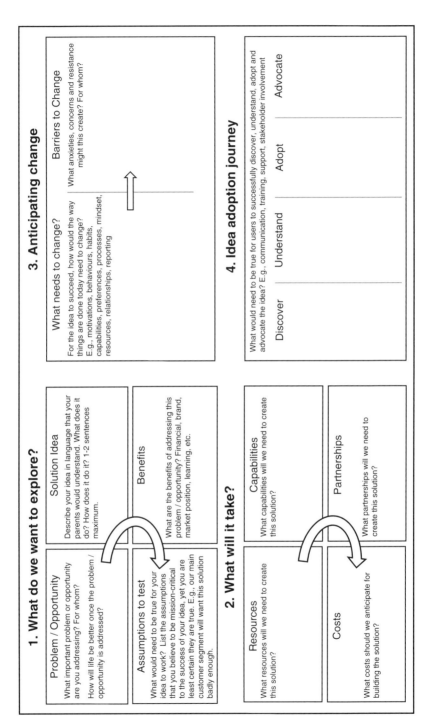

Summary

So, make assumption-hunting and validation a reflex response in your team. Developing your ability is this area is one of the biggest accelerators to your innovation performance.

Having identified the assumptions that matter most, now it's time to test them.

29 If You Only Read One Chapter …

How anyone can design and run low-cost, low-risk, high-return experiments.

In the 1980s, an IBM voice recognition scientist had a brainwave.

He imagined a world where we could hit 'delete' and do away with computer keyboards. If IBM computers understood *spoken* words, why would millions of office workers need to drum keyboards ever again?

Logically it made sense. Commercially, it was mouthwatering. But the development costs were potentially staggering. How could they be sure that their audacious vision would work?

It's the question facing every executive who is presented with a new idea that needs investment: 'How do I know if this will pay off?'

Here's what IBM did.

They set up a room containing a desk, a computer screen and a chair. Test subjects were invited in and told that this was a prototype computer that didn't need a keyboard. 'Take a seat and talk to the computer. Let us know what you think.'

The guinea pigs obliged and squeaked in delight as their words appeared on the screen.

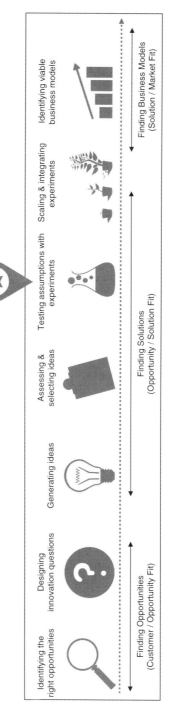

© *Elvin Turner.*

Here's what they didn't know. A few doors down was another office. Inside was a typist wearing headphones that were connected to a hidden microphone inside the test room. Every word that the test subjects uttered arrived in her headset. She typed what she heard, and the words appeared on the screen back in the test room.

The users loved it! Successful test, right? Not so fast.

As IBM extended the duration of experiments, the testers' throats became sore. What's more, as they worked through different use-case scenarios they realised that this solution wouldn't work for people dealing with confidential matters in open spaces.

And the noise! Multiplied by a few dozen people in a confined space, suddenly the people couldn't hear themselves think.

IBM continued its product development, but not in that direction, sparing them considerable effort, resources and reputational damage.

Democratising Innovation

In an increasingly unpredictable world, inside organisations where innovation typically has little structure or pathway, and where risk aversion is high, experiments are as close to a silver bullet as you can come.

An experiment is a small, cheap, rapid test that creates data to inform decision-making. Invest a little, learn a lot.

In my own experience, it's one of the few innovation tools that makes 95% of executives lean forward and want to know more. Why is that?

A well-designed experiment simultaneously achieves many important things.

It Reduces Risk and Fear

Shrinking the scale reduces the stakes and everyone sleeps better. 'If this fails, the pain is tolerable,' is the unspoken commentary.

It Activates More Disruptive Ideas

Risk aversion stops many ideas from getting out of the brainstorm alive. If the starting point is a tiny validation experiment, it's a lot safer for many more bold ideas get to first base.

Idea Pathway

One of the biggest blockers to idea execution is knowing what to do next with an idea: there's no process, especially for ideas that fall outside the current operating model. Experiment design is a simple and scalable approach that anyone can follow.

Pay-As-You-Go Innovation   Experiments receive investment according to the data and learning they generate. That stops ideas receiving overinvestment which can create problems of its own. Stopping a million-dollar juggernaut project is much harder than a thousand-dollar test.

Competitive Advantage   Every experiment that you run delivers unique data that only you own. Industry research reports are helpful, but everybody else buys them too. Experiments give you insights that can help you make better decisions than the competition.

Executive Confidence   Experiments remove a large amount of the guesswork associated with backing bold new ideas. Whilst instinct and gut-feel still have a place, data from the experiments provides a solid foundation upon which investment decisions can be made.

Innovation Efficiency   Because data reveals the truth about our ideas, the wrong ideas can be escorted to the shredder quickly and objectively. Google rewards people for finding the failures as fast as possible, knowing that 90% of their bold ideas are shredder-bound from the outset. Better to find them early.

Innovation at Scale

When everyone knows how to design and run an experiment, the innovation shackles can be removed. With some basic boundaries in place, everyone is free to pursue the ideas that they believe make most sense in their context.

Employee Engagement

I've found experiments to be one of the most powerful ways to increase employee engagement. Usually the innovation focus is on either making a difference to customers or changing the way we work for the better. Both tap into purpose and progress and are intrinsically rewarding in their own right.

At the end of one experiment design workshop, a manager approached me and said that the day had reconnected her with the reason she got into the business in the first place. It's powerful stuff.

Working with Experiments

So what exactly is an experiment, and how do you design and run one?

Experiments are like edging out onto a frozen lake.

No one knows whether stepping on to the ice is the right choice to begin with. So we poke it with a stick. Feels OK? We carefully take a small step on to the ice.

No one wants to go under so we tentatively slide our toes forward, poke some more, and gain confidence as we learn whether or not the ice will bear our weight.

Every step delivers decision-making data. No crack? Move out a little further. Slight fracture? Move in a different direction or head back to the edge.

Experimentation is exploration – discovering the right direction and distance of travel *as you go*. Small steps forward, minimum resource commitment for maximum learning.

Eric Ries, entrepreneur and author of the seminal innovation book *The Lean Startup*, calls these experiments 'minimum viable products' (MVPs). But this approach isn't restricted to products. As I've introduced the concept to organisations, I've found that MVPs can be used to test any idea that comes preloaded with a degree of uncertainty.

Minimum viable products: Dream big, start small, move fast. Illustration © Richard Johnston.

In fact, after running the experiment numbers inside one international bank, it turned out that 70% of MVPs were focused on what seemed to be dull, inward-facing projects. I was puzzled, as the group had been given free rein to reimagine the bank's future.

Then I realised that these experiments were all bent on dismantling the bureaucracy that would crush any ambitious customer-facing ideas. No point in working on great ideas that are destined to suffocate.

Having seen such a wide variety of experiments across multiple industries and business functions, I now prefer the term 'Minimal Viable *X*.' The principles to exploring uncertain new approaches to anything apply universally. What's more the words 'minimum viable' often trigger a wonderful side benefit: They provoke questions about the bloatedness of many parts of organisational life and often spark a desire to target overly complex or laborious ways of working, for example

- Minimum Viable *Meeting*
- Minimum Viable *Process*
- Minimum Viable *Project*
- Minimum Viable *Spreadsheet*
- Minimum Viable *Sign-Off*
- Etc . . . .

Designing an Experiment

Remember that experiments are for testing assumptions. If we clearly understand cause-and-effect in a given context, you probably don't need an experiment. That said, I'm increasingly seeing them used as a stakeholder engagement tool to help nervous executives sign off budgets on standard run-the-business projects.

So with your idea in mind, and your list of 'leap of faith' assumptions in hand, you're ready to start designing an experiment.

Here are the basic steps:

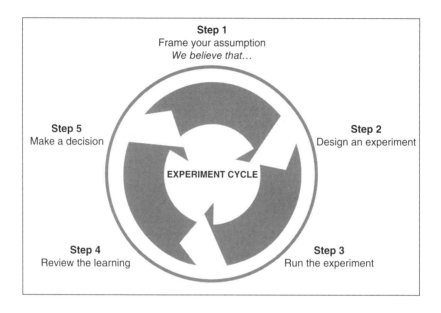

Step 1: Frame Your Assumption

Take the biggest 'leap of faith' assumption that your idea's success depends on and turn it into a statement.

For example, let's say that we've discovered that 50% of customers fail to complete their transactions on our website. Our insight tells us that they get frustrated with the amount of time and steps needed and so bail out of the transaction early.

Our idea is to reduce the number of steps from five to two but the engineering and back office changes required are significant.

So if the time and steps actually make no difference to the number of transactions, we'll waste a lot of time and effort.

Our assumption is, 'We believe that reducing the time and steps involved in the checkout process will significantly increase the number of completed transactions.'

It's good practice to define 'significantly' here. Otherwise we can validate assumptions with an increase of 0.1%. What level of increase would make it commercially worthwhile? We'll look at this more in a moment.

Step 2: Design an Experiment

Experiments help us understand how true our assumptions are.

With your assumption in mind, challenge your team to come up with several ways of testing the assumption.

The traits of a good experiment are:

- Small
- Cheap
- Fast
- Learning-rich (which requires clear metrics and success criteria).

Small Experiment design is a creative act and, like anything, takes a little practice to master. At first, your experiments will probably be far too big. Imagining a great yet tiny experiment isn't always easy.

Here are a few examples of common experiment formats that created a good enough learning experience for some organisations to validate their assumptions:

- A blog that invites comments (Groupon).
- A 'smoke test' landing page that invites potential customers to sign up (Buffer).

- A pre-order page, Kickstarter campaign or letter of intent (Oculus Rift).
- An explainer video with email sign-up (Dropbox).
- 'Wizard-of-Oz' service – appears to be automated but is happening manually behind the scenes (Zappos).
- A no-feature 'pretotype' – a wireframe or physical mockup (Palm Pilot).
- A one-feature prototype (Go Pro).

Cheap A good technique for keeping experiments small and cheap is a little cruel at first but pays dividends in the long term. Ask a team to design a test. Whatever they present to you, tell them to try again but this time using half the resources required by their first idea. Same learning, half the resources. I do this as standard practice in workshops. After an initial look of disbelief, teams always manage to come back with a smaller, better experiment.

Also, try asking people to develop and run experiments with no resources. In many instances it's possible and the requirement to beg and borrow resources helps to develop some entrepreneurial hustle that many organisations lack.

Monitor this closely though. Sometimes experiments genuinely do need additional resources to move forward. If the hustling of resources means the performance of another part of the business is impacted, squirt some help their way.

One outcome of cheap experiments is that they are usually ugly. Get used to this. If people want your idea badly enough, they'll see past the ugliness and recognise the beauty of the progress it delivers them.

Reid Hoffman, founder of LinkedIn once said, 'If you are not embarrassed by the first version of your product, you've launched too late.'

Software company Basecamp calls this 'bread-boarding'. It's a term borrowed from the electronics industry and describes prototyping basic product ideas on a simple circuit board – but with no consideration for user design, at least yet.

Uber launched ugly. Despite having an app, users still had to call or send a text message to an Uber employee who would then desperately call other car companies to find you a ride.

That said, balance ugly with some elegance. Too ugly can be off-putting and cause an otherwise good experiment to deliver an inaccurate result.

Fast   Speed of learning is often described as the only remaining source of competitive advantage. Whether or not that's true, the faster that you can test assumptions the less money you'll burn on the wrong ideas.

But speed doesn't mean rushing. That leads to poorly designed experiments that simply waste resources.

Back to our checkout example. How might a small, cheap, fast experiment look that is trying to understand the cause-and-effect relationship between the number of steps in the checkout process and completed transactions?

Think in increments. If moving from five steps to two is a big engineering investment, what if we measured the impact on moving from five to four steps? That's a much smaller, faster, cheaper way to test cause-and-effect dynamics.

Which step sees most bail outs? Perhaps, like our frustrated elevator travellers earlier, it's not really a time issue, it's boredom.

So you could run a couple of different experiments in parallel: one that has something entertaining or informative happening on the screen as users wait for background churning to take place; and another one that consolidates two stages into one. Start with the least complex.

As I said earlier, designing experiments is a creative exercise so invest the time in developing something smart: small but oozing with data.

Learning-Rich Did it work? Were we right? To what extent?

One of the biggest dangers with experiments is post-rationalising the outcome of a failed experiment and continuing with it too long.

'Well, of course *that* happened because … '

Just like in a science laboratory, a good experiment defines an expected outcome. If this, then that.

Building on our checkout example, our expected outcome might be, 'We believe that reducing the checkout process from five steps to four steps will result in 10% more completed transactions.'

Clarity upfront helps decision-making later. If precision is difficult, make predictions across ranges to begin with, e.g. between 10–30%. Once you have established some benchmarks, you can become more precise.

Who gets to choose the metric? To help overcome bias, fantasy and politics, do this in a group. Ask what outcomes are needed to prove the assumption to be correct. Individuals write down their thoughts privately and then share them with the group. The conversation that unfolds will reveal all kinds of hidden assumptions, and after some negotiation you'll agree on a suitable metric.

Talk Is Cheap, So Make Learning Costly One more point about learning which is especially important when testing for user desirability. Customers are renowned for saying that they would definitely buy a new product but then failing to show up once it is launched. There are many reasons why that can happen, not least how the original research question is framed.

It's easy to say yes to something when it costs you nothing. That's why the most valuable learning comes from experiments where there is a value exchange. The customer only gets the value if they're prepared to 'pay' something. It's a much more reliable indicator that customers will actually buy your product once it's available.

Money is always good. Asking potential customers to sign up and pay for a solution upfront is a great way to flush out hidden reticence. If they say no, ask what would need to be true for them to say yes to a pre-order. It usually creates a treasure map of hidden assumptions.

That's what makes Kickstarter such a powerful platform. No one builds anything unless the market pre-orders in sufficient quantity to fund it. It's a strong indicator that you're on to something, for a particular market segment at least.

However, tread carefully when extrapolating market expansions from very early data. Products and business models that appeal to very early adopters often need modification for the broader market. Look up *Crossing the Chasm* by Geoffrey Moore if you want to know more.

But experiments don't always have to be about money. One of the most famous start-up experiments was conducted by Drew Houston, CEO of Dropbox. When he was trying to understand the potential demand for his cloud storage service, he required people to hand over three kinds of value before they got anything in return. If they wanted it badly enough, thought Houston, they'd play along.

The first value exchange was customers watching a video that Houston posted online. The video appeared to be a product demo (in fact it was just a clever animation), which gave viewers a realistic experience of what it would be like to own the solution.

The user cost? Four minutes and 39 seconds of their valuable time. As YouTube video traffic tends to bomb after 60 seconds, anyone watching the whole video would be indicating a reasonable level of interest, thought Houston.

Next, some clickbait. After the video played, a button appeared inviting potential customers to download Dropbox. 'Who knows what I'll actually download … malware, a virus?' were likely user thoughts. The risk is low, but there's risk all the same. People would only click that button if they were sufficiently interested.

But the click was a trick. The final desirability test appeared on the web page that loaded next. It announced that Dropbox didn't actually exist yet ('Great, you just wasted five minutes of my life') and invited users to sign up to an email list if they were interested in being beta users.

First, I watch a four-and-a-half-minute video, then I attempt a download, next I find out I've been lied to, and now you want me hand over my email address to a potential scam? Exactly.

Only those desperate enough for this kind of solution would sign up. Everyone else (those most likely to say, 'Sure, you build it and I'll buy it!') dropped out of the journey clicks ago.

Less than 12 hours after posting the video, Houston had acquired 70,000 email addresses – 70,000 people who had to *show* they were interested, not just *say* they were interested.

So when designing experiments that are testing potential demand amongst early adopters think about testing across three levels.

© *Elvin Turner.*

Step 3: Run the Experiment

Having designed an experiment with an expected outcome it's time to put it live.

One of the biggest watch-outs here, especially with experiments that you're running in person, can be interfering with the process.

Your experiment is optimised for specific 'lab conditions'. If users don't do what you expect them to, it can be tempting to 'help' them. 'No, you need to click on *that* button … that's it.' 'Don't skip this bit, it's important.' 'Try using lower case and see if that works.'

You're not trying to *make* your experiment work, you're trying to *learn* how it works, unaided. In the real world you won't be there. So set the experiment off and watch what happens. We need to deal in reality.

Step 4: Review the Learning

The experiment is done, now it's time to review what happened. Even though the data should tell its own story, I strongly suggest inviting outsiders to help your team review the data. Fresh pairs of eyes bring valuable objectivity.

I know from coaching hundreds of experiments that often my most valuable input is looking at the results of the first experiment. It's so tempting to retrospectively justify unexpected outcomes that risk derailing ideas. It's also easy to miss some of the hidden gold in the data that reveals you're on to something promising.

That said, in most cases, teams can generally work through the findings and discern some helpful next step conclusions. But consider bringing in a friendly outsider to keep you on the straight and narrow.

Unforeseens   Despite what I said earlier about being tough on specific metrics at this stage, it is important to factor in the influence of unforeseen elements that often occur during experiments.

'We expected outcome X but hadn't anticipated side effect Y to occur during our experiment.'

Even more puzzling is validating an assumption with one cohort of experiment testers, only to get a completely different result with a second cohort.

This can feel like failure but it's actually a bonus. You're finding missing pieces of the puzzle that you didn't know you needed to find.

You've started discovering 'dependent variables'. The things that have to be true for the predicted outcome to occur.

When Airbnb runs tests on its website, it knows that answers will vary according to the weather. Nothing to do with the product, it's all about the context.

So, during the process of experimentation, look out for dependent variables that influence cause-and-effect that you may have previously overlooked.

The reality here is that sometimes you have the right idea, you're trying to validate the right assumption, but you're running the wrong experiment. Finding the right experiment can sometimes be a journey of experimentation in its own right.

So don't be in a rush to ditch your idea after one run of an experiment. Spend some time assessing the context and the cause-and-effect dynamics and persevere a little longer to see whether some tweaks in the experiment change the outcome.

As you can see, despite the desire for a scientific pursuit of undeniable truth, experiments need wiggle room. It wouldn't be exploration if we knew all of the answers in advance.

Step 5: Make a Decision

It's decision time. Based on what you've learned, you likely have three choices in front of you:

1. **The experiment validated our assumption**
   Build out a slightly higher fidelity, slicker version of the experiment that allows you to test another related assumption. Or, if you've learned enough, move on to the next most important leap-of-faith assumption (although ideally, where possible, you're already doing this in parallel).

2. **The experiment invalidated our assumption**

The data was overwhelmingly clear that our assumption is wrong. Don't shred it too quickly though. As I said above, it could be the influence of dependent variables or other factors that your experiment hadn't considered. In many cases you may want to tweak the experiment and run it again.

3. **The experiment was inconclusive**

Some parts of the experiment worked as planned, but others didn't. Again, look for dependent variables. But also look for other signals that might be indicating that your idea is on the right track, but needs to pivot in a slightly different direction.

A journey of exploration is rarely a straight line. Continual course correction as we test our assumptions is a natural part of the experimentation process. If it's all too easy, someone somewhere is probably not dealing in reality.

The learning that you have gathered is a huge confidence builder for executives. My experience is that leaders are typically asked to back bold ideas with little real evidence of their likely success. Ideas that come with a level of data-driven validation are much easier to make decisions about.

In fact, once experimentation had become standard practice inside Pernod Ricard, Managing Director Denis O' Flynn inverted the usual approach to exploring bold new concepts. 'Don't bring me an idea. Run an experiment and bring me some validation,' was his mantra.

Don't Lose the Learning   Regardless of your decision, you're sitting on valuable learning. In most organisations, especially with ideas that turn out to be wrong, the learning dies with the project. Huge mistake! Knowing *not* to do something saves another team reinventing the same broken wheel later.

What's more, hidden amongst the remains of experiments there are often gems of insight that will be of use to other teams around the organisation. Make the deliberate sharing of learning a requirement of every experiment. It's a huge opportunity, not least when combatting a culture that fears failure. Celebrating the courageous team endeavour, and the learning from an idea that turned out to be wrong, is a helpful ally when trying to turn the tide of risk aversion.

Idea Funerals Some companies that are passionate about overcoming risk aversion hold what they call idea funerals or memorials. Senior executives applaud the effort and the journey of teams, recall the reasons why everyone believed the idea to be worthy of exploration from the start, and share the lessons learned. It may sound morbid but it's the sign of a healthy culture.

Most organisations, however, bury their failed ideas in secret. Cover-up cultures, driven by fear, tend to view failures as a career-limiting embarrassment and are disposed of without ceremony. Unfortunately, the courageous souls who worked on the ideas are often castigated, which does little to motivate future innovators.

But in the real world, unless you can predict the future with perfect accuracy, a degree of failure is inevitable.

That's why companies like Netflix, Amazon, Google, Pixar and a host of other super-innovators have chosen to make 'smart failure' a source of competitive advantage.

And a culture of experimentation is an important part of the pathway that every company can choose to create.

Scaling Experiments When an assumption is validated, and the data suggests that it makes sense to scale an idea to the next level, how big do you go next?

There is no simple answer, but as I said earlier, there is a helpful rule of thumb, developed by Mark Bjornsgaard of System-Two. It's called Tank, Pond, Ocean.

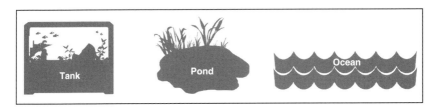

© *Mark Bjornsgaard.*

Experiments start in the tank. A small, safe, controlled environment. Spotify talks about 'minimising the blast radius' of early experiments: testing a new idea with one team or a single cohort of customers.

If the experiments validate their initial assumptions, it's time to move from the tank to the pond, a slightly bigger environment where different dynamics will be at work. Perhaps this is working with five teams, or a larger group of customers.

Again, if the idea iterates successfully in the pond environment, it's time to graduate to the ocean. This is the idea at full scale.

Undoubtedly there will still be learning, but the core idea is sound.

Teams find this metaphor helpful when they are navigating where they are on their journey. In reality, there may be some thimble, paddling pool and lake stages that need throwing into the mix. But beginning an experiment journey with these stages in mind is very helpful for stopping ideas from scaling before they are ready.

'Nail it, then scale it,' as INSEAD assistant professor Nathan Furr says.

Experiments: Innovation Tipping Point or Starting Point? Experiments are innovation rocket fuel. In fact, even though they show up quite late in this book, in many instances I recommend that organisations start with them. Why? Because most companies find innovation just plain difficult. Either it's ad hoc, seen as too difficult to systemise and measure, or is politically problematic because of a recent failure.

Experimentation on the other hand brings simplicity, flexible structure, safety and energy. It is easy to train people at scale very quickly and give them a simple toolkit to get started. I've done this many times, in many contexts and have seen consistent results. It works.

And for these reasons, experimentation is often the perfect Trojan horse to stimulate an appetite for the wider, more strategic innovation capability building that I advocate through this book.

Start smart. Run an experimentation experiment. One team, one experiment, one month. No one need ever know. But they'll probably want to …

Watch-Outs Whilst earlier I described experimentation as the closest thing you'll find to an innovation silver bullet, there are some road bumps that can show up along the way that it is worth being aware of.

'Experiment Police' People love experimentation. If I have a tough audience during a workshop or leadership training session, I know that the experiment slot will win them over. However, watch out for the 'experiment police', especially early on.

These are people who like the experimentation process so much that they go off to study it more deeply. I love this, but it can backfire.

In the early days, you just want people to get started with experiments, build their confidence and instil the principles as instincts and reflexes. It doesn't take long for a training programme conscript to become an ardent convert.

However, like all methodologies there are levels of sophistication. There is always a more precise experiment or a better metric. I fell into this trap myself early on. People would come back to me with experiments that weren't really experiments at all. They were just smaller versions of the entire solution, not a tiny test of a big assumption about one aspect of the solution. And yet management was still excited about the 'sea change' in innovation that they saw taking place.

After a while I stopped complaining to my clients that the 'people weren't doing it properly'. I was right and wrong. No, they weren't perfect experiments, but in their context, the tests were a huge improvement on where they were before. They were still spending far too much too soon on ideas, but everything is relative.

So keep an eye out for purists. Give them the bigger picture and consider making them innovation coaches. As people's familiarity with experiments build, turn up the sophistication.

Bridget Gardner from Pernod Ricard UK handled this issue well. As part of an all-employee training programme she developed a community of 'innovation ambassadors' who were embedded in teams across the business. Every few months we would gather them together, discuss experiments, introduce additional tools and build the group's capabilities.

Mind Your Language Nothing creates employee cynicism like a nice bit of jargon. So when you begin working with experiments, be careful what you call them. For example, I've found that the term 'MVP' (minimum viable product) can be a mixed blessing. Some companies love it, others hate it.

Decca, one of the world's oldest yet most innovative record labels, calls its early experiments 'petri dishes'.

© *Richard Johnston.*

It's a small thing, but it can become a big thing. Early on you're looking for traction, so remove any possible reasons for rejection and choose words that work.

Fake Experiments Some people, when they realise that senior executives are experiment fans, get lazy. They realise that the only way for your idea to get attention is to run an experiment. So they do what they would have always done and simply start referring to it as an experiment.

This is an important watch-out. Despite what I said earlier about avoiding experiment purism early on, you do need to look out for fake experiments because they can be harmful. As soon as people start to see overweight 'experiments' entering the system, there can be a temptation to back off the small and cheap dimensions of a true experiment.

Gradually, the resource, executive attention and associated politics begin to creep back into the process and things begin to grind to a halt. The term 'experiment' loses its meaning and you've taken a few steps backwards.

So ensure that those who sign off on experiments are looking out for icebergs masquerading as ice cubes.

Having a greater level of scrutiny above a certain budget threshold can help here. A cross functional 'funding board' is often useful, not only to get broader input on the experiment's progress, but also to stop senior functional heads pushing through 'experiments' in their own areas for reasons of political or personal preference.

Make It Normal, Not a Campaign   Most people in large organisations have change fatigue. They smell a new change programme a mile off and in many contexts it breeds resistance. Even though experimentation usually breeds energy, it is not immune.

For that reason, I sometimes recommend the tank–pond–ocean approach instead of a more formal introduction to experimentation. Find a team that is hungry to do more and help them become successful experimenters. Before long, other teams start peeping over the dividers to see what they're up to and also want a piece of the action. And so on.

It's a more viral, demand-driven approach and can feel less imposed, less corporate. It can also prevent the boredom that people feel after a change campaign has been running for a while. There's an implicit expectation with change programmes that at some point we will have, well, changed, and so we won't need to do this 'thing' anymore. Organisations can't afford for experimentation to go away. It needs to be business-as-usual for ever. So be mindful of people's expectations from the start and make it a new normal.

Brand Damage Fears   One of the most frequent concerns about customer-facing experiments is the potential for brand damage. 'We can't put *that* in front of customers!' It's a valid concern but many companies have been overcoming it for a few years now. Two approaches have become especially common:

- **Pop-up brands**

  Run the early experiments under another brand. If the idea gains traction, bring it in-house. If not, pull the plug. This is a very common approach in many sectors.

- **Start a beta programme**

  Many companies now offer customers the opportunity to join a 'beta programme'. This means that they get early access to products and services that are still under development. Google and Microsoft have been doing this for years.

  When people's expectations are properly set, glitches and problems are part of the ride and don't negatively impact the brand.

  Usually, the people who sign up for these programmes are early adopters and actually enjoy the process of helping you craft the product. They get a buzz from being on the inside and finding out about things first. It's a win-win.

A Growing, Global Community   One of the great benefits of experimentation is that there is a large, enthusiastic community across the globe that is regularly sharing new tools, tips and experience on how to work with experiments.

A quick web search on 'lean start-up' will get you started, but here are a few places and books that I recommend starting with:

Online   www.strategyzer.com

www.precoil.com

www.leanstack.com

https://medium.com/@johnpcutler

https://grasshopperherder.com/

https://leanstartup.co/

Books *The Lean Startup* (Eric Ries)

Value Proposition Design (Alex Osterwalder)

The First Mile (Scott Anthony)

Scaling Lean (Ash Maurya)

Lean Enterprise (Jez Humble, Joanne Molesky & Barry O' Reilly)

Sense & Respond (Jeff Gothelf & Josh Seiden)

Disciplined Entrepreneurship (Bill Aulet)

Experimentation is possibly the most powerful galvanising force in corporate innovation today. It doesn't really matter whether you choose to start your company's journey into innovation with them or let them emerge after developing an innovation strategy.

Either way, you'll find them invaluable in sparking and sustaining the motivation for innovation and increasing the efficiency and effectiveness of your company's creative pursuits.

30 Show Me the Money?

How to give leaders the confidence to back bolder ideas.

Big ideas often shrivel because it's too easy to say no to them.

The low, perceived ROI (Return on Inconvenience) is one reason.

But a greater one is the misconception about how to correctly measure the potential value of ideas. Here's what I mean.

I once sat in a circle of 20 up-and-coming media executives who were pitching some early ideas to their higher-ups. When I say early ideas, I mean 24 hours old.

The intention was for these young bucks to get some seasoned industry wisdom on their proposed opportunities. But a familiar scenario played out.

One by one, each idea was dismantled and discouraged. What was supposed to be an inspiring, entrepreneurial hothouse left the delegates somewhat disillusioned about the real innovation ambitions and future of the company. The reason? The continual refrain, "Show me the money."

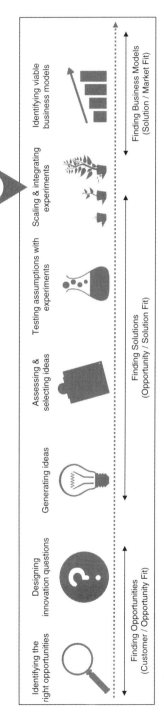

© *Elvin Turner.*

RIP Bold Innovation?

Very early stage, disruptive ideas have a very short life expectancy in most organisations because they can't promise leaders the hard, financial numbers that they are used to in the day-to-day business. The reality is that it's far too early for that.

It's the reason why venture capitalists mostly ignore the revenue projections of eager start-up founders. They know those projections are somewhat fantasy until the idea gets out of the building and meets a real-life customer and all of their unforeseens.

That said, there are some early stage numbers and indicators that can help build executive confidence around bolder ideas.

When I'm helping organisations build their innovation capabilities, I recommend they train their people in three areas.

1. The Company Numbers

When people understand how and why money flows around the business the way it does, it helps them think from the perspective of the leadership team. That's a good thing in a general sense because it helps them become better businesspeople in many dimensions.

But it's doubly helpful when people are considering what ideas to pursue and how to present them to leaders, because they start from a place of shared understanding and realism.

Regularly sharing company financials with employees and helping them understand the "So what?" is essential here. Providing training on the basics of financial management is also worthwhile. It needn't be expensive (I bought a great course from Udemy for $10), and it'll increase the quality and credibility of new idea conversations.

2. Pitch Decks and Canvases

Sometimes new ideas are too easy to turn down because the concept and the potential value are badly communicated. I've sat in on many internal *Shark Tank* or *Dragon's Den*-style events and been part of the conversations when idea pitchers leave the room. So often the decision-makers are left confused about what the idea actually is, let alone the business case.

Help out everyone here with some common resources:

i. A common idea pitch deck – Give people a template of the 10 slides that would cover the essential details about the idea. This might include:

- The nature and scale of the problem/opportunity
- The proposed solution (why this, why us, why now?)
- A proposed business model
- A proposed go-to-market plan
- Competitive analysis
- Likely capabilities and resources required
- Financial projections and metrics
- The core assumptions – known and to be tested
- The proposed next step, success criteria and metrics
- The ask (what help do they need?).

This ensures consistency in approach, creates a common language, provides commercial rigour, and creates a shared expectation of what's needed for an idea to be taken seriously.

And be flexible. Remember that at the early stages, not all of the answers are available. They can only be discovered by experimenting forward.

ii. Some organisations prefer not to use slides but opt for canvases – one-page visual overviews of the key ideas, facts and assumptions.

Use the summary framework at the end of the "Finding Assumptions" chapter as a starting point. Alternatively, the Business Model Canvas or Ash Maurya's Lean Canvas are good options for market-facing ideas. They are free to download and intuitive to use (although it's worth watching some basic tutorial videos on YouTube to get the most from the tools).

3. Learning Before Earning: Early Stage Metrics

Money is usually a very unhelpful early measure for new ideas.

As the chapters on experimentation show, to begin with, the primary task is testing assumptions about whether the idea even makes sense and whether it helps customers make important progress.

Customer/opportunity fit is the first pursuit, followed by opportunity/solution fit. At that stage, a trickle of money can become a more reasonable expectation, but it's only when we find a business model (solution/market fit) that the money becomes more certain.

Fortnite, Epic's runaway success video game, seemed to have appeared out of nowhere but was actually a six-year development journey. Uber, Airbnb and many other so-called unicorn companies followed in the same footsteps. Had money metrics been the emphasis too early, none of them would have survived.

So in the early stages of an innovation journey, what kinds of metrics can leaders justifiably ask to see to help them understand whether an idea is worth continuing to support?

Metrics around learning matter most, especially those that validate assumptions. This means that teams need to communicate clearly with leaders about the experiments that are being run, what they are trying to learn, and to what end.

Depending on the nature of the experiment, examples of early stage metrics might include:

- Rates and types of response to email or social media campaigns
- Information request rates
- Landing page sign-ups
- Letters of intent or pre-orders (using varied price options).

Once you have a working product, however simple, broader ranges of metric can be tracked. These vary according to the nature of the product, but where digital analytics are possible, consider:

- Conversion rates
- Daily active users (a good proxy for pre-revenue growth rates and often the most interesting metric for start-up investors)
- Monthly active users (demonstrating repeat usage)
- Conversion rates from free trials to paying customers
- Revenue growth rates (e.g. monthly and annual recurring revenue)
- Customer acquisition cost
- Customer churn rates.

The main principle is to measure for customer traction. How can you learn with ever greater certainty that you are solving the right problem for the right people in the right way?

Killing 'Zombie' Projects

This can also be helpful for reviewing ideas that persist for too long, so-called 'zombie projects', with the hope that at some point they will turn into revenue earners. Instead of being killed off, they hover in the background, sometimes for years, waiting for a decision to be made on their destiny.

When we track pre-revenue metrics, we can make much better and faster decisions about their value-generating ability. This is especially useful for dealing with executive pet projects that everyone knows should be put to sleep, but they continue limping on.

One other useful metrics category is around resource usage. It is healthy to have a regular reality check on resources used so far, how effectively they have been used, and likely resources required for the next proposed phase. It keeps maintained focus and accountability over scare innovation resources.

Measuring for Reality

If your organisation needs a faster flow of more disruptive ideas, think hard about the impact of metrics in the early stages. Don't allow unrealistic metrics to shut down ideas too soon. Coach your leaders in different kinds of early-stage expectations, and coach your people how to build experiments that deliver confidence-building data.

31 Dead on Arrival

Big bureaucracy kills bold ideas fast. Learn how to keep your ideas alive for long enough to know whether they really should scale.

Being a disruptive idea isn't easy. You're probably going to fail, and everyone wants to kill you. It's a tough gig.

But suppose you're one of those ideas that genuinely *should* make it out of the building alive? This chapter is about keeping ideas breathing long enough to find out whether they really were destined for greatness.

Helping Decision-Makers Make Great Decisions

So why are so many original ideas crushed prematurely? In the previous chapter we looked at how a better business case can help extend the life of an emerging idea.

But that's often only half the story. Literally.

In my experience many disruptive ideas are shut down too soon simply because they are either misunderstood or misrepresented.

I've been part of corporate *Shark Tank* and *Dragon's Den* events and watched executives nod and smile during idea presentations, and then shrug their shoulders to one another when the idea pitchers leave the room. They didn't get it, so the ideas got a straight 'no'.

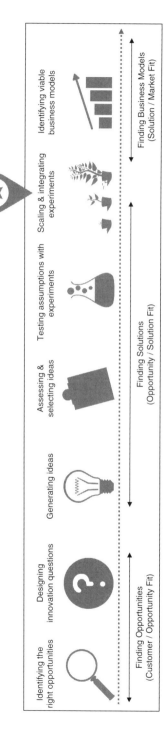

© *Elvin Turner.*

Either that or the ideas festered in a corner for months because managers didn't know on what basis to make a decision. Or, in more consensus-driven cultures, there's no decision because no one wants to upset the idea pitcher.

If your ideas have ever suffered these fates, you'll know how easy it can be to feel disillusioned about leaders not being willing to take risks or try new ideas. But often executives are left with little choice.

Their confidence level is often a function of the *experience* that the idea owner creates around the idea. That includes storytelling, but it also involves anticipating likely feelings, biases, interest and energy of decision-makers, and responding accordingly.

And this extends beyond the initial pitching of an idea. It continues through every phase of an idea's development journey. Every idea is one meeting away from being prematurely flushed.

So how does an idea owner help time-poor, hassled, status-quo-measured managers make the best possible decisions about their ideas?

The starting point is to reframe your job description. You're not just the idea owner, you're a campaign manager. Your job is to engage hearts and minds behind the potential benefits of the idea, but not duck the gritty reality of what's needed for it to succeed.

And of course, the idea might *not* succeed. Idea owners have to walk a difficult and paradoxical line. On the one hand, they need to be passionate enough to push an idea forward, creating 'moments of truth' for decision-makers to engage with the idea and give high-quality feedback. But on the other hand, they must temper that passion with a cool objectivity and be willing to drop ideas when the data says that the idea doesn't actually make sense.

Be a Thought Leader

If you aren't deliberate about creating the conditions under which people can make great decisions, your idea is very likely to fail. You have to own the job of upgrading people's thinking.

Whole books have been written on the topic of stakeholder management so I'm focusing on the two main aspects that I've found that give teams a much greater chance of keeping the right ideas alive for longer:

- Idea journey mapping: Anticipating the journey that a successful idea will need to travel, paying specific attention to the mindset shifts that stakeholders may need to make.
- Stakeholder experience design: Helping stakeholders make the best possible decisions about your idea.

Idea Journey Mapping

'What would need to be true for this idea to succeed?' is perhaps the most important question you can ask throughout the life of an idea. The more accurately we can map a holistic view of the dependencies on an idea's success, the more likely it'll avoid an early grave.

Yet it's a map that will continually change. As you test an idea's assumptions and gather new data, your idea will inevitably evolve. And as it evolves, so must your journey map if it's to support your idea's survival adequately.

So where should you begin?

First, find a cross-functional group to help you. If you're trying to create a realistic journey map you can't afford to make assumptions about how other parts of the organisation will support you. I've seen many ideas fail because the idea owners assumed that IT or logistics could bend into their project timeline, only to find that the required capacity wasn't available when needed.

So assemble the group, explain the idea, the problem it solves, and its current assumptions. Then, sketch out the anticipated idea development journey, approximate timeline, and key milestones on a white board.

Now add the dependencies that you are aware of: decision-making points, resources, collaboration, and capabilities required.

Then say to the group, 'These are my assumptions about *how* this idea will need to develop, but I know I only have half the picture. What am I missing?'

Depending on the responses, you might want to encourage feedback with questions including:

- What concerns do you have about this approach?
- How could it fail?
- Whose support will it need, and at what point?
- What specifically will I need those people to do?
- How might they respond to that request?
- Who would carry most influence in whether this idea succeeds or not?
- If this idea was successful, what would need to be true for it to integrate into current ways of working?
- What new ways of working would be necessary for it to succeed?
- Which important KPIs might this idea affect (in the short-term and long term)?
- Who might feel threatened by these new ways of working?
- How could we minimise that feeling?
- What experience would they need to feel 'safer' about this idea?

Be open to what you hear and be prepared to design a journey that appeals to more than people's logic. Depending on the level of change that your idea may require inside the organisation (or amongst customer behaviour), you will need to consider managing factors such as stakeholders' habits, routines, comfort zones, biases, politics, and deep-rooted fears. This is largely emotional territory, not logical, and we underestimate its influence at our peril.

Based on what you learn, create a more detailed journey map with key milestones and the major belief shifts that may need to take place with different individuals or parts of the organisation.

It can be helpful to clearly articulate the current beliefs of these stakeholders and why they hold them. Then write down the beliefs that they would need to hold in order to support your idea, and then begin planning what would need to be true for them to make that belief shift.

Based on this framework and belief shifts, you're in a position to begin planning how you'll engage with specific stakeholders over the short, medium and longer term.

Build a Coalition

A word of warning though. In this process it can be easy to create a map that includes so many people that it feels overwhelming. I would suggest applying the 80/20 rule here. Which 20% of these stakeholders can facilitate 80% of the progress that you need to make?

And while you're at it, think about your 'minimum viable decision-making group'. What's the smallest number of stakeholders who need to be involved in the service of developing the idea at greatest speed?

For more disruptive ideas, this often means focusing on senior leaders whose opinion will ultimately hold most sway across the organisation.

'You have to build a coalition,' says Harvey Wade, Managing Director of Innovate 21 and former innovation executive at Cisco and Allianz. 'Your coalition is what gets other people on board. It can never be just you against the world.'

Stakeholder Experience Design

Having mapped the journey, you're in a stronger position to plan the kinds of experiences needed to help people make great decisions.

Much of what you'll be doing orients around communication, so for simplicity I'm going to talk about two key aspects: *what* to communicate and *how* to communicate it.

What to Communicate

A friend of mine likes to say, 'The most important question in the world is "So what?"' It's certainly the case when helping stakeholders grapple with new ideas. Speed-to-so-what is a crucial metric in any presentation.

In the previous chapter we covered the essential 'so what' elements to include in a pitching meeting:

- The nature and scale of the problem/opportunity
- The proposed solution (why this, why us, why now?)
- A proposed business model
- A proposed go-to-market plan
- Competitive analysis
- Likely capabilities and resources required
- Financial projections and metrics
- The core assumptions – known and to be tested
- The proposed next step, success criteria and metrics
- The ask (the help you need)

Depending on the stage of your idea, you'll need to adjust these accordingly. But in addition to these elements, there are some more subtleties to consider at this point.

The Hidden Power of 'Why' 'According to molecular biologist John Medina of the University of Washington School of Medicine, the human brain craves meaning before details. When a listener doesn't understand the overarching idea being presented in a pitch, they have a hard time digesting the information.' So says Carmine Gallo in her *Harvard Business Review* article 'The Art of the Elevator Pitch'.[1]

At a stakeholder presentation it can be tempting to launch straight into the idea, especially when under time pressure. After all, that's what you're there to discuss, right? Well, mostly.

Our ideas only make sense in context, and if we skip through that too quickly, our idea may never land properly with the audience. Cutting to the chase should never mean cutting out the context.

Problems Beat Ideas A central part of setting the context is framing the opportunity or problem. If stakeholders agree that you are trying to solve an important problem, but your current idea fails along the journey, the problem remains on the table demanding to be solved. Pitch your idea but own the problem. The future will thank you for it.

Why This, Why Now? Creating a sense of urgency is a core tool in the change management toolbox. You can achieve this for your idea by covering issues such as:

- What are *real* and important customers saying about this problem/opportunity?
- What's changing, what's under threat, what opportunity is emerging? What 'undeniables' are we facing?

---

[1] https://hbr.org/2018/10/the-art-of-the-elevator-pitch

- What realistic scenarios could unfold if we wait or do nothing?
- What is the scale, size, moment and likelihood of impact of those scenarios?
- What evidence can we see today of those scenarios emerging?
- Where have we seen comparable scenarios play out in other industries and what happened to the protagonists?
- How are our competitors responding to the problem/opportunity?

Be an Educator   Don't assume too much knowledge on behalf of your stakeholder audience, especially if your idea relates to new technology. In a pitch meeting, ego can often prevent stakeholders from declaring that they don't understand the fundamentals of an idea.

If they don't get it, they can't make an informed decision.

So doing your homework about likely levels of understanding is very important. It's also one of the benefits of having pre-meetings with stakeholders before a pitch meeting (which we'll cover in a moment). When you know the comprehension journey that people will need to go on, you can design your pitch accordingly.

This is always a delicate balance because over-explaining can get impatient executive fingers twitching. Some executives get ideas quicker than others. They just need the headlines. But others have a different learning style and need to experience it differently. Better to have a couple of fidgeters in the room with everyone on board, than a room full of headscratchers because you didn't create the right learning experience for everyone.

Join the Dots   I said earlier that we can often jump too quickly from the problem we're solving to the specific solution that we're pitching without adequately explaining the context. It's not the only cognitive leapfrogging hazard that can derail a pitch meeting.

When we go from problem to specific solution without sharing the other ideas that we discounted along the way, we can trigger questions in the minds of our audience that create decision friction:

- *Is this the first idea that they came up with?*
- *What other ideas did they consider?*
- *I bet they didn't consider XYZ …*
- *If they did consider other ideas, where are they now?*
- *What makes this idea the best option?*

What they are really wondering is whether you have considered all possible options and whether this is really the best way forward.

Product development expert, Teresa Torres, puts it like this:

We are communicating our research findings as truth without preparing our stakeholders for that truth. We also aren't giving them a chance to integrate their knowledge and expertise when interpreting the findings. We aren't allowing our leaders to co-create research conclusions with us.[2]

Stakeholders will often feel more comfortable about new ideas if they feel that they have had some stake in developing them or guiding them. So, in addition to joining the dots to show how you came to settle on this particular idea, be sure to ask for their advice on how the idea could be improved, and how it should move forward.

How to Communicate

Let's move on to look at the *how* of communicating with stakeholders, which is often the make-or-break element.

---

[2]https://www.producttalk.org/2018/06/managing-stakeholders/

Clarity   I was recently talking to a lobbyist who was pitching an international development idea to several foreign governments. When he shared the idea with one government representative, she responded, 'That's perfect. Simple enough for the minister to understand.'

It wasn't necessarily intended to be a joke about the minister's intellect. It was more a reflection of his lack of time and specific expertise, something that is also true for most executives.

As idea owners we can often struggle with simple. It can feel as if we're not doing our idea justice. Surely it deserves a few buzzwords to give it some extra sizzle! But simplicity in service of clarity is essential when we are helping people make the best decisions possible about ideas.

Here are some examples of companies that have done a great job at crystallising the value that they offer into a few words:

- Evernote: 'Remember everything'
- iPod: '1000 songs in your pocket'
- Weebly: 'The easiest way to make a website'
- DeskBeers: 'Crafted beer, delivered to your office'
- Square: 'Start selling today'
- Tortuga backpacks: 'Bring everything you need without a checking-in bag'

When we read these statements, they seem obvious. That's the point! But don't underestimate how difficult this can be. The reality is copywriters will have spent hours fine-tuning hundreds of different statements to finally reach this level of simplicity that simultaneously presents the solution whilst subtly pointing to the problems that they solve. I know, I've been that copywriter!

So how do we know whether we're being clear enough with our messaging?

The start-up world offers some helpful tools here: The 'mom test' (would your mother understand what you're pitching? If not, simplify your message), and the 'five-second test' (if you had only five seconds to scan a web page could you accurately explain what it was offering?) are two favourites.

But whatever your approach, you are well advised to try out the messaging of any idea presentation with a wider audience before you go into a pitch meeting. You will always be surprised at what people don't quite understand and, if you're open to feedback, you will always come out with a better message.

Tristan Kromer of Grasshopper Herder[3] recommends a simple approach that he calls a 'comprehension test':

- In 1–3 sentences, write down your idea, explaining the value (or progress) it delivers to a specific audience.
- Show your explanation to a colleague (or potential customer) for a few moments and then take it away.
- Ask them to explain the idea and its benefits in their own words.

If the participant's explanation is more or less the same as yours, that counts as a success. If it's quite different, that's a failure.

If 80% of your test subjects succeed you know you're communicating clearly. What's more, as they use their own language, you'll start to hear words reoccurring which you can adopt to make your message even clearer.

Clarity is king and as an idea campaign manager, this has to be a top priority for you. So, if you know that you're someone who struggles with simplicity, find a 'language buddy' who can help you speak better Earthling.

---

[3] https://grasshopperherder.com/comprehension-vs-commitment/

Brevity   Clarity's stablemate is brevity. You may have noticed that some of the examples that I shared above were extremely short. One of the superpowers of brevity is memorability. Short is more likely to be sticky. When you're relying on others to help oil the organisational wheels in favour of your idea, it's a powerful ally.

But brevity is contextual. In my experience you generally need four lengths of message depending on the outcome that you are aiming for, and the context.

The Five-Second Story

This is your key 'campaign message'. It's the value that your idea aims to deliver told in one sentence. It's the one thing that you want your audience to remember. If you had to compress the whole idea into a memorable, pithy tweet, this would be it. This will show up in pretty much all of your communications.

If you were pitching Google, it would be these 77 characters: 'Google organizes the world's information and makes it universally accessible.' It's more about the 'why' and the 'what' than the 'how' at this level.

A fun resource to help you build your story-crunching muscles is *Film in Five Seconds* by Matteo Civaschi and Gianmarco Milesi. It's a book containing dozens of Hollywood movie storylines that have been simplified down to a few key frames. This order of simplification is a superpower.

30-Second Elevator Pitch

When a key stakeholder is approaching along the corridor you need to be ready to pitch. A five-second story isn't enough, and anything longer than 30 seconds could start to feel like an imposition. So, a classic elevator pitch needs to roll off of your tongue at the drop of a hat.

Your objective with the elevator pitch is generally to gain an invitation to share the idea in more detail. Here's what your elevator pitch should contain:

- The problem/opportunity that you're working on.
- The headline benefits and outcomes that you think your idea could deliver.
- Request to book 20 minutes to tell him/her more.

Notice that I didn't include anything about explaining what the idea actually is. That's deliberate. If they are interested in the problem and the benefits that you're proposing, they'll lean in and ask you to describe the idea. That's a good initial level of engagement and suggests that even though they are en route to somewhere else, they have a couple of minutes of flexibility to throw your way.

If you launch straight in with your idea, there's a chance that they'll begin to switch off or immediately start to make inaccurate conclusions about it that shut down their engagement. Of course, if they invite you to tell them more on the spot, you can either push for a meeting or take the risk and go for it.

For eventualities like this, I strongly recommend having something visual pre-prepared on your phone. When people can see something tangible, they click with ideas faster.

So consider having five slides or photos on your phone that you can quickly whip out and talk them through in 60 seconds.

This could be a simple flow chart showing how the problem you're solving shows up and how your idea overcomes it. Depending on the stage that you're at, show sketches of prototypes, users working with prototypes, graphs showing data trends from experiments, quotes from early users – whatever you have that brings meaning and colour to your idea.

If you are invited to meet, make sure that you include your five-second pitch in the meeting name. That'll help you stand out and remind the stakeholder of your corridor encounter.

Also, add a couple of bullet points in the notes section of the invitation to remind your stakeholder of the problem that you're solving and the benefits you're aiming to deliver. If you can, attach your slides or photos as an aide memoire. You need to do everything you can to prevent that meeting from being torpedoed if a fire lands on the stakeholder's desk on the day of your meeting.

Five-Minute Impromptu Pitch

In an ideal world you'll never use this pitch. In the real world it could be the making or breaking of your idea.

Here are the two main scenarios where I've seen it used:

i. **The 'could you just join this meeting?' scenario**
   Completely out of the blue, one of the stakeholders that you've been warming up calls and asks you to step into a meeting that's in full flow. The problem that you're working on has come up in conversation and the stakeholder thinks it would be good to bring you in.

   All eyes are on you as you enter the room. You may not have the opportunity to use slides and you don't necessarily know the level of knowledge or the agendas around the table.

   Start with your elevator pitch to create a baseline of understanding and then use the next few minutes to explain how the idea would work in practice, how the benefits would show up, the assumptions that you're testing, and the wider group of stakeholders that are supporting you.

Undoubtedly questions will follow, questions that you would likely cover in your 20-minute meeting pitch (we'll cover this next). Most likely these will be questions around feasibility, viability, and resources. If the conversation heads this way, you might ask to grab your laptop so that you can refer to your 20-minute pitch. This is reasonable under the circumstances.

Again, depending on the stage of your idea, take anything you can that brings your idea to life, especially anything visual or physical. Remember that you're at base one with these people and your aim is to help them move from awareness of the idea to a level of understanding that helps them make the best possible next-step decision.

ii. **The 'sorry you only have five minutes after all' scenario**

You're waiting outside the pitch meeting room and it's clear that the stakeholders' current meeting is running late. Your 20-minute pitch slides are primed ready to go on your laptop. Finally, the door flings open and you're invited in. 'Sorry, we overran and we're dialling in Japan in five minutes. Can you give us the headline version?'

Always assume that this will happen.

If it doesn't, awesome. But if you're caught off guard and left needing to rush through 20-minutes of slides in five minutes, most likely you'll lose everyone.

It's much better to nail a five-minute pitch, leave them curious, and come back with more time next time. You'll also gain a lot of credibility because few people can pivot so significantly at a moment's notice and present unflapped.

20-Minute Meeting Pitch

This is your opportunity to share the idea in sufficient detail for stakeholders to make a considered, next-step decision. It's likely that you'll face questions in this meeting about unanticipated issues, and that you may need to return having clarified those issues, but this is the main event that you've been working towards. (Most likely you'll have several main events at significant journey milestones.)

Whilst meetings to discuss your idea in detail are likely to run for longer, consider 20 minutes a maximum pitch length to aim for. TED conference speakers aren't allowed to present for more than 18 minutes, so consider your pitch to be your own personal TED talk. In fact, have a look at TED's own speaker guidelines;[4] they're full of useful ideas on how to capture your audience's attention.

But even though you have 20 minutes, less is still more.

Your pitch should cover the essential 'so what' elements that I mentioned in the previous chapter on building good business cases. But resist the temptation to dive into too much detail during your pitch. Allow that to emerge from the questions that will inevitably follow. Attention is a scarce commodity in business. You must do everything you can to protect it. Too much detail when people are still trying to get their heads around what your idea *actually means* can be a turn-off.

Know Your Audience

Obvious, but worth stating: do your homework on stakeholders. What's important to them *right now*? Whose lead do they follow? What kind of questions do they normally ask about new ideas? What is guaranteed to turn them off? Are they numbers people, stories people, visual learners? What's their likely level of understanding about the problem that you're addressing and the solution you're proposing?

---

[4]https://storage.ted.com/tedx/manuals/tedx_speaker_guide.pdf

Find the people who know your stakeholder well, and who have your stakeholder's ear, and ask for their advice. Listen hard to what they say and calibrate your pitch accordingly.

Make It Experiential

Most corporate communication is endured rather than enjoyed. And this is one of your biggest opportunities as an idea steward.

Executives are used to sitting through vanilla presentations that are stuffed with words, graphs and default PowerPoint clipart. It's facts over feelings, logic over magic.

So when someone shows up with a well-crafted, engaging 'idea experience' it immediately stimulates a higher level of engagement.

What are the ingredients of such an experience? In their book *Made to Stick*, Chip and Dan Heath, state that ideas become 'sticky' when they embody six crucial characteristics: simple, unexpected, concrete, credible, emotional and laced with stories.

It's unlikely that your idea pitch will include all of these elements if you are creating it late the night before the meeting. Just as ideas usually improve through iteration, each of these elements will improve the longer you work on them.

That demands a different way of thinking about the role of communication with ideas. Remember, you're a campaign manager. Work back from the outcome that you are trying to achieve and ask: 'What would need to be true for those executives to make the best decision possible about this idea?'

If your idea is going to reach its deserved lifespan, I recommend beginning the communications and experience design from day one. Then come back to it every week to see how it could be improved in the dimensions that the Heath brothers suggest. Great Hollywood scripts go through dozens of drafts. Your pitch experience design shouldn't be any different.

Based on the hundreds of idea pitches I've seen, here are some suggestions on how to create engaging experiences for your audience:

i. **Be visual**

We know this, yet rarely act on it. When something looks great it gets our attention. Some of the best pitches that I've seen were wireframed by an idea team but then developed by a designer. I strongly suggest that you do the same. If you don't have access to one internally, find a freelancer and ask them to spend half a day making it look amazing.

If you have zero budget, use a tool like www.canva.com which gives you direct access to editable, professionally designed visual materials.

Visualising an 'idea story' can become something of an art form. In fact, it's the genius of great advertising. So if you're up for the challenge, always ask yourself, 'If we could only communicate this idea with a single image, what would it be?'

These days there are no excuses for showing up to a pitch with a clunky PowerPoint deck. Your idea likely deserves better and good idea stewardship demands it.

ii. **Experiencing vs showing vs telling**

People need to 'get' your idea quickly in a pitch setting. Typically, that means adequately articulating:

- The problem that you're solving, and for whom
- The context in which it shows up
- Why it's worthy of this group's attention (the prize)
- Your solution
- How the solution works.

At all times in the meeting you are trying to avoid 'cognitive friction' – people not really understanding what you're communicating, and them not necessarily asking for clarification.

Because we all learn in different ways, relying on PowerPoint to *tell* people your idea is likely create a baseline of understanding, but it may not be enough.

Often, the fastest way to help your idea 'click' for people is to give them an experience of it. Put an early prototype in their hands; create a fake app experience using PowerPoint; do whatever you can to *bring the idea to life*. When people experience an idea, they are much more likely to be able to imagine it in use and in context.

In the early days of idea experimentation, the experience that you create is inevitably going to feel a little rough-and-ready. This can put people off, believing that it won't be taken seriously unless it's a finished product. My experience is that decision-makers are much more likely to click with an idea that they can see and feel, even if it does require some imagination.

If a physical experience isn't possible, *show* the idea instead. Create mock-ups of the imagined product in use, in context. Show interfaces, sketches, customers using or responding to the idea. Show customer journey stages, where the problem is encountered and how your idea shows up. Do everything you can to make the idea feel real. This gives the audience the best possible chance to provide useful, informed and accurate feedback.

iii. **Words**

Use as few as possible. Get to the point. Choose evocative words. Avoid jargon.

If you're pitching a brand-new concept, help people to connect with it by aligning it with something familiar. When the sharing economy began to explode, a standard shorthand for many new ideas was, 'It's like Uber for … '

What familiar, product, service or experience could you compare your idea to help people understand it immediately?

iv. **Lead with 'data stories'**

The most responsible way to make decisions about yet-to-be-proven ideas is with data. Sharing the cause-and-effect relationships of your experiments provides an objective platform for discussion. This helps to keep subjective opinions in check and guards against the unhelpful influences of overexcitement, politics and fear.

Data helps to validate important assumptions about our ideas. It doesn't replace gut-feel, instincts or experience, but it brings objective evidence that helps build stakeholder confidence around decision-making.

Yet great data can also kill an idea stone dead. I once coached the head of data at a global organisation who was frustrated that his higher-ups weren't backing his team's experiments, even though the data pointed to a compelling investment case.

I asked him to show me some examples of what he meant and quickly saw the problem. His numbers showed hockey stick growth, but exactly *what* was growing was a mystery. He was all numbers and no stories. I literally had no idea what his idea was or what it meant.

So lead with data, but turn data into stories. Put the customer in amongst the data, point to human behaviours and cause-and-effect shifts that occurred when you iterated an experiment.

v. **Progress not PowerPoint**

When your idea is already moving and you're preparing for an update meeting remember this: people don't really care about your slides. They want to see progress.

What has happened since the last meeting? How has the idea developed? How are customers responding? Is it trending or tanking?

So, while it's useful to have some slides in your back pocket, your major focus should be on *showing* your progress. It comes back to helping people experience the idea and watching how other people are responding to the idea (i.e. customers and users).

Take your slides to an update meeting, but most likely you won't need many (or any) of them.

vi. Emotion

Show authentic passion about your idea when you pitch. If people don't feel that you really care, they are unlikely to.

vii. Let someone else pitch

Even if you carry infectious enthusiasm for your idea and you are the company's subject matter expert, you may not be the best person to pitch it. With your stakeholders in mind, ask, 'Who will carry most credibility with this group?'

Whether we like it or not, we all have a personal brand. As idea owners, to give our ideas the best possible chance of making it to the next stage, we have to be brutally honest about whether we are the best people to pitch it. That will likely involve asking people we trust to give us honest feedback about whether we should step back from certain pitches for the sake of the idea.

Sometimes the best person to pitch your idea is a customer. I once heard of a senior manager who arranged for her monthly one-to-one with the CEO to coincide with a customer meeting. Only she didn't tell the CEO. And this wasn't to be an ordinary customer meeting. It was a workshop to discuss an idea that the CEO had specifically forbidden the manager to work on.

With the workshop in full flow, the CEO arrived for the one-to-one and initially assumed that he'd come to the wrong room. The manager quickly ushered him in and introduced him to the customers. The penny began to drop but the now-trapped CEO was forced to sit and listen.

To cut a long story short, when the CEO had first-hand experience of customers' enthusiasm for the idea, his mind was changed, and the idea went forward.

Whilst I don't necessarily recommend adopting this potentially career-limiting approach, there's a lot that can be learned about creating the right experience for stakeholders, in service of helping them make the best possible decision for the idea.

Where Possible Work One-to-One

Pitching ideas in a group setting can put your fledgling idea at the mercy of unhelpful group dynamics: politics, groupthink, following the opinion of the most senior person in the room, to name but a few.

To give your idea the best possible chance of getting the most appropriate feedback, meet stakeholders one-to-one. Sure, it's more time-intensive, but it's more likely that stakeholders will ask the questions that they may feel too vulnerable to ask amongst peers – especially around their real level of understanding.

Working one-to-one also helps you gauge the level of interest and the support that each stakeholder is likely to give your idea. What's more it creates more space for stakeholders with specific expertise to contribute more value to your idea. This is especially true for more introvert stakeholders who may stay quiet in a group setting yet have valuable insights to offer.

Even if you do have to pitch the idea in a meeting, get some one-on-one time with as many stakeholders as possible in advance. Ensuring that stakeholders fully understand the idea *before* they enter the meeting means there's a much lower risk of them rejecting it because they hadn't fully grasped its potential value. It also gives people time to reflect on the idea more fully than a pitch meeting may allow, meaning the quality of your input is likely to improve.

You'll find ideas on how to prepare for these kinds of one-to-one meetings in the chapter *You Are a User Experience.*

When You Can't Get a Senior Enough Audience

Sometimes, your idea can't reach first base because your line manager isn't prepared to sponsor it any further up the organisational chart.

This can be extremely frustrating, especially in environments where circumventing the hierarchy is a career-limiting decision.

The irony is that senior leaders often complain that there are too few bold ideas emerging from employees. The ideas are usually out there. They just lack a survivable route to the boardroom table.

There are two approaches that I have seen work well in most organisations that have tried them:

1. **Quarterly pitch days**

    Employees are invited to pitch new ideas directly to the board, rather than going through the usual channels. The following factors can make these days most likely to succeed:

    i. Provide guidelines on the most important problems or opportunities that the ideas should focus on. This avoids people wasting time on well-intentioned ideas that don't move any strategic needles.

    ii. Ask people to pitch experiment results and recommendations rather than brand new untested ideas. Even some rudimentary testing brings some helpful rigour into the process and gives the executive audience some data points with which to make better next-step decisions. (If you take this approach, you'll need to give people some basic training on how to run cheap, fast and effective experiments.)

    iii. Ask people to dream big but start small. Incremental ideas generally make it through the system anyway, so invite bolder, more disruptive ideas which only an executive audience is likely to be able to sponsor.

iv. Give people supporting resources to help them develop great pitches.

v. Have a filtering process that includes direct input from a board member. Realistically there will be a limit to the number of ideas that the board can hear in one sitting, so invite people to send in their ideas in advance. But always give considered feedback to those who submit ideas that don't quite make the cut. There's nothing more demoralising than receiving a reply-to-all/'computer-says-no'-style email after working on an idea for a long time.

vi. Create a Pitch Book for the executive sponsors; the book should clearly explain each idea in 100 words. If the executives can refer to this during presentations it helps counter the impact of poorly presented ideas that are actually worthy of consideration.

vii. Ensure the board is actually prepared to back some ideas to the next stage. That may mean having some dedicated 'seed capital' budget available. Otherwise the whole process is just theatrics and loses credibility very quickly.

viii. Have some fun in how the event is staged. Some companies do this off-site in a funky venue, or after hours with a bar. Some create specific branding for the event and purposely aim to make it feel more like a start-up environment. Be authentic though. If it smells fake people will only show up for the beer.

2. **Idea management systems**

If employees have a central place to submit ideas that are regularly reviewed by the board, there's a greater chance of bolder ideas emerging. There are mixed views on the value of allowing employees to submit ideas anonymously, but in the early days of building a culture of innovation I've seen its merits.

In one global advertising agency, only creative directors were deemed worthy to propose 'big' ideas. That severely constrained the flow of creativity from the several thousand other employees that were spread around the globe.

When the company implemented an anonymous idea management system something magical happened. An account manager would put out a request for ideas and employees would vote on those that were subsequently submitted. More often than not, the ideas rising to the top of the pile were from junior account executives hidden in an office far from the centre.

The life of a new idea is a precarious one. But with careful 'campaign management' you can increase its chances of staying alive long enough to know whether it really is the game changer that you hope it is.

32 Your Great Idea Isn't Enough

Great ideas only work with a great business model. Here's how to start designing one.

A zombie's favourite bloom must be the corpse flower, so-called because of the smell of rotting flesh that it exudes (really).

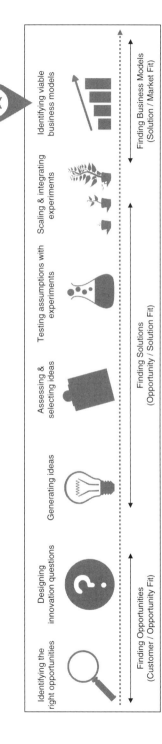

© *Elvin Turner.*

It only flowers once every 40 years and is only found in the equatorial rainforests of Sumatra. It only shows up in a very specific context.

Ideas are the same: they need a specific context in which to work.

But often, our excitement about an idea overshadows the need to explore and design the unique context in which that idea can thrive.

One crucial dimension of context is the business model. The best idea in the world is almost useless without the right business model. I say 'almost' because even at the early stages, some ideas can have potential value as intellectual property that can be licensed.

Three Exchanges

If your idea is customer-facing, it is very likely that a three-way value exchange needs to take place:

- *Creating* value for customers
- *Distributing* value to customers
- *Exchanging* value with customers.

The key to discovering solution/market-fit for an idea is designing a business model that allows these three value exchanges to show up simultaneously, efficiently and profitably.

But this doesn't only apply to new products. The most innovative companies treat their business models as a source of continual experimentation and evolution. They have to. They recognise that yesterday's formula for profitable relevance subtly changed overnight, and therefore so must their business model. Business model innovation is a source of competitive advantage in its own right.

'Every successful company, whether it knows it or not, owes its success to its business model,' says business model expert Mark Johnson.[1]

This is especially true when it comes to disruptive innovation.

'Nine times out of ten, innovation at scale is about a better business model, not a better app,' says Rafael Orta, a former eBay and Tesco executive, now chief product officer at moneysupermarket .com. 'When you look at the companies that are winning in the digital era, their underlying advantage is a different business model, and that's not going away.'

Whether you're searching for a business model for a new product or evolving an existing model, how do you go about it?

Business Model Power Tools

One of the most useful tools to appear on the innovation scene in the last 10 years is the Business Model Canvas. I introduced it in Chapter 7, so head back there for an overview.

---

[1] https://hbr.org/2018/12/digital-growth-depends-more-on-business-models-than-technology

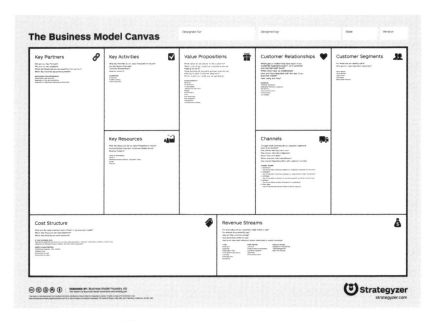

Illustration designed by Strategyzer; Creative Commons Attribution – Share Alike 3.0 Unported Licence.

Like the concept of minimum viable products, the Business Model Canvas has helped many organisations amplify their innovation capabilities for several reasons:

- It is intuitive and easy to work with immediately.
- It provides a common language and format for people to discuss business model ideas.
- It helps teams deal in reality and quickly uncover unforeseen issues.
- It has attracted a large global community of practitioners who frequently share their best practices online.
- It's free to download and use.

In the first instance, use the Business Model Canvas as a brainstorming tool. With the product/solution idea in mind, set your team the goal of developing several different business model prototypes. It can be tempting just to satisfy yourself with the first model that emerges. But that's the equivalent of stopping a brainstorm after one just idea.

And just like the outcomes of a brainstorm, any prototype business model that you choose to take forward will be an iterative development journey. Your canvas contains a mix of facts and assumptions which need to be validated.

This means that your progress towards discovering solution/market-fit must be an aligned, bifocal pursuit: the learning from your solution experiments and your business model investigations must inform one another.

Designing 'Unfair' Advantages

If your validation journey looks promising and an initial business model is emerging, begin designing a second layer of sophistication: 'unfair' advantages, barriers to entry that make the model difficult to copy. That extends the window for growing market share and the opportunity for charging premium revenues.

Unfair advantages at the *solution* level protect your competitive position to a certain degree. A business model that *also* contains unfair advantages provides a deeper level of protection and should be deliberately pursued. Examples of unfair advantages to explore include:

- Exclusive agreements with key partners and distributors (Apple's iPhone).

- Exclusive licencing of strategic technology assets (Dow Chemical).
- Acquisition of niche companies to access valuable resources, talent and capabilities (Cisco).
- Pricing, e.g. giving away the product for free because value is extracted in other ways (Waze).

Every organisation is different, so make the pursuit of unfair advantages a creative endeavour tailored for your unique context.

Business-Model-Innovation-as-Normal

The best innovators make business model innovation a deliberate, ongoing practice. So if your solution makes it to launch, build in regular business model reviews for two reasons.

First, to ensure you are continually recalibrating the model in line with inevitable market changes and internal priority adjustments.

Second, to look for ever-better business models that are more profitable and difficult to copy. A useful way to do this is to use the canvas to provoke disruptive questions that the competition would hate you to answer, for example:

- How could we increase sales without the need for distribution partners?
- How could we automate 90% of the customer relationship without sacrificing customer intimacy?
- How could we develop the solution with superior resources that competitors couldn't access?

Work through each of the nine boxes on your Business Model Canvas and design questions that focus the simultaneous pursuit of maximum stakeholder progress and maximum profitability. Look back at Chapter 19 'Catalytic Questions' for more ideas.

Alex Osterwalder, the originator of the Business Model Canvas. Illustration © Richard Johnston.

Friction vs Flow

Another area to monitor is the health of business model dynamics. For the nine boxes to perform optimally and integrate effectively, certain dynamics will need to be present. For example, what would need to be true to minimise business model friction in areas such as:

- Decision-making speed
- Collaboration between internal functions
- Process efficiency
- Resource allocation (quantity and speed)
- Supply chain dynamics

- Regulatory compliance
- Quality of partner relationships.

Tracking the cause-and-effect dependencies that knit your business model together is crucial. These non-negotiable performance drivers are just as important to your business model as the nine boxes on the canvas. So, having identified them do three things:

1. Establish 'vital signs' metrics for the major dynamics. What is the minimum performance threshold that the business model can tolerate before performance is impaired?

2. Monitor the performance of these dynamics and their dependencies.

3. Communicate them clearly to stakeholders whose role and performance has a direct or indirect impact on these dynamics and dependencies. Maintain healthy relationships and communication with these stakeholders and collaborate with them to maximise the flow of value across the business model.

Competitor's Business Models

Another use for the Business Model Canvas is to map competitors' business models. Studying existing models and anticipating likely moves is a valuable part of business model innovation. Using the Business Model Canvas makes this a fast, collaborative and more accessible conversation to have on an ongoing basis.

It can also be useful to help anticipate competitors' responses to your strategic moves.

Growing Business Model Instincts

One piece of advice I give to all teams that I work with in this area is to become business model students. As you go through daily life, notice the brands, offers, product launches around you and consider some of the necessary elements of the business model. What would need to be true for that product or offer to succeed?

Why is this so important? Because when business model thinking becomes instinctive amongst your people, the strategic intelligence and imagination of your whole organisation lifts. Innovation capacity rises by default and strategic new ideas have a greater chance of bubbling up naturally, rather than having to wait for orchestrated meetings.

It also nudges innovation in the open-source direction: many more brains working on the problems and opportunities that matter most.

What if once a month your team meeting set aside 20 minutes to discuss what you've each noticed about business model dynamics – yours, competitors' and any organisation doing something different – and then experimenting with anything useful that emerges? Or whatever regular rhythm or format works for you.

It's all part of pursuing an everyday innovation reflex.

Part Three
Building Your People's Innovation Capabilities

Most organisations want more innovation but few equip their people to actually deliver it. This section provides practical strategies, roadmaps and case studies to help your people out-innovate your competitors.

33 Enabling Ingenuity

Equipping people to turn on bolder innovation.

Innovation as a Core Competency

Most organisations simply don't teach people what innovation is, how it works, where their personal strengths may lie, or how to do it well. Yet they expect ingenuity on demand.

A training video on brainstorming that's playing in the background whilst doing your email isn't going to move many innovation needles. Harsh, perhaps, but sadly true in many organisations.

And whilst innovation sometimes benefits from serendipity, great innovators don't leave such high-stakes outcomes to chance. They train and coach people in innovation and help it show up in daily life through processes, rewards and metrics. It is cause and effect. It's a core competency for all.

Train Less, Do More

Innovation often has a mystical reputation for being unteachable. Or is a power that leaders instinctively develop by virtue of their seniority. Neither are true.

I've watched nervous employees bloom into confident innovators inside dozens of organisations. But don't expect it to come from a training programme. Not on its own anyway.

'Learning innovation is 2% instruction and 98% application,' says Andy Billings, Vice President of Profitable Creativity at Electronic Arts Inc. Based on the many contexts in which I've seen innovation capability develop, I would agree.

Yet when many companies decide to train their employees in innovation capabilities, the model is usually flipped. People attend a course and are expected to apply the learning as they would after an advanced Excel workshop. There's a big difference between practising a skill that neatly fits into the day job and its reward structures and introducing new ideas that actively challenge the status quo.

Successful innovators have been on a mindset and behaviour transformation. It happens over time and needs a combination of motivation, capabilities, opportunity and resources.

Training that Works

I receive many requests to design and facilitate innovation capability programmes. Before discussing the content of any course, I strongly recommend two design principles as a minimum starting point.

1. Create a Context and Expectation

Ideally, the training should be part of a bigger picture to help people understand why this is an important use of their time. If they don't care enough, they won't engage. So as a minimum, ensure every programme is framed around these questions:

- What specific needles does the business need to move, and why?
- By when?

- Why have these people been chosen? Why now?
- What outcomes are you expecting of them?

2. Create Space for Dedicated Application of Learning

The most effective innovation training programmes expect delegates to produce something tangible with their learning. By implication this means that the classroom experience is only the beginning. This isn't an optional, vague add-on; it's a rigorous, integral part of the development process.

Regardless of the audience, when both of these components are in place there is a much higher chance that people's innovation capability will tangibly increase.

So what should a training programme include? It will vary according to a company's specific context and strategy, but as a minimum, I would recommend the following for executives and managers.

Executive Development by Stealth

Most leaders that I meet have had very little training and development in innovation. There seems to be an unwritten assumption that if you've made it this far, you must know how to do it. That's probably true if we're talking about incremental innovation, but that's not what most organisations are asking for.

So it's not uncommon to have leaders sponsoring innovation programmes with no real experience in what it takes – organisationally and personally – to deliver more transformational levels of innovation.

It's a delicate business trying to convince leaders that they would benefit from innovation training that they will *genuinely* apply. Many say they can't justify the time. Others' pride won't allow them to admit a gap in their knowledge. Some genuinely believe they've ticked the box because of a half-day innovation module they once attended. Others still fear the responsibility of leading more disruptive innovation on the other side of the programme, and so rail against it.

So my approach is to not talk about training at all.

I facilitate 'innovation strategy off-sites' instead.

It's what David Reay, senior vice president of Sony Music Entertainment, calls, 'The education of executives by stealth'. I like that.

With executives, I find that it's a much more productive approach to use innovation tools as *facilitation aids*, rather than *training topics*.

For example, a business model canvas only requires five minutes of explanation before a team can work with it for the first time. During the hour's conversation that follows, I can drop in coaching cues and make suggestions about how the approach could be sustainably embedded into the rhythm of the business.

Across a couple of days, it's possible to give leaders experience with a range of tools that help them think more strategically about innovation, and that provoke important discussions that rarely otherwise make it on to the agenda.

Outside of the meeting, individual executives often want to probe deeper into other tools and approaches that might be useful for their teams.

With the right design it's possible for many great outcomes to emerge from these workshops:

- Applied 'stealth' training in innovation strategy tools that live beyond the meeting.
- Increased understanding and agreement about the systemic dependencies of a higher performing innovation.
- The ways of working that the team must embrace for innovation to succeed.

- The metrics that innovation must deliver – all of which tie neatly into the tools that people will be trained in later (e.g. experiments).

- A collective sigh of relief that innovation isn't such a black art after all.

Emerging Leaders and 'High Potentials'

When working with more junior executives it's possible to employ more conventional approaches to learning. If a business wants to quickly activate managers with innovation capabilities, the journey that I have found bears most fruit is to quickly help them achieve the following within a 60–90-day period:

- Frame a strategic, catalytic question around a significant, relevant business challenge.

- Lead the idea generation and selection process.

- Design and run multiple solution experiments.

- Design a business model prototype.

- Prepare a compelling 10-minute overview of the innovation journey with a strong commercial recommendation on how to proceed with the idea.

Employee development programmes can come in all shapes and sizes with varying time and budget requirements. Every company is different, yet in the specific context of developing the next wave of leaders, I've found that some common steps work well in most contexts:

1. Identify and recruit delegates (ideally those with a combination of ability, drive and social skills).

2. Work with delegates' line managers to set their expectations on the support levels required, and the amount of time that delegates will need to spend on experiments.

3. Identify and brief senior programme sponsors who can provide delegates with coaching and advice through the innovation journey.

4. Agree strategic issue areas with sponsors and line managers to frame delegates' solution exploration.

5. On-board delegates with the programme journey.

6. Design a 3–5 day innovation 'bootcamp' that immerses delegates in three areas: innovation strategy, innovation tools, and innovation culture.

7. Give time and space for delegates to apply the tools during the 'bootcamp' – leaving with experiments to run back in the business over 60–90 days.

8. Give coaching support for delegates as they navigate their experiment journey.

9. Provide a playback event for delegates to share their learning and recommendations with sponsors.

10. Debrief and next steps on normalising innovation in their local context.

Delegates generally want their ideas to succeed on these programmes, but that's not the point. Experiencing the highs and lows of *leading* the journey with the help of the tools is what solidifies the learning and prepares them for ongoing application. It gets them to first base in capabilities and second base in mindset.

Going Deeper

After the programme, I recommend that delegates facilitate an innovation performance process for their teams, helping to shape the context and teach the tools that make innovation a more inevitable and repeatable outcome in their local contexts. That might include:

- Facilitating the creation of a team innovation strategy (if it's appropriate at their level, and one doesn't exist already).

- Identifying the most important team innovation priorities/questions to answer in the next 12–36 months.

- Facilitating a conversation about how to create more capacity for innovation in the team (time, collaboration, resources, etc.).

- Facilitating innovation tool training for the team (teaching is a great way to consolidate learning).

- Initiating team projects for the questions that matter most.

- Providing coaching for other team members.

- Co-designing measures with the team to track progress and accountability.

This goes much deeper than simply training people in concepts; it provides first-hand experience in applying the tools, extends the delegates' learning to their immediate teams, provides experience in building sustainable innovation capacity in their teams, and increases the overall innovation capability of a much wider group of people.

Sony Music's Innovation Programme

'Amplify', Sony Music Entertainment's award-winning innovation leadership programme, has put hundreds of managers through a similar development process. Teresa Kotlicka, one of the company's talent experts, helped design and facilitate the programme, and suggests that there are two key elements that make the difference.

'We realised early on that delegates have to be taught to fall in love with their *problem*, not the proposed *solution*,' says Kotlicka, referring to the wrong kind of 'idea love' that I mentioned earlier. Failing to learn this crucial skill early on has significant knock-on effects when delegates later discover that they have been investing in the wrong ideas all along. 'It's an important lesson to *learn* in a safe environment on the programme and then *apply* for the rest of their careers,' says Kotlicka.

Working with leadership development consultancy DPA, the Amplify programme accomplished this with sessions that specifically helped delegates identify the flawed assumptions in their ideas very early on. The process can smart a little at first, but asking that essential question, 'How am I wrong?' soon becomes second nature. And it does wonders for keeping the ego in check.

Turning Concepts into Instincts

Kotlicka's second recommendation concerns making learning stick beyond the programme. 'You have to design application time into the programme so that concepts can become instincts for people,' explains Kotlicka. 'When people develop a radar for unproven assumptions, or can spot the coalition of stakeholders that's required three steps ahead, you know they are in a much better place to serve the business than if they simply walked out of a classroom with a bunch of beautiful PowerPoint slides.'

I often see great ideas die because they are misunderstood by executives or misrepresented by their owners. Sony Music addressed this with the help of two expert storytelling coaches, Rob Salafia and Ole Tillmann. This ensured that delegates were able to represent their ideas with impact, passion and creativity at all stages of the innovation journey.

Paying It Forward

'As the name suggests, "Amplify" is "a pay-it-forward" programme,' says David Reay, senior vice president at Sony Music Entertainment. 'We designed it so that delegates could become innovation agents across the global organisation, activating their own projects but also equipping and encouraging others along the way. We now have a human innovation network with a shared language, experience, mindset, ambition.'

Rewiring Capabilities for Innovation

But building innovation capabilities isn't only a matter of enhancing innovation process skills. It's also about rewiring existing capabilities in better ways.

Achieving any significant innovation outcome requires cross-functional collaboration, something which many large organisations struggle to achieve. And it's a reason why many organisations now create temporary cross-functional teams or 'swarms' around innovation problems to help them deliver better results faster.

'At the heart of digital innovation is the small, cross-functional team,' say Jeff Gothelf and Josh Seiden in their book *Sense and Respond*. 'You'll typically find a balanced group made up of the diverse capabilities you need to launch a digital product or service and to quickly interpret the insight generated by the resulting two-way conversations.'

This is standard practice inside 'born digital' organisations and becoming more common elsewhere. But if such structural flexibility isn't yet possible inside your organisation, you can still benefit from its wisdom.

Start an 'Idea Advisory Board'

I encourage people to create informal, cross-functional 'idea advisory boards' for their ideas. This isn't a formal team, simply a group of cross-functional colleagues willing to give specific, early input over a coffee. 'What would need to be true from your perspective for this idea to work? How could it fail? What am I missing? Is it solving the right problem?' Most people are happy to help with such requests. For many it's often an interesting diversion from the day job.

The same group can often be helpful for granting important 'favours' through the project: access to information, introductions, sounding out senior colleagues on aspects of the idea, access to resources, and so on.

It's a simple way to start building a network of capabilities around your idea to help validate it and accelerate the decision-making process downstream.

Don't Do Everything Yourself

One of the temptations that I often see companies fall into is believing that they need to build everything themselves, and if they can't, then the idea can't be worth pursuing.

I've watched many ill-equipped but enthusiastic teams burn themselves out trying to build an app that a freelance coder could have developed in a few hours.

More and more, especially for disruptive innovation, the role of the organisation is to facilitate appropriate collaboration between diverse capabilities, many of which may lie outside the organisation, not build everything internally. It seems obvious and yet is often overlooked in the panic to innovate quickly.

Networking giant Cisco uses an ecosystem approach to innovation which is a useful rule of thumb to consider. The company's holistic view on how to create the most value most effectively combines five complementary approaches:

i. **Build:** Creating their own products and intellectual property.

ii. **Buy:** Acquiring companies for their technology and talent.

iii. **Partner:** Developing solutions in partnership with other technology companies.

iv. **Invest:** Supporting strategically interesting companies or hedging bets.

v. **Co-develop:** Plugging into the global network of technology developers and, where appropriate, supporting them with incubation resources.

Every company needs to design its own approach to sourcing and networking appropriate capabilities. A key part of that is strategically choosing what *not* to do and developing strong competencies in the orchestration of networks of capabilities.

Future Capabilities

Tracking future market trends also presents questions about the strategic capabilities that will be needed in the future. Part of the organisational innovation mandate is to explore, not only the capabilities that you'll need in the future, but also how they will transition and integrate into the organisation effectively.

Get Started

Innovation needs know-how. There's no escaping it, which is why the best innovators make it a strategic, ongoing concern. It doesn't have to break the bank, but typically you do need to prime the pump with some capability foundations.

For more resources, take a look at www.belesszombie.com/turniton.

Part Four
Time, Money and Talent: How to Resource Innovation

B usiness-as-usual makes little provision for bolder innovation. This section helps you rethink how resources are managed and allocated so that the future has a greater chance of showing up.

34 Who Does It and Who Pays for It?

Smart strategies for resourcing bolder innovation.

Where your treasure is, there your heart will be also.

Matthew 6:21

'W e gave ourselves an eight-out-of-ten for talking about innovation, but a three-out-of-ten for doing anything about it,' says Denis O' Flynn, former UK managing director of drinks giant Pernod Ricard. As we saw earlier, O'Flynn managed to shift this balance, but not without a concerted focus on some key aspects of resourcing.

Nothing speaks louder about true innovation motivations than how time and money are spent.

Glossy, end-of-year financial reports may ooze snappy, investor-friendly innovation soundbites. But ultimately resourcing reveals reality.

I once asked a manager inside a global publishing company to estimate the approximate split of resources allocated to enhancing today's business versus exploring tomorrow's. '110% on today,' was his reply.

It turned out that he was only half-joking. Yet it underlines the tension facing many organisations that need to build a bigger future. The inertia of the status quo and its iron grip on resourcing can often feel irresistible, even to CEOs.

So how does an organisation begin to better recalibrate resources – time, money, capabilities, means, rewards and energy – around innovation?

Owning and Funding Innovation

A helpful starting point is to agree an overall resourcing model that can bring a lot of clarity to how and where innovation shows up. This ultimately boils down to answering two key questions:

1. Who owns innovation (central vs distributed)?
2. Who funds innovation (dedicated vs ad hoc)?

Without clarity on these issues your innovation performance will flounder. The jaws of the status quo machine are unforgiving towards anything that smells vague in either dimension.

The figure below shows a model from Robert Wolcott and Michael J Lippitz[1] that can be a helpful navigation aid to explore the right approach for your organisation and its initiatives.

---

[1] https://sloanreview.mit.edu/article/the-four-models-of-corporate-entrepreneurship/

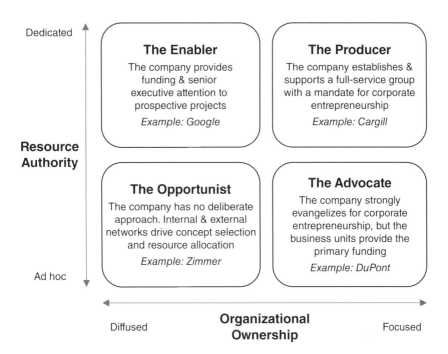

Source: MIT Sloan Management Review, October 2007

Most organisations will trend towards an Opportunist model in the absence of any other deliberate intent. With the right culture and engagement from senior leaders this model can work but is perhaps the most vulnerable of the four described. Typically, few dedicated processes, resources and senior sponsorship exist, making innovation somewhat sporadic, arduous, disconnected and inefficient.

At the other end of the spectrum, Producers are highly deliberate and organised in the way they plan and deliver innovation. This favours companies in pursuit of more disruptive levels of innovation, whether that's exploring brand new technologies or designing new markets. In recent years it has become popular to set up corporate innovation 'labs' to serve this purpose.

Advocates are less likely to dream quite so big. They are generally havens for less adventurous innovation because they operate at a business unit level where the overriding motivation is for continuous growth from the core. That's not necessarily a bad thing but works best when closely connected to a Producer team. They can pilot disruptive ideas and hand them over to the Advocate teams once their desirability, feasibility and viability have been somewhat road-tested.

The Enabler model is well suited to organisations where well networked knowledge workers regularly come up with new ideas and need access to resources to develop them. Consultancies and technology companies tend to prosper with this model.

Ultimately, you need to choose a model that best serves your strategy. You may choose to run a mixed economy, with innovation initiatives of different strategic importance being owned and funded in different ways. That's fine. Just pick something, see what you learn from the approach and then iterate your model accordingly.

Which approach you choose is perhaps less important than *whether* you choose. Having clarity about which resourcing model would best support your innovation strategy, and then organising accordingly is a huge step forward. Most organisations that I encounter are accidental Opportunists whose innovation performance would improve if they simply became more deliberate in their focus.

So, how does your organisation think about who funds and owns innovation? Which of the profiles chime most clearly with who you are today and who you need to become tomorrow? What shifts would need to occur for you to be successful in those dimensions?

If the answer is unclear, I strongly suggest initiating a leadership conversation to pursue a dedicated approach to resourcing.

Having that strategic framework in place is undoubtedly helpful. But navigating the ongoing resourcing of innovation has its fair share of challenges to overcome. Here are some of the most common that I encounter with some suggestions on how to move beyond them.

1. Funding the Future: Provoke a Point-of-View

How you choose to structure resource allocation is a matter of innovation strategy.

But perhaps the bigger question is not *how*, but *how much?*

Whether it's a distributed model of funding and managing innovation, or a centralised approach, the million-dollar question is, 'How much is enough?'

Answering that question can often feel too difficult, too ambiguous and too politically charged to broach. But it doesn't have to be.

In the innovation strategy section, I suggested an outline for a leadership workshop to help jumpstart what can be a cumbersome conversation about the future. Combined with a discussion about the approximate, future resource requirements (see the 10/20/70 split in chapter five), it can create some useful starting points. For example:

By (year A), we need (outcomes B+C+D) which will require a resource split of approximately (X% / Y% / Z%).

I realise that this sounds overly simplistic but in many settings it's exactly the kind of provocation that executive conversations need to get started.

It creates a point of view for people to respond to: *Do I agree? If not, why not? Which proportions feel more appropriate? Why? Which assumptions are driving my thinking?* Much of this inner dialogue remains hidden, tacit and often unprocessed in the collective executive grey matter. A point of view forces more of the iceberg to the surface.

My rule of thumb is always to start these conversations simply and go deeper as required.

So, how much innovation resource is needed for your company to deliver its long-term strategy?

2. Letting Go of 'Your' Money

Unsurprisingly, in almost every conversation around resourcing innovation, teams realise that they need to shift resources from today's business into tomorrow's. This is rarely popular, as someone, somewhere gets to have a smaller budget next year.

Sometimes this conversation can be resolved collectively by the senior team; but more often than not, a CEO needs to make some tough calls about whose budget will be reinvested into the future.

But rather than anticipating an annual stand-off, establishing some different rhythms and rituals around resource allocation can lead to some less painful conversations that benefit everyone. Here are four effective approaches to experiment with:

i. **End-of-life-as-normal**
    Some companies make it a policy to dispose of a percentage of their portfolio every year, freeing up investment budget for innovation.

    Product lines or investments that contribute little strategic value are prime candidates. Of course, this needs to be done sensitively and with wisdom; but most companies can easily point to areas of the business that are well past their sell-by date.

    Resources are finite, so being deliberate about regularly disposing of low-performing assets is a valuable strategic discipline. And when this process becomes the norm, the leadership team is prepared for the conversation and less defensive about letting go. It's disposable sustainability.

ii. **Scrap budget meetings, start strategic resourcing meetings**
    When people hear the word 'budget' they immediately think about 'new' money for the new year. But that neglects a much more valuable conversation that focuses on the optimum allocation of *all* resources, not just money.

'What is the greatest return-on-strategy that our collective resources could deliver?' is a good way to frame such a conversation. Of course, this includes money, but it also considers how *all* available resources could be reconfigured to optimally support the existing portfolio of opportunities.

This is a much more strategic and holistic conversation than one that focuses on mere dollar bills. For example:

- Are 80% of your best people working on 80% of your most valuable opportunities (existing and emerging)? If not, how could that balance be redressed?

- Who are the most promising entrepreneurs inside the company and are they aligned with our high-growth initiatives?

- How many disruptive technology projects are on hold because of bottlenecks in the IT department, and how could we liberate them?

- Where are you seeing most exhaustion in the company (let's be real here)? Who could you rotate in and out of positions?

- If we divided roles into categories according to their strategic importance (e.g. A roles, B roles and C roles), what percentage of C roles could we resource in more cost-effective ways?

It's really a resource innovation meeting that moves the mindset from resource *ownership* to resource *stewardship*.

A quick watch-out here though. I've sat in on meetings that look through both ends of the same telescope – executive meetings at one end and meetings with the people doing the work at the other. Both have different views about current resource levels and what might be needed in the future. And both are right in some measure. At some point, bring the two worldviews together to avoid a car crash that results in all-round frustration.

iii. **Don't be so anally annual**

Twelve-month planning and budgeting cycles may have been appropriate for the twentieth century, but today they create serious constraints on agility and innovation.

According to a 2016 HBS survey, most executives are frustrated with standard approaches to planning because speed of change makes their painfully crafted documents redundant far too quickly.

Alessandro Di Fiore, CEO of the European Centre for Strategic Innovation, advocates 'agile planning' as an alternative. This approach, which organisations are increasingly adopting, creates a 'strategy marketplace' where dozens of agile teams around the company are in regular conversation with business leaders.

The purpose of the discussions is a two-way strategy/ resourcing calibration: agile teams feeding their data into the centre to help validate the relevance of current strategy, and the centre ensuring that the collective team picture is consistent with the overall strategic direction.

Moving away from annual planning cycles makes commercial sense and it also breaks up the budgetary bun fights that consume weeks of executive energy in the run-up to new financial years.

There's no doubt that a marketplace methodology requires more executive attention than the traditional planning techniques. But in an age of rapid change, such an approach ensures that resources are continually aligned with innovation that tracks with market relevance.

iv. **Speed of reallocation**

The speed of change also means that the ability to dynamically reallocate resources is an important source of competitive advantage. In fact, research from management consultancy McKinsey shows that companies who regularly reallocate resources against strategy are likely to be worth 40% more over a 15-year period than those who don't.[2]

This is another example of where scenario planning can be a powerful strategic aid. When we consider likely future scenarios, not only can we imagine our likely necessary response, we can also estimate the *speed and implications* of our response.

- What would it take to dynamically reconfigure and respond to a specific market shift within 90 days?

- What impact would the reconfiguration have on our business if it began tomorrow?

- What potential friction points can we identify and 'rewire' now so that the transition would be smoother and faster?

Anticipating the 'speed of how' is a valuable resourcing capability that every company can benefit from. And because significant shifts will require systemic responses, it is another technique to build a collective mindset around 'our resources' not 'my resources'.

3. Talent-As-A-Service?

When a company is trying to turn on innovation quickly, I'm often asked who should be involved. The question behind the question is, 'Who can help us get quick wins?' And depending on the context, this can often be a good way to create some early momentum for innovation while a more robust, strategic approach is being developed.

Very often, the talent or 'high potential' population is volunteered because these people are perceived to have the smarts, the drive and the ambition needed to make it happen. And in many cases, that's a good instinct.

[2]https://www.mckinsey.com/business-functions/strategy-and-corporate-finance/our-insights/how-to-put-your-money-where-your-strategy-is

With the right training, support, opportunities and time, I've seen hundreds of these people catapult corporate innovation capabilities in a short space of time. It can be dynamite. But that's not always a good thing.

It's no secret that the talent community generally delivers disproportionately. Scientific studies have shown that on average 20% of the workforce delivers 80% of organisational output. That ratio stretches further as job complexity increases.

Inevitably, being a scarce resource makes talent susceptible to overload and burnout. So before inviting a talent group into an innovation capability programme, set some clear boundaries in advance.

This is especially true if you are expecting them to run an innovation project alongside their day jobs. Too often I see leaders positioning these projects as 'stretch' assignments when in fact they become 'snap' assignments. To deliver the project they work even crazier hours often to the detriment of the day job, and the innovation project. Most people don't do their best work between 9 p.m. and 2 a.m.

As an example, at short notice, a large corporation once invited me to deliver a 90-minute introduction to experimentation to a group of 30 high potential managers. It was part of a six-month leadership development programme and my role was to coach them through the experiments that they were to work on during the programme.

I assumed that the cohort already knew about the journey ahead of them. But after my first mention of the experiments, sharp intakes of breath echoed around the room and whispered conversations broke out everywhere. It was evident that I had just delivered a newsflash.

From that moment on I'd lost them. And the Q&A that was planned over dinner had little to do with my talk. I was bombarded with questions about deadlines from despairing managers, one of whom was almost in tears, because of the breaking-point strain that they were already under from their day jobs.

Bad form.

Talent-as-a-service is an easy but costly mindset to adopt. Talent-focused initiatives *can* work but they need a healthy dose of resourcing reality to prevent people from burning out.

When you set people off to find the future, they have to want to come back.

4. 'Make-It-Happen' People

Whilst talent may be the golden resource for activating innovation, there is an equally important, yet often unsung resource, that is crucial in the early days of building innovation capabilities.

'Everyone needs a Bridget,' says Denis O' Flynn, referring to Bridget Gardner, Pernod Ricard's UK head of employee development.

From 2013, Gardner's role was … unique. From 30,000 feet you would identify her as the architect of the company's *Project Ingenuity* initiative that aimed to catalyse innovation performance across the firm. But at closer quarters you would see what it really took to activate innovation at scale:

- Co-ordinating innovation training for all employees.
- Negotiating a 'treasure chest' for backing bold ideas.
- Cleaning up after innovation 'car crashes'.
- Massaging bruised executive egos.
- Counselling failed experimenters and encouraging them to go again.
- Creating a deliberate innovation communications programme to demonstrate progress and momentum.
- Building a network of specialist innovation coaches …

… to name a few.

O' Flynn isn't overstating the importance of these crucial roles. In every company that I've seen innovation take off quickly and sustainably, someone somewhere was tirelessly fighting the cause.

Sometimes it's a team (for example, at Sony Music it was David Reay, Laura Ellis, Aileen Coombe, Teresa Kotlicka and Nathan Knight). Sometimes it's an individual (at Wiley it was organisational design expert Mark Ryan).

However the role is managed, these people are essential to success. They are commercially astute, organisationally savvy, socially adept and have a deep care about company success.

Track them down, plug them in, and look after them well.

5. Creating Innovation Resources for Free

At the end of an innovation training programme I always ask delegates: 'OK, so who has spare time to go and put this innovation toolkit into practice?' Awkward silence.

Lack of dedicated time is a top-three innovation blocker in most organisations.

But the good news is that delegates have yet to leave those workshops without finding the extra time that they need. Very often it's possible for people to find up to a day of additional time per week to dedicate to innovation, if they so choose.

I hear your scoffs of incredulity. But it's true.

Often, we have allowed the organisation to happen to us. We have gradually succumbed to a kind of corporate chloroform that renders us helpless. We look around at the myriad of issues that conspire against our productivity and find it hard to see a way out.

It needs a catalytic question to act as a dose of smelling salts.

Provoke a possibility and ask what would need for it to become true, and see where the conversation leads. The opening question is less important than the place that it takes you – to the *real* question and destination that you need to reach. Often you just need a starting point. Here are some starters for 10:

Meetings

- How could we spend no more than 2 hours a week in meetings?
- How could they be the best two hours of the week?
- How could we prevent unwanted meetings from appearing in our diaries (i.e. when colleagues put them in the diary without consulting you)?

Interruptions

- How could we reduce our susceptibility to digital interruptions?
- How could we stop people from interrupting us so that 2–3 hour productivity windows become the norm?
- How could we ensure that we take regular enough breaks to re-energise through the day?

Email

- How could we reduce the time we spend on email by 75%?
- How could we stop looking at email after 6 p.m.?
- What kinds of emails do we want more of and less of? How could that happen?

Automate

- What common, low-level tasks could we automate?
- What tasks would happen faster or better if we automated them?
- What tasks (or parts of tasks) do we assume can't be automated, and how do we know that we are right?

Finally, once new ways of working have been established, what metrics and incentives would prevent us from falling back into old habits?

If you're prepared to pursue these kinds of questions on an ongoing basis, I guarantee that you'll free up at least a few hours a week that can be applied to innovation. Even by challenging the assumption that meetings need to be an hour long by default, and experimenting with 20, 30 or 40–minute meeting formats can be a game changer for some people.

'Work expands so as to fill the time available for its completion,' says Parkinson's Law. It's a resource-sucking reality. What new laws does your organisation need to counteract it?

6. Other Ways of Resourcing Work

As we saw in chapter 33, Cisco has a systematic way of aligning innovation challenges with the right capabilities.

Companies can take a similar approach to resourcing and avoid the temptation to overload the system with work that would be done better using alternative resources.

Ravin Jesuthasan, managing director of Willis Towers Watson, believes that leaders need to 'liberate' work from the organisation so that it can be carried out in the optimal location, wherever that may be in the world.[3]

He advocates eight potential resources that organisations should explore thoroughly before assuming that work should happen in-house:

- 'Gig' workers (for short-term assignments and projects)
- Volunteers (e.g. crowdsourcing innovation or promoting brands on social media)

---

[3] https://hbr.org/2019/08/the-8-ways-companies-get-work-done-and-how-to-align-them

- Smart automation (to replace highly repetitive, rules-based work)
- Robotics (physical automation)
- Independent contractors
- Outsourcers
- Alliances
- Employees (either part-time or full-time)

How deliberately do your people consider all available options before committing resources to projects? Encouraging them to think more broadly can often reveal more efficient and effective ways to resource work, and free up capacity for innovation.

Many organisations believe that they can't afford innovation. And many individuals believe that they are too busy to innovate. Yet with some creative approaches to resourcing, these imprisoning misperceptions can be shifted and innovation performance can rise.

Part Five
Innovation Culture for Realists

Culture has been defined as 'what is ordinary'. Yet most companies demand extraordinary innovation to emerge from their status quo set-ups. This section shows how to move beyond a one-size-fits-all culture to where bigger ideas can emerge and thrive on a repeatable basis.

35 Calibrating Culture to Outcome

The building blocks of an 'innovation-as-inevitable' culture.

T he further we move from the core, the higher the risk of failure. It's just as true for Google as it is for you. Yet the future gives us no choice but to deliberately lean into uncertainty to find our sources of future relevance.

Different types of innovation inevitably carry different risk profiles. But one of the most common traps that companies fall into is trying to mix low-risk and high-risk innovation in the same context. It very rarely works. Here's why.

Your company is likely to be set up to deliver repeatable certainty. There is a range of well-known products and services, an established business model to protect and a well-understood customer base to serve. That context is perfect for incremental innovation; there are plenty of known cause-and-effect relationships where investment risks are low and tolerance for failure is scant. And so it should be if we're doing a good job in a well-understood context.

But try dropping an idea for a brand new proposition into that climate. This fledgling idea kind of makes sense on paper but it uses emerging technology that we don't really understand, serves a category of customer that we're not too familiar with, would require some support capabilities that we don't have, and would be driven by a business model that is hard to predict.

That idea, 99 times out of 100, will die fast or drown by death of a thousand watering-down committees. And yet it might have been an important new revenue stream.

Innovation outcomes are highly dependent on their contexts. So, as well as allocating deliberate levels of resource, be equally deliberate about creating contexts where the right kind of innovation pursuit can thrive. The diagram opposite describes some fundamental dynamics in each of the three innovation contexts that we looked at in the chapters on innovation strategy.

The Explore zone is high risk and failure is frequent. So, here, people need to be rewarded for speed and quality of learning about an idea's desirability, feasibility and viability, not earning revenue. That comes later.

In the Explore zone, if people are measured on creating products that must quickly deliver revenue will radically reduce their creative ambition and lower the ceiling on your disruptive innovation. You get what you measure for.

The reality of creating a self-renewing organisation is that the further from the core the idea, the more likely it needs to be explored away from core operations. And for good reason: stable, day-to-day operations should rightly be focused on delivering today's results, not squeezing out resources for unpredictable experiments that are likely to fail and disrupt business-as-usual.

	Exploit	Extend	Explore
	Existing teams	Handovers (fuzzy crossover phase)	Dedicated NPD teams
	Core business	**Growth business**	**Emerging business**
	Defend & extend core business	Scale up the most promising new business ideas	Incubator: discover potential new sources of growth
	Profit funds tomorrow's growth		
	Transitioning declining businesses		
	Major innovation focus Operational efficiency	**Major innovation focus** Business model development	**Major innovation focus** New product development
	70%	**20%**	**10%**
	Highly predictable	Somewhat predictable	Highly unpredictable
Outcomes and KPIs	• Productivity improvements • Cost reductions • Plant efficiency scores • Monthly profit against budget • Net income growth • Return on capital	• Unit sales • Revenue growth • Gross margins • Market share • Installed base • Efficiency of incremental capital	• Speed of validated learning • Beta testing / pilots • Securing new partnerships • Finding problem/solution fit • Successfully harnessing resources of the organisation
Transitions	**Indicators** Solution / market fit (traction) **Actions** Hand over to business teams **Watch outs** Scaling too soon	**Indicators** Problem / solution fit **Actions** Collaboration with business teams **Watch outs** Investing too soon	
Culture	Efficiency; no surprises; incremental	Hustle; taking smart risks	Exploratory; learning; high failure
Resources	Self-implemented innovation	Established & supporting teams	Full-time innovation teams
Capabilities	Execution; value chain analysis	Growth; go-to-market; adaptability	Curiosity; product development
Leadership	Delivery oriented	Entrepreneurial	Visionary & experimental

Funnel labels: No. of products · No. of pilots · No. of ideas

Table © Elvin Turner.

There are different ways of tackling this, each with their own pros and cons. If creating an environment that is dedicated to Explore innovation isn't feasible in the short term, just ensure that you are deliberate about protecting the context in which bolder innovation shows up. This includes factors such as rewards, time, capabilities, resources and customers.

Rewards: Rewarding people for high quality learning, not sales-ready products. It's too early for certainty. At this stage you need people to figure out whether this is an idea that we should invest in further. Usually it's not. Google knows that 90% of its Explore ideas will be wrong, so they make the efficient finding and flushing of them a superpower.

This may require adjusting people's reward packages accordingly, even aligned to specific projects. For example, if the expertise of a particular salesperson is needed to help co-create a new concept for 90 days, their day job bonus for that quarter shouldn't be at risk.

Time: Protecting people from having to respond to 'urgent' short-term demands from other parts of the business. This is a very common innovation killer – either stopping projects dead in their tracks or delaying them to death.

Often, this comes down to a contracting agreement with an individual's line manager. They ultimately call the shots on what employees dedicate their time to. Ideally, meaningfully incentivise the employee *and* the line manager to deliver the intended project progress on time.

There is a wider point here about resourcing the whole company too thinly. Few people that I meet have sufficient time built into their roles that allows them to deal with unforeseen circumstances. The more-for-less culture has people stretched to the limit in many companies, and unexpected eventualities either lead to longer hours or cutting corners.

In most companies, thinking time, learning and innovation all have to line up behind regular 'fires' landing on desks, some of which are legitimate, many of which are consequences of problems caused by overstretching resources elsewhere.

In my own research, the 'fires landing on desks' syndrome is the single largest cause of innovation slowdown.

You can see the advantages of having non-core innovation taking place outside the context of daily business!

Capabilities: Ensuring people have the capabilities for running low resource/high learning experiments. We covered this in Chapter 29.

Resources: Access to appropriate resources (e.g. specialist external skills, prototype budgets). Some companies address this by having a 'treasure chest' that employees can pitch for and which acts as seed corn funding for projects. The *Shark Tank* or *Dragon's Den* model of pitching project ideas in return for resources and autonomy to pursue innovation is a popular approach in many companies.

How resources are allocated will largely depend on who owns and runs innovation, as we discussed in Chapter 34.

Customers: Access to trusted, early adopter customers (or 'lead users') who are prepared to experiment with new product concepts and ideas. The sales force, which 'owns' the customer relationship is a regular block to early innovation initiatives that need customer exposure. Their nervousness is understandable, but their motivation is rooted in a preservation of the status quo and steady incremental growth.

This is a delicate balance, but proper contracting and relationship management with customers who actually want to take more risks with emerging ideas is entirely possible. But it needs a dedicated ongoing approach with the direct sponsorship of the sales director.

Designing Context

When people are proposing new ideas, get them to be clear on their anticipated requirements in each of these areas. This will help you get clarity on the context that they need to succeed and allow you to make the best decisions around which ideas to back and when.

If this is an area where you know you need to develop, start small. Pick one team where Explore innovation is likely to show up most frequently in the future. Work with them to co-create the indicators of a healthy Explore innovation context.

Then put them into practice with a real project and see what you learn. Iterate, then go again until you find what works best in that context. Then get that team to coach two other teams, and so on.

An excellent resource for going deeper in this area is *Beyond The Idea: How to Execute Innovation in any Organization*, by Vijay Govindarajan and Chris Trimble.

Leaders who aren't deliberate about creating the right context for different types of innovation will find their company trends towards lowest common denominators. Innovation will bump along the floor delivering the obvious quick wins that everyone else is doing.

Breakthroughs come more often when people feel safe to take risks. Your safest route to the future is a deliberate, executive-sponsored calibration of culture to innovation.

Let's look in more detail about how to create a culture where more disruptive innovation can show up.

36 Be More Human

Original ideas rarely emerge from mechanistic bureaucracy. Serious innovators work with their people's humanity, not against it.

Every one of our films, when we start off, they suck ... our job is to take it from something that sucks to something that doesn't suck. That's the hard part.

Ed Catmull, founder of Pixar, in *Creativity, Inc.*

For most organisations, the journey of creativity is hugely inconvenient.

We like instant solutions. We want cordon bleu but expect it out of the microwave in 60 seconds.

Often the hardest innovation truth for leaders to grapple with is that big ideas aren't born ready. They're born ugly.

And for more big ideas to show up, they need deliberate, persistent incubation and iteration. But it's unpredictable, and that's an inconvenience to a corporate machine built for repeatable certainty.

Ugly Pixar babies *Frozen* and *Toy Story 3* evolved into $1 billion+ box office hits (not to mention the merchandising revenues). But each one was a long, deliberate and necessarily messy pursuit of greatness.

And what's true for Pixar is true universally: if you want higher order creativity, you can't escape the ugly duckling journey. It takes time and there are rarely shortcuts.

But there's more.

Human Creative Performance

For human beings to create beautiful and original swans, certain things need to be true.

Whilst great innovators deliberately create the conditions in which ingenious ideas are more likely to emerge and thrive, there is no escaping the fact that creativity flourishes when it can be discontinuous, messy and can invite serendipity.

What's also inescapable is creativity's humanity. Businesses are more optimised for robots than humans, trading mostly in logic. But necessarily, creativity and innovation are a more unpredictable cocktail of logic, magic and emotion.

Great ideas evolve when people are allowed to care deeply, take risks, put themselves on the line, fight for something, feel something, dare something. That's what it takes to put a dent in the universe, to coin Steve Jobs's phrase.

Let's be clear: creativity in the workplace is biological warfare.

© *Richard Johnston.*

The ability of human beings to dream up and pursue break-through ideas is directly related to their psychological, emotional, physical and spiritual state.

Human performance and creativity dip when they encounter stress, anxiety, fatigue and hopelessness. Sadly, as numerous studies confirm every year, these elements are on the rise in society at large.

And creativity is no different. Energised and motivated people engaged in meaningful work in trusted environments do amazing things. Stressed out, worn out people don't. We need to be real about this.

People and Process

The journey and humanity of developing beyond-the-obvious ideas are inseparable and inescapable.

The journey needs time and patience. The people need care and encouragement.

And that's why it's difficult for businesses who are in a rush to stay alive. Trying to deliver today whilst discovering tomorrow is an inevitable performance car crash.

We've already talked about separating work into categories of increasing uncertainty: Enhance, Extend and Explore.

But there's another complementary concept that companies can use to help optimise the performance of the journey and its people.

It's called space.

37 If Culture Feels too Woolly, Switch to 'Space'

How rethinking culture as 'space' can make it more tangible for innovation.

Creativeness is correlated with the ability to withstand the lack of structure, the lack of future, the lack of predictability of control, the tolerance for ambiguity, for planlessness.

A.H. Maslow, Maslow on Management

'Space is the shared intention to grow something, whatever it takes,' says Gemma Metheringham, long-time creative director for women's fashion brand Karen Millen, and now leading 'Label/Mix', a start-up for UK clothing retailer Next.

Space is a deliberate combination of direction, mindset, capabilities, time and resources to achieve a specific outcome.

Most organisations run a one-size-fits-all space. But as we found out earlier, the thing companies need more of – disruptive innovation – rarely shows up in this context.

Two Different Spaces

'If you're going to be the best, you have to distinguish between what I call the "performance space" and the "rehearsal space",' says Emily Bollon, a coach on the TV show *X-Factor*, and award-winning director of gospel choirs. 'The performance space is all about excellent execution. It's a choir on stage nailing a song with no margin for error.'

'The rehearsal space is completely different,' she continues. 'It's about continually building collective technical capabilities and experimenting with new performance ideas. That means a lot of mistakes are inevitable, so I have to create a climate of bravery, vulnerability and mutual trust.'

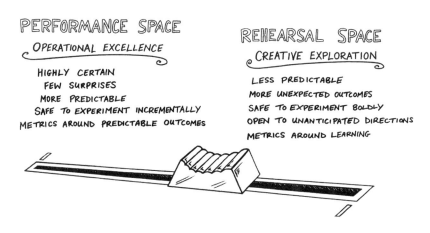

© Richard Johnston.

Defining the Levels

Different types of creative work will require different blends of performance and rehearsal state.

The role of the leader is first to understand the required outcome of a piece of work. Then she must intentionally design and establish the right combination of team mindset, capabilities, time and resources to fuel the journey that's required. Inevitably that will be a process of trial and error and is best done with an open conversation with a team.

For example, when kicking off a new project, draw the slider (as in the diagram) on a flip chart and ask people what kind of space they'll need for different types and phases of project work. Then ask how it will feel to work in that space. What will we need more of and less of from each other to succeed?

Then make it someone's task to remind the team of the optimum state they need during those stages of work. I would go as far as to make it the first point on a meeting agenda or the first slide in the accompanying slide deck.

At the rehearsal end of the slider, there will be a lot of experimental work. Nothing should leave this space until it has reached a certain level of maturity. But it's a place to explore, try out new ideas, practice and refine. And most likely you need a lot more of it.

At the other end we have the day-to-day contexts where there can be no margin for error. Products and services in our customers' hands that must deliver on promises; legal and financial processes; and health and safety procedures.

And in between we have a wide range of contexts where it's a bit of both. A standard weekly meeting, for example, needs to feel safe for people to speak candidly about issues and problems. But they also need to turn up with great data with which good decisions can be made.

When a team can instinctively flip between performance and rehearsal states, it is well positioned to deliver today whilst designing tomorrow.

Streaming Space

Spotify, the music streaming company, understood this early on. It gives every team complete autonomy to determine the required creative space. Defining an outcome and then allowing the team to design the optimum space that their journey will require – resources, ways of working, and much more.

Unless we're intentional about correctly calibrating the space according to the type of creative journey (especially when pursuing more disruptive ideas), we'll find that people default to standard operating behaviours which crave certainty and crush creativity.

Once we understand the nature of the space we need, how can we ensure it delivers the necessary creative outcomes?

38 Bold Ideas Aren't Born on Stage

How to create more 'rehearsal space' and find bolder ideas.

Different outcomes need different drivers, and because this book is more oriented to helping teams uncover more disruptive ideas, what follows is calibrated in that direction. The headings apply regardless of outcome, so adapt them to suit your needs.

Vision: Become a Broken Record

Most leaders do an OK job at kicking off a project with a sense of vision, but then it rarely gets mentioned for the remainder of the project. Well, why would we? We all heard it once, why would we need to repeat it?

But in the context of innovation and change, you need to become a broken record. It's a key ingredient of sustaining motivation especially if the team is encountering a lot of frustrating and unexpected dead ends through trial and error experimentation.

© *Richard Johnston.*

'What is this all for and how far we are along the journey?' will be a constant, unspoken refrain amongst your team if you don't continually remind them.

Your project charter is helpful here. Get it out at the start of every project meeting. Your people need to be able to recount it in their sleep; it'll be fuel for the journey.

Mindset

Exploration thrives on curiosity and optimism. On an unknown journey with an unclear outcome you'll need heaps of both. Yet the initial project sizzle can fizzle quickly for several reasons:

- The wider organisation puts up barriers to the work.
- Experiments have a high failure rate which can gnaw away at optimism, especially over longer periods of time.
- Team conflict when collective passion isn't focused towards a clear, shared purpose.
- Unclear processes and decision-making.

One of the most important team-leader jobs is to check in with the team's mindset and address anything that could be pulling them off course.

Resources

Creative exploration is an unpredictable journey and high failure rates come with the territory. That has some specific implications on resourcing:

- **Lean exploration:** Most ideas in the exploration space turn out to be wrong to some extent. So, investing big at this stage makes little sense. Instead, cheap, small, rapid experiments should take priority. Spend a little, learn a lot, is the mantra.

  An exception to this is research and development. Discovering and developing new technology in many fields is expensive and there are few shortcuts. But don't be tempted to lump every experiment into the R&D bucket for convenience. Great innovators test early assumptions quickly and cheaply wherever possible.

- **Time:** If ideas are born ugly, they need time to evolve to a point where informed decisions can be made about whether they justify further investment. Depending on the newness of the idea (newness to you and newness to the market), build in sufficient time for ideas to incubate and iterate. How long? It's a case-by-case decision, and often commercial realities force projects to move faster than you would prefer.

On the whole, teams aren't given sufficient quality time for creativity to show up as a superpower. Yet looking longer, dreaming bigger, and thinking deeper than the competition are all choices than any company can step into.

Run some team experiments around this. Get your people to discover the innovation rhythms that deliver the best results for them. Then share them with other teams and ask them what's working for them.

Diversity

Most teams believe they can figure it out themselves. After all, that's half the fun of creative work. While that's true, a bigger truth is that teams that invite diverse input perform better than those who don't.

There are two main reasons:

- **Expertise and experience:** It's impossible to have a 360-degree view of every part of the ecosystem that your idea will potentially inhabit.

I've seen so many teams waste months of effort developing a solution, only to fail because they didn't seek the input of functional experts around the organisation.

Marketing has a great new product idea for a summer launch but fails to liaise with logistics, who are already overcommitted for the summer period.

Sales develops a brilliant lead-tracking app that will integrate with the current IT system. Only, IT is about to switch platforms and the app will soon be redundant.

It's very often very simple stuff, but the enthusiasm to get started often blinkers teams, to their ultimate detriment.

- **A sideways perspective:** It's no secret that increasing the diversity of a group means a broader range of ideas is likely to emerge. Mixing young guns with old heads is a tried-and-tested approach to finding breakthrough ideas. But it turns out that some diversities matter more than others.

  'Deep-level diversity', which refers to psychological factors including personality, values and abilities, has a greater impact on performance than demographic diversity (gender, age and race).[1]

  When you're in exploration mode, put a requirement on your team to invite these aspects of diversity into the idea generation and testing process.

Creative Conflict

Most people hate conflict. Yet it turns ugly into awesome and is a foundational capability in the rehearsal space.

One of the most brilliant advertising executives that I ever worked with was always looking for a fight. His methods weren't always endearing, but people knew that his underlying motivation was the pursuit of genius. 'Good enough' was anathema to him, and in an industry that pays for bold ideas, his instincts were often right.

Innovation giants know this and have made a conscious decision to make creative conflict a source of competitive advantage.

Pixar, one of the most successful movie companies of all time, has the philosophy built into its DNA. Its movies are so good, specifically

---

[1] https://hbr.org/2017/06/does-diversity-actually-increase-creativity

because they are in pursuit of incredible ideas, not 'good enough' ideas.

Pixar calls its approach 'plussing' – the collective pursuit of making everybody's individual work as corporately valuable as possible.

Everyone's work is out for collective review and suggested upgrades on a daily basis. As a new employee, it stings at first to have yesterday's work pulled apart by peers, yet ultimately improved. But after a while it becomes second nature in pursuit of collective excellence.

It takes great vulnerability and trust for people to put ideas on the table that they know will be challenged and chiselled. Even if it *is* for the greater good.

'I would never hire anyone that I couldn't debate with, it's a creative necessity,' says Gemma Metheringham who heads up Label/Mix in the UK. 'But that means I need to create an environment where people feel safe and not fearful of the consequences of disagreeing with an idea's direction.'

Google famously identified 'psychological safety' as the single-most important characteristic of its highest performing teams. It's a trait that I also see in every team that is over-indexing on creative output.

We'll look more at building team safety later. But in the context of building creative conflict capabilities, change consultant, Jo Twiselton, recommends a useful tool for leaders. 'Creative sessions can simultaneously excite and terrify us,' she says. 'The buzz of sharing an idea mixed with the fear of its rejection can put us all in a state of mild anxiety, which isn't always conducive to giving helpful feedback.'

To avoid shutting down the best dynamics of a rehearsal space, she recommends instilling a habit in teams that becomes second nature *before* people give feedback on an idea. 'Make it a habit to ask, "Will this feedback be helpful or harmful?",' she says. 'That question helps people to reconsider or reframe their feedback in ways that build people's confidence to be vulnerable and share unconventional ideas.'

Another creative superpower is to care enough about your idea to push it through cynical environment, but not to be so emotionally attached to it that you aren't open to important, objective input. So, while you're building this team conflict capability, be careful with language. Focus feedback on ideas, not people. Every time we use the word 'you' or 'your' in relation to the idea, we trigger an involuntary emotional response – usually defensive, and often likely to provoke a feeling of personal attack.

Start gently and as the team's trust builds, people will become more resilient to more raw, direct feedback.

Trusting Instincts

'People are also more likely to engage in debate if they know that they will be listened to, and their creative instincts will be trusted, even if they are not understood by the rest of the team in the moment,' says Metheringham.

She tells me of several projects where colleagues pitched ideas that didn't quite land with the wider team, yet because individuals' instincts were trusted, they were allowed to continue working on them.

Sleep and Decide

Finally, be prepared to be wrong, sleep on ideas that you don't have consensus about, and appoint an arbiter for the final decision, says

Metheringham. 'You have to be open to changing your mind, but ultimately someone needs authority to make the final decision. At that point, we lock-in and get behind the decision.'

For many teams, working in a rehearsal space will be a new experience. So be prepared for a bumpy early journey as people figure out how to take risks, encourage disruptive thinking, have their preconceptions challenged and be more vulnerable.

Preparing Your Space

At the start of every project, have a team conversation to define the specific space that your journey is likely to need.

Step 1: Performance Space vs Rehearsal Space

Draw a horizontal line and write Performance Space on the extreme left, and Rehearsal Space on the extreme right. With your project in mind, have a team conversation about where it should sit on the line. Use your project charter to help you identify the level of certainty that you have about different aspects of the journey. This is a key factor in where your project should sit along the line.

Once you have agreed a position along the line, make a note of any important questions, ideas, potential roadblocks or accelerators that emerged during your conversations.

Step 2: Space Performance Drivers

With your agreed space in mind, discuss the profile of the performance drivers that you'll need. The table below will help you get started, but depending on the nature of your project you may want to draw a timeline and list the different drivers that your project may need at different stages.

	What's Needed?	Risks	Risk Indicators
	What will you specifically need?	What could put this driver at risk?	What signals would indicate the driver is at risk?
Mindset			
Resources (time, budget, materials, equipment etc.)			
Capabilities			
Outside expertise & experience			
Team culture			
Rewards & motivations Leadership			

© *Elvin Turner.*

These elements will be crucial performance dependencies for your team, so add them to your manifesto and review them regularly.

New Normals

'Culture is ordinary,' said British intellectual Raymond Williams. It's what we think of as normal, and usually goes unnoticed.

Ordinary produces the expected. The more disruptive our creative pursuit, the greater the requirement for an extraordinary context.

Few teams are so deliberate about defining, cultivating and guarding the specific 'space' that will foster the outcomes they need.

But the unavoidable truth is this: if you need to change the game, you probably need to change the space.

39 Next-Level Creative Culture

The power of 'kindred connections.'

Whenever I'm inside an organisation that has a strong reputation for innovation, I always sense an irresistible force magnetically pulling people together and forward.

That force isn't accidental. It's well understood by the leaders of these organisations and it is carefully cultivated as a source of competitive advantage.

It attracts the best people, retains them, draws out their best work, and motivates them to reach beyond their grasp. All key ingredients for a culture of innovation.

So what is this force? I call it a 'kindred connection', a fusion of three elements that forms an almost unbreakable bond between people and organisations:

Connection to the purpose of the organisation

We're doing something here that matters.

Connection to meaningful, progressing work

I'm getting stuff done that matters.

Connection to other people on the same 'journey'

These people get it and are 'on it'.

At its simplest, innovation rock stars create environments where people can *do something* that they care about *with people* that they care about. It's mission-making. It's tribal. It's kindred connection.

Connection to Purpose

Company purpose is who we are, what we stand for, the difference we're making, and for whom. That's not difficult information for any organisation to share with its employees on a regular basis. It's corporate communications 101.

Yet you'd be amazed how many people that I meet every year who have no real idea what their employer *actually does*. I'm not kidding.

In management coaching sessions, one of the biggest barriers to meaningful business-related conversations is a lack of awareness about strategy, decision-making processes and who does what.

If people don't know what we do, why we do it, and how we are continually making a difference, their level of engagement is likely to be moderate at best. In an environment of continual change, that's not a deep enough connection to sustain high performance.

Making Meaning

Connection to purpose isn't a problem at Decca. The 90-year-old record company has launched numerous industry legends, and produced the biggest track of all time, Bing Crosby's 'White Christmas'.

'Decca is about making meaningful music,' Becky Allen, president of Decca tells me in the company's hip, new headquarters in London's King's Cross.

One could easily write that off as a cute platitude, but I quickly feel its truth as Allen's leadership team gathers for an off-site that I'm attending. Unlike many such meetings, people are not cramming in a few last-second emails or consoling one another over the edict that was sent out last night.

These senior executives are geeking out over 'the craft' within some demos that they were listening to on the tube, and overnight news of some emerging artist who got a great Instagram shout at a gig, and wondering if the label could do anything to help ease the homeless situation in the area close to where we're meeting today. And it continues at every break throughout the day.

I know a geek when I see one (I love geeks) and I quickly realise that these people are sold-out, in relentless pursuit of making music that matters.

This is confirmed later in the day when we're discussing a 'DNA manifesto', something to help crystallise, communicate and amplify their culture. 'Can I read something out?' someone half-coughs. 'It's just something I quickly hashed together last night.' He takes the floor. 'It's called, "We are Decca."'

We are the sound makers, the ground breakers

The come-up-for-more-breath-takers

We're the sound of your soul

We're a sign for the times

A tribe of imagineers

Elsewhere just can't find

Been here since the start

We go back, but look far

If there's a sound not yet made

You know it's coming OUR way

You see, we've pledged no compromise

Makes sense to mix fools with the wise

We're the future of sound, the status quo wrecker

Ain't none can compare

Because we are Decca

If I'd dropped a match the whole place would have exploded. The team went bananas.

Now that might not be your cup of tea. It doesn't matter. What matters is that *your people* need to feel *something like that* to care enough to fuel the innovation journey that will get you to your future. If your team's likely response to a culturally appropriate equivalent is a polite clap, a connection to purpose is unlikely to run deep.

The Decca feeling is a kindred connection to purpose, and it starts with leadership.

Play It Loud

I meet up with Allen a few weeks later to discuss her approach to creating that deep connection to purpose. Since the workshop she has become one of only a handful of women to make *Billboard Magazine*'s 2019 'International Power Players' list.

'Decca is a label that likes to surprise people. We like the unexpected,' she says. 'If we're going to deliver that promise sustainably it means we'll need to take a lot of smart risks. And that means people need to care enough, and feel safe enough, to step into potential failure. It has to be worth it.'

But what creates the care?

First, somewhat unsurprisingly, is a deep love for music. Just like any industry, if people care enough about the subject matter, they'll find a way to make a living from it. But that alone isn't enough.

Second, there is the deep motivation that's provoked by an artist's commitment. 'Most of our artists are masters of their craft,' says Allen. 'I'm often blown away by the price that artists pay to be the best in their field. It draws out an admiration and a passion to do whatever you can to help them succeed.'

Whilst this may feel unique to the entertainment industry, there is a wider principle here that any company can apply. Research has shown that when staff meet customers in context, their empathy levels increase which has a knock-on effect to customer service performance. Run an experiment and see what happens.

The third area is what I read between the lines after being around Allen and her colleagues over the next few months. Her actions and reputation betray a deep and genuine care for whoever is around her. And that undoubtedly contributes to the strong followership that she has. 'I'd leave my job tomorrow and work for her,' someone from a sister record label blurts out to me in the elevator one day.

But one expression of that care particularly caught my attention. And it's a leadership trait that is crucial for building kindred connections.

Allen is a 'star maker,' not only for artists but for her people. It breaks down into three areas:

Instincts: Allen recognises the potential in a person at an early stage, sometimes before the person has seen it themselves.

Generosity: Spotting the gold in someone is one thing; drawing it out of them is quite another. It takes deliberate time and effort to take people on that journey. That requires a generous spirit, especially when the journey gets bumpy.

Humility: As the stars grow, their abilities begin to overtake the mentor. Pride causes many a car crash in these situations, yet Allen graciously defers to others' perspectives, ever willing to learn, it seems.

She is the brand's purpose in action, finding great talent and taking them to the top of their game.

Of course, not every journey will have a neat and happy ending; we're dealing with human beings after all. But Allen carries around a philosophy that helps her stay resilient to failure and to stay the company's number one creativity cheerleader.

'One of the best pieces of advice that I ever had was from my childhood trumpet teacher,' says Allen. 'Play it loud, play it wrong, or not at all.'

In a world where businesses need greater levels of disruptive innovation, that sounds like good advice.

Connection to Personal Progress

I once worked for a 30,000-person company at the peak of its Silicon Valley powers. For a while, it was *the* place to be.

But try as I might, for the whole year that I worked there, I didn't get *anything* done. I mean *nothing*. Sure, I sat in on tons of conference calls, went to lots of meetings, went along to some great corporate jollies. But actual progress against a target? Zip.

Did anyone seem to care? Not really. We just moved the numbers around, blamed the blockers in another silo, and set new targets for the next quarter. Zero progress in a whole year. I couldn't wait to leave.

Five years later the company was on the ropes and was bought for a bargain. But five years is a lifetime now.

A leader inside a 4500-employee airport technology company told me that a 12-person company in Silicon Valley had eroded 50% of its market share in just 18 months. This company had been around for decades. When I fell victim to the painful torture of their procurement process, I started to see how things might have started to go wrong for them.

People need progress. Great people want to do great work. If they can't they'll go elsewhere, and with the 'war for talent' showing no signs of abating, there are plenty of available options.

Not All Work Is Created Equal

But great work doesn't mean *all* work. No one will complain that they didn't spend enough time reading the emails they were copied into today.

The most consistent theft of important, meaningful work that I encounter is thinking time. And here's the irony: *people* are crying out for it to fuel their motivation, and *your future* is crying out for it for survival. But there's a drastic shortage in most organisations.

Think of a Number

Have you ever asked yourself how much quality thinking time your role actually needs? Or perhaps, how much better your performance might be if you could trade off some transactional work for more strategic and creative thinking and problem solving?

This line of enquiry is the stuff of daydreams for most people who desire it but can't imagine how it could possibly happen. But as we learned in the earlier chapters, this is *exactly* what innovators like Amazon do. They make deliberate choices about the time and energy needed for certain types of value creation and plan accordingly.

There's no reason why every team couldn't take a step in a similar direction. I'll look at some specific approaches to doing this in the section on Resourcing.

But *what* we do is less than half the story. I believe *how* we do it is more important when it comes to building kindred connections.

How We Work

'Real work happens at a desk.' These days managers know that they can't openly agree with this binary statement. Yet the actions of many reveal their true convictions. The 'real work' mindset remains one of the biggest, silent blockers to innovation, and a constraint on how deeply kindred connections can run.

True, *some* work is done best at a desk. Yet the most valuable work inside high performing innovators happens *wherever* it needs to. Recent research backs up this approach showing that average productivity for 'work from anywhere' employees was 4.4% higher.[1] Few breakthroughs occur in front of a computer monitor with one eye trained on the inbox.

At its root, this is an issue of trust. Absence may make the heart grow fonder, but it also quickly triggers doubt and suspicion amongst managers who can only equate employee productivity with presence.

---

[1] https://hbr.org/2019/08/is-it-time-to-let-employees-work-from-anywhere

During a corporate innovation push inside a well-known UK company, I sat in many meetings where the board struggled with the idea of moving towards more flexible working patterns that would support more creative and strategic thinking.

Finally, in one meeting, an exasperated executive blustered, 'Yes, but what would they all be getting up to if we started letting them work from home?' Everyone was thinking it. And many still do.

If leaders genuinely want to free people to do more of the creative work that their future needs, they need to address the trust crisis that is present in so many organisations. Of course, there are certain types of work that are arguably best done in person in the office. And I would advocate a decent measure of office presence, not least because of the important relational bonds that it strengthens.

But when leaders trust their people to make the right choices about where and when great work needs to happen, motivation and trust boom. In turn, that fosters deeper connections with both managers and the brand.

How many people in your organisation drive home smiling, thinking, 'My boss trusts me deeply'?

Companies wanting to make progress in this direction have some options, including:

- Executive education about the conditions under which human beings do their best work (Ron Friedman's book *The Best Place To Work*, and *Culture Code* by Daniel Coyle, are great resources to start with).

- Challenging executive mindsets that people should 'just get on with it – we never had these "perks" and look where it got us'.

- Normalising experimentation around optimal ways of working. Data from experiments about performance improvements is difficult to argue with.

I remember watching a conversation between a conservative executive and a marketing manager once. 'Your new campaign is great! Where did the inspiration come from?' asked the executive. 'We jumped on a cruise boat and ran our brainstorm speeding along the River Thames,' came the reply. Confounded silence.

- Learning best-practice ways of working from organisations that were 'born digital' such as Spotify and Airbnb, and creative giants such as Pixar and Lego.

- Measuring for outcomes, not attendance. In theory we do this; in reality there's often a cognitive penalty applied to those seeking more flexible approaches to work. They're not deemed to be 'serious'.

Pursuing trust is essential for deepening the connection people have with their work. If, deep down, they know they aren't trusted by colleagues, there is a limit to the depth of connection they can make.

Even in a progressive company like Decca, old habits die hard, and the performance state shift that Allen is continually pursuing will require many people to un-learn the habits and reflexes that persist from twentieth-century ways of working. It's hard work, but essential work. And rewarding work.

Kindred Connection to Others

'These people get it, and are on it,' is how I described this component of kindred connection earlier.

When we're on a mission with people who care as deeply as we do, and demonstrate their commitment with consistent integrity and excellence, most days are good days. And on good days, great work can happen. But it can run even deeper, as Dr Alice Cook, a senior emergency room specialist in the UK, tells me.

'Working in a high-stakes environment, often with inebriated, addicted and violent patients, means that a sense of crisis is never far away,' she says. 'But if your team has your back, and you've worked through difficulties together, you all come out stronger.'

That level of connection isn't automatic, it is grown. As you saw in Chapter 38 on rehearsal spaces, calibrating culture to the level of creative outcome and risk must be deliberate.

So how do we develop those connections?

According to psychologists, there are three primary drivers of close friendships: proximity, familiarity and similarity. In other words, the more that we share time, space and interests, the more likely a friendship will develop. (Hence my earlier affirmation for at least *some* work to happen in the office.)

Simply working in the same space will take you so far. But every company does that, so where's the advantage?

The real magic happens when we pursue depth.

Getting More Naked

Let's remember the real outcome of what we are pursuing on this journey toward more kindred connections: People who are passionate enough to explore an uncertain journey together that will be characterised by risk, ambiguity and failure.

That means creating a safe place to be real, and to be vulnerable. It means being free to say how we really feel, to matter-of-factly point to the emperor's birthday suit, to admit to a paralysing fear, and to call someone back up to a position of dignity when they stumble.

Like everything I'm suggesting in this book, start with very small steps towards the edge of your team's comfort zone. It's getting more naked, but one sock at a time.

So how do we go deeper?

I have helped teams do this in two ways: conversationally and experientially. Conversations are free, so let's start there.

Kindred Conversations

We don't need psychologists to tell us (even though they've proven it), that when we share personal details with others, we feel a closer connection. Yet in the workplace, it isn't always opportune or appropriate to have those conversations. And sometimes, we just plain don't want to. Vulnerability, and fear of shame, is a scary place for most people.

But it doesn't have to be that way. What I'm not talking about here is revealing deep, dark secrets. That's not the point.

This is about letting people see a slightly bigger picture of who you are, what makes you tick, and why. And the 'why' is often electric because it involves stories, and people *love* stories.

I once facilitated a spiritual development programme for a group of Christians who had known each another for some time. But this group wanted to go on a journey that would require a vulnerability upgrade. So, to warm people up, I asked people to share a simple story about how they first became a Christian.

Oh. My. Goodness.

What I thought would take a couple of hours took over 10 hours (across a few meetings) and the impact that it had on the group connection was incredible. What happened? Over time, the stories graduated from handshakes to heartbreaks, from simple informational transmissions to powerful, deeply personal testimonies.

One of the beauties of telling stories is that people can volunteer whatever level of information feels safe. But there's an interesting dynamic: when someone wades out a little deeper and offers something that the group is unlikely to know, it sets a confidence precedent for the rest of the group to follow, if they want to. And they usually do.

Whilst in many instances along the innovation journey I caution against leaders speaking first in meetings, this is a great time to do the opposite and pitch the tone early. There's no compulsion for people to follow suit, but chances are they will paddle out further than they would have done otherwise.

Designing Conversations

Intentionally building kindred connections means designing pathways for the right kinds of conversations to go deeper. That generally means two things:

1. **Creating safe opportunities for those conversations to happen**
   Vulnerability is generally a function of safety. The leader's job is to understand from people how 'safe' looks and feels, and then create that experience. This could include location, who is present, what will be discussed, and what happens to disclosures outside of the meeting.

2. **Designing conversations that stretch comfort zones and provide opportunities for greater disclosure**
   I would always emphasise to people that they are in control of how vulnerable they want to be in conversations. However, with the right conversation guidelines, most people are willing to be more open that they might have expected to be at the start of the conversation.

Designing conversations is a subtle skill and whilst this is a generalisation, my experience is that women have better instincts around where to start them. Male designers can often be in too much of a hurry to cut to the chase. Yet, ironically, it's the men who often take longest to 'warm up' during the actual conversations.

There are three main levels to this kind of conversation:

Level 1: General, informational questions: 'What', 'how' and 'when' questions. These are ice-breakers.

Level 2: Gentle 'why' questions that give the opportunity to go further and reveal general motivations.

Level 3: Finally, questions that explore underlying values, assumptions, beliefs and expectations.

Sony Music once brought in a guerrilla negotiator to help its leaders develop deeper kindred connections. Working with consultancy DPA and events company Shelton Fleming, Sony Music built a 'pop-up guerrilla terrorist camp' in a forest outside London.

The leaders were dropped off at the camp where they met Simon Walsh, a humanitarian aid expert whose work in the jungles of Colombia requires him to negotiate with guerrillas.

After learning his methodology for stepping into fearful but necessary situations, the leaders paired off and were given a handful of related questions to explore together. The questions led the delegates to share stories of workplace situations that provoked fear at different levels, and to explore some underlying root causes, and overcoming strategies.

This wasn't therapy, it was gentle, guided exploration, entirely under the control of the individuals. And it was phenomenal to watch people talk privately, yet openly about deep issues for the first time. In a fake guerrilla camp. Yes, it was a little surreal.

Obviously, there's no need to go to these lengths to facilitate a conversation (this was in the context of a week-long innovation leadership bootcamp). I've facilitated comparable conversations in sweaty meeting rooms.

It's the sensitive and deliberate design of conversations that's the key.

Shared Experiences: No Pain, No Gain

That said, great conversations in the context of a powerful shared experience take kindred connections deeper, faster.

But like conversations, different depths of connection occur with different flavours of experience.

Those that include a collective struggle to overcome something, or involve a degree of pain, deliver deeper levels of connection. This can happen in the context of a workplace crisis. Get to the other side and something relational shifts in the team.

This is borne out by research that asserts that shared pain is an important 'social glue'[2] that increases group cohesion and collaboration.

But waiting for a crisis to show up that may go off in a direction that doesn't necessarily build deeper connections, perhaps isn't the most proactive strategy. Deliberately engineering them in pursuit of greater innovation performance is a tried-and-tested practice inside great innovators.

Show Time

I had first-hand experience of this during a leadership programme in the Swiss Alps for a global electronics company. For reasons that

---

[2]https://journals.sagepub.com/doi/abs/10.1177/0956797614545886

would take too long to explain, my role on the programme was to pose as a tourist. I was to discreetly follow delegates around as they completed difficult assignments and listen in on their conversations to track their progress.

Some delegates did not enjoy certain aspects of the week-long programme at all. The low-light for many was being told that 100 school children were arriving in the town square in three hours and were expecting to watch a circus performance from the leaders. In full circus costume. I could feel the silent earthquake of rage inside the senior executive that I was standing next to at the time.

Whilst I'm not necessarily advocating the humiliation of senior teams (I hasten to add that the circus wasn't my idea!), it was interesting to observe management dynamics within that company over two years later. Those who had been on the programme had a much deeper connection with one another than with other managers.

In fact, for new leaders entering the company, programme alumni had to make special efforts not to become an exclusive clique. This stuff works but needs careful management.

Camp Rock

Decca's leadership team took a slightly different tack in 2019. Rather than use pain to deepen kindred connections, they voluntarily chose to live together in tents for four days. Now that's commitment. And potentially painful, I guess.

The context had a sweetener though: the camp site was the Glastonbury Festival, the UK's primary outdoor music event.

Allen's team confidentiality contract was clear: 'I'm a 45-year-old married mother of two. I don't get out much. What happens at Glastonbury, stays at Glastonbury. Is that clear?'

Passion Trumps Paychecks

I once met veteran Hollywood script coach, Bob Dickman, in a Los Angeles hotel. Squinting over the top of his glasses he asked me, 'You want to know the golden rule for all Hollywood scriptwriters? It's three words: Make. Me. Care.'

Passion trumps paychecks when it comes to innovation.

Every company is different, but the requirement is the same. A kindred connection to purpose, work and each other is essential fuel for sustainable innovation. That level of care rarely develops on its own, but with intentional focus it can and should be systematically developed.

Care is connection, and kindred connection is competitive advantage.

40 Innovation Fight Club

What it takes to fight for bold ideas in a culture that wants to kill them.

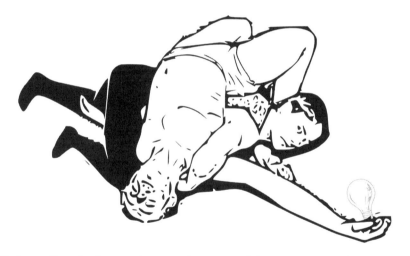

I deas often find an early grave because of the emotional chain reactions that they provoke.

By definition, a disruptive idea means inevitable change, which in turn stirs up fear and fights.

Want your idea to survive? Don't get drawn into the fight. It's often how *you* respond to other people's defensive reactions that determines the success of your idea.

This is Innovation Fight Club, the norm inside most organisations.

Membership isn't inevitable though, especially if there is a clear line of sight between strategy, progress and ideas, and if those ideas are validated with objective data from well-designed experiments.

That said, we all know that innovation isn't simply a matter of following logic. In many cases, subjectivity, feeling, mood, energy, agendas, and different priorities can cause someone to push back against something with an unfamiliar whiff.

And sometimes that reaction comes from simply not connecting properly with the idea because it was badly presented, badly timed, or the recipient didn't have the time or bandwidth to adequately process it.

Good stakeholder management can help here. But ultimately, the better prepared we are for the different stages of battle that we will probably face, the more likely we are to succeed.

So how do we do that?

Be More Greek

First, fall in love with your ideas. Wait? Isn't it conventional wisdom *not* to fall in love with your ideas so that you avoid being blind to objective input? Yes, but that's only part of the story.

The Greeks have six different words for love. Each emphasises a different aspect of love, whereas English, somewhat unhelpfully, mashes them all together.

- *Eros* is fiery and powerfully irrational.
- *Philia* is deeply loyal and sacrificial.
- *Ludus* is playful, teasing, sometimes flirtatious.
- *Agape* is selfless, both to close friends and distant strangers.
- *Pragma* takes the long view and is patient and tolerant.
- *Philautia* is the love of self, which, unchecked, can become narcissism.

When we talk about being in love with our ideas, we generally mean *eros*, sparking feelings and emotions that distort our thinking. But a more holistic take on love is a balance between passion and prudence.

More often than not, real love is making a choice, *despite* a feeling.

It's the battle between head and heart, one of the greatest paradoxes of creative work. We need to be passionate enough about an idea to push us through the grinding battle that it often provokes, yet prudent enough to know when to change direction or lay down an idea altogether.

So help people to distinguish between falling in love with ideas rather than being infatuated by them. The former will encourage wise choices and a less stressful journey. The latter? Road rage.

Love, but Don't Make It Personal

Sometimes, we become so captivated by our ideas that they subtly cross the line from being part of our job to part of our identity. That is dangerous ground because when our idea is attacked, we take it far too personally. We've started caring more about our idea than the problem we're solving, and the interests of the organisation.

As innovators, our job is to *steward* ideas. Take them seriously but hold them lightly.

One of the best ways to do this is to assume that *all* ideas are probably wrong to some extent from the outset. The reality is when working with disruptive ideas at least 90% are in fact wrong. The most innovative companies know this and make the rapid discovery of a *wrong* idea something worthy of celebration. It may feel a little glass-half-empty, but it's not really.

Remember the bigger picture here. We've found a problem worth solving yet we have limited resources to solve it. Better to discover a wrong trajectory sooner so that we can direct resources towards an idea that *will* solve the problem. We need to care more about solving the problem than pumping up ideas that will ultimately explode.

'Feedsmack'

Along the journey of idea development, we'll regularly encounter two kinds of difficult feedback: negative noises from naysayers, and critical feedback that is actually correct and which takes the wind out of our sails.

Both sting, but there's something worse. Our idea fails suddenly and unexpectedly. That can knock us hard, sometimes so hard that it can cause us to retreat and avoid innovation and risk taking in the future. Which is why I went to meet someone who knows something about getting back up after a knockdown.

Learning to Take a Punch

Malcolm Hassan. Image design © Luke Turner

Malcolm Hassan used to train cage fighters.

And as a former training partner to some of the UK's most successful boxers, Hassan knows something about how it feels to be punched hard. But more importantly he knows what it takes to recover fast.

'Learning to take a punch starts a long way before anyone actually hits you,' says Hassan. 'It all begins with mindset. You have to want to be there in the first place – mentally, emotionally and physically.'

'And it's really important for knock-downs. Where you were mentally before you were knocked down determines whether you'll get back up again. You have to be tuned into your reason for being there: your core, your passion.'

This passion is what keeps people moving forward with bold ideas in the workplace despite continuous knock-backs from colleagues.

So how do boxers recover when they are unexpectedly floored?

'A knock-down happens so fast and can hurt so much that it's easy to let shock and fear paralyse you,' says Hassan. 'You can go into a shell and if you let that happen, you'll start making bad decisions.'

'So you have to immediately take control, re-focus and override your emotions. There's a drill: Stand up, hands up, back to basics, focus, make it to the bell.'

Hassan suggests three recovery techniques that are easily transferred to the workplace when dealing with tough feedback or failures. In the boxing ring, these steps happen in a matter of seconds. Thankfully, in the workplace we usually get a little longer:

1. **Refocus:** 'When you're back in your corner, first, you refocus. Check-in with yourself,' says Hassan. 'Recognise what happened and how you're feeling but then get your perspective back fast. You have to put whatever has just happened behind you and rebuild your self-belief. In between rounds, breathing deeply and slowly in your corner helps.'

Business psychologist David Riley concurs. 'When we've just been hurt in the workplace, one of the fastest, proven ways to recover is to acknowledge our feelings,' he says. 'So often we're taught to deny or hide emotions, but resilience is built on reality. Name the emotion, either to yourself or someone you trust, and it'll soothe the sting sooner.'

2. **Listen:** 'Your corner man is there to help you focus,' continues Hassan. 'Listen to him. He sees things that you don't: patterns, ways to beat your opponent. If you're wise you'll listen. But if your ego or pride gets in the way and you choose not to listen, it can cost you the fight.'

It may be hard to accept, but most feedback or failure will contain some element of truth that you have to confront. Sometimes it's the reality that you missed something or made a mistake. Often it's an unforeseen situation that no one could have predicted. No one is at fault, but it can still feel frustrating.

Either way, as the idea steward, your job is to be objective about the facts. Push ego aside, consider the feedback, and identify what's true and helpful. But don't fall into self-condemnation. Experimentation is learning, and learning involves moving from one level of understanding to the next: from less wrong to more right.

3. **Act:** 'Then the bell goes. Gum shield in, on your feet, hands up,' says Hassan. 'Now you have a choice. Do you act on what your corner man said or go your own way? If you trust him and you're smart, you take his advice, regardless of how loud your emotions are shouting. But if your ego is bigger than your brain, you'll ignore him and probably lose the fight.'

Losing the fight could be causing an idea to fail because you chose to ignore important feedback from someone who irritates you. Or your mind and your will are subservient to your emotions and you 'follow your heart'.

This is where experimentation can be helpful for two reasons. First, if you follow the data from experiments it can act as a powerful, objective counterbalance to emotions. Second, if you do make a wrong call, the iterative nature of experiments means that you probably haven't lost much by driving into a ditch.

Yet, like much of the innovation journey, this is an imperfect science. Occasionally your instincts kick in, you *do* follow your heart, and it pays off. But this is the exception, not the rule.

Organising for Audacity

But wouldn't it be better if there were, well, fewer punches altogether? Innovation *is* an argument with the status quo, but does it have to hurt quite so much?

Great organisations recognise the humanity of the innovation journey and do their best to make it hurt less.

Here's Astro Teller, head of Google's disruptive X organisation.

'At the end of the day, we all have to pay the bills and want the people around us to think highly of us,' said Teller in a *Wired Magazine* article.[1] 'So it's human nature to gravitate toward the paths that feel psychologically safe. That's why, if you want your team to be audacious, you have to make being audacious the path of least resistance.' And that requires a deliberate 'rehearsal space'.

---

[1] https://www.wired.com/2016/04/the-head-of-x-explains-how-to-make-audacity-the-path-of-least-resistance/

Google's 'X-Man' Astro Teller, Captain of Moonshots, X Illustration
© Richard Johnston

For giffgaff, a disruptive UK mobile operator, this philosophy begins at the top with CEO Ash Schofield. When employees bring him new ideas his regular refrain is, 'Play it to a 10', meaning, push it further, make it edgier, dream a little longer.

'If people aren't bringing me big ideas, I'm likely to get agitated,' the softly spoken Schofield tells me. I wonder how that looks a little later when I learn he is a karate black belt.

But that's not the giffgaff way. With a culture built around mutuality, giffgaff is one of the safest places in the industry to try something bold. And Schofield's gentle but uncompromising focus on delivering today whilst exploring a bigger tomorrow is a compelling example to learn from.

Learn to roll with the punches when you need to, but better still, create audacity-friendly, strategically aligned, low-stakes rehearsal spaces. When people feel safe to dream big and step out with a small, low-risk experiment, you'll find that edgier ideas are more likely to emerge and blossom.

41 Driving with the Handbrake On

Overcoming organisational innovation friction.

'If I need a $1 length of rubber tubing to fix an urgent customer problem, there's a 10-person sign-off process waiting for me.'

This is the tired voice of an engineer employed by one of the world's largest construction companies.

It remains the worst case of bureaucratic obesity that I've ever encountered, and it was crushing any motivation to innovate.

Yet a different version of a similar story is told every day around the watercoolers inside most organisations.

Numerous studies have shown the connection between employee engagement and customer satisfaction. As Jennifer Robison of engagement specialist Gallup says, 'A world-class culture inspires your most talented employees to create superior customer experiences.'[1]

People progress affects customer progress affects financial progress.

---

[1] https://www.gallup.com/workplace/257744/future-workplace-depends-purpose.aspx

Friction Burns

Ultimately, the focus on customers and employees must be the same. Make them awesome. Understand the progress that they need to make and remove any friction that impedes that progress.

The people charged with designing and delivering profitable user experiences every day, are often suffering from multiple 'friction burns' in their pursuit of daily progress.

More organisational friction means less speed, but perhaps more importantly, more friction means less capacity and energy to proactively find and remove friction from your customers' lives.

In other words, more employee friction, less customer innovation.

If you want people to try new things and take more risks, they have to care. And nothing drains people's 'care tank' like bureaucratic friction.

Finding the Crazy-Makers

In my experience there is a clear connection between the number of big ideas moving through the system and the level of engagement people have with their work. No care, no dare.

What kinds of friction could be showing up inside your organisation? Some companies employ armies of change and transformation consultants to help answer that question, often with mixed results.

But if you want to quickly find the biggest sources of friction that are stitched into your organisational fabric, here's a simple test. Ask people to anonymously complete this sentence: 'It drives me crazy when …'

Before long you'll likely have a long list of the things that stop people doing their best work. Processes, policies, systems, decisions, people, plans … each, no doubt, established at some point to deliver useful progress to the organisation. But over time, as the wider environment has changed, they have become more of a constraint than a conduit.

Of course, 10% of the feedback will be whining from people who should probably be looking for another job. But it's a quick-and-dirty way to find friction that is impeding great work from good people. Get managers to ask the question regularly and empower teams to solve the problems themselves.

It can be an instant people-engager, too.

I recently facilitated a workshop to help a cross-functional team create a 'friction heatmap' for one of the company's services. Our task: Identify what gets in our way, rank its impact, and address the biggest causes.

Halfway through the session I realised that this wasn't an innovation exercise at all. It was much needed group therapy. People were finally able to express their frustrations about the barriers to progress they encountered every day, and in an environment where they could do something about it. And they did.

It wasn't a self-pity party. These were good people trying to do a good job for a company that was inadvertently getting in its own way. And despite a fairly gruelling 8-hour session, they left recharged, refocused and re-energised for what they had joined the company to do.

A Culture of Friction Removal

For Fiona Conway, director of retail customer operations at Santander Bank, friction is a sworn enemy. One of her leadership mantras is, 'Bring me your problems, all of them!' That's quite a statement when at the time of writing the UK banking sector is wrangling with dozens of regulatory changes with extremely tough deadlines.

But Conway knows what she's doing. She's a performance turnaround specialist inside the bank and I learn that her teams have some of the some of the highest engagement scores amongst the organisation's 20,000 UK employees.

'If there's any issue that affects a colleague's performance, a customer's experience, or the brand's reputation, people need to know that I'm interested,' says Conway. 'If people know that I'm interested in solving problems, they are more likely to follow suit.'

And that means friction points come under the spotlight quickly.

But not just the simple ones. Conway's team has a reputation for serially tackling some of the bank's most complex issues.

The secret of their seemingly fearless pursuit of friction monsters? A relentless question: 'What's the right thing to do here?'

Whatever the situation, it's the same the drill. Ask the question. Pursue the *right* solution commercially, ethically and relationally. And it's backed up from the top.

'Anyone who knows me knows that if you're doing the right thing, for the right reason, in the right way, I'll always have your back,' says Conway. This is backed up by some smart reward metrics which are a 50/50 split between what employees do and how they do it.

Over months and years, 'do the right thing' has become an instinctive response, deeply embedded in the language and rituals of Conway's transformation unit.

It's a culture where friction has a hard time surviving and where there is confidence and agency for people to raise difficult issues and pursue innovative solutions.

Pulp Friction

How could your organisation develop a similar approach to finding and pulping friction?

Leaders who need more innovation and growth must see themselves primarily as *progress enablers* for their people. Friction damages prosperity in almost every dimension of company life. And because we often learn to endure it, rather than tackle it, friction can engender an 'inefficiency-as-normal' culture.

But what if your company set and rewarded 'friction removal targets' in the way that it does sales growth targets?

I believe that this kind of mindset is so important that, like Santander, a board-level executive should oversee it. The financial package should be aligned with results, and he or she should sit in on a minimum number of team meetings where trench-level friction is being discussed. Often there is a two-way reality distortion between teams and executives about how work gets done, so this is a good reality check in both directions.

Before you do that, try running a friction discovery and removal experiment for 30 days with a smart, keen up-comer. See what you learn, then choose your next move to take it further. You've nothing to lose. Except to start experiencing how it feels to drive without the handbrake on.

No doubt it will require ongoing, cross-functional support, but being deliberate is the key. Determine to pursue better progress for your people and the innovation tide will rise.

Streamlining People Progress

Spotify, the music streaming service, realised this a few years ago. Its leaders decided that the best way to reduce friction and boost employee engagement was to let go. Hand control to the people and allow them to determine the best way of getting work done.

The company turns its strategy into specific outcomes (units of progress). Cross-functional teams of 8–9 people (called squads) are then given accountability for achieving an outcome but with complete autonomy for *how* they want to achieve it.

The philosophy is that smart people on the ground typically know best how to solve problems. When the company gets out of their way, trusts them with results, and provides assistance as and when it is needed it, work gets done faster, better and with more engaged employees.

The approach has now been adopted by many other companies, including the bank ING. It maximises employee motivation and minimises friction in the value creation process. It's what Professor Julian Birkinshaw and Dr Jonas Ridderstråle call 'adhocracy' in their book *Fast Forward*.

Everything Is Awesome

As I said at the start, people progress affects customer progress affects financial progress. Our focus on customers and employees must be the same. Make them awesome. Diagnose friction, innovate flow.

Give people the mandate, tools and rewards to safely identify and remove friction, wherever they find it.

Help them make better progress than their counterparts inside your competitors.

Then there's a greater chance of them being more engaged, more productive and more innovative than them, too.

Run Your Own Anti-Friction Workshop

The battle against friction is constant. Here's how to get started:

1. **Initiate the conversation**
   Raise the issue of friction in your next team meeting. Let people see how important it is to you and commit to pursuing a team performance state where friction is minimised. People need to know that you care about the problem of friction, but also that

you care about its consequences: their motivation, productivity and well-being.

2. **Measure the impact**

Ask people to identify the greatest sources of friction in their work. This is often best done in a solution-focused workshop setting. Here is a broad workshop outline that I use:

   i. Identify the most important value that you need to create as a team (or objectives that you need to achieve).

   ii. Map the sequential stages of those value creation processes.

   iii. Identify where the greatest sources of friction lie and the impact that they have on performance (especially if there is a knock-on effect to customer experience).

   iv. Identify root causes of that friction (to be validated outside the workshop).

   v. Prioritise the most important problems to solve.

   vi. Form teams to explore and solve the friction problems – allowing for incremental fixes and radical new approaches that could transform performance. This will often require cross-functional collaboration and is a good opportunity to build mutual understanding of one another's operations challenges.

   vii. Embedding new ways of working that prevent the friction from returning.

3. **Normalise the conversation**

Make friction an everyday conversation (weekly and monthly meetings as a minimum). The faster we can identify emerging barriers to progress, the less chance they have to rust through performance and motivation.

I would also suggest having a more formal 'friction review' every quarter. Good intentions about regular conversations can fade over time. So be realistic and book in quarterly check-ins so that friction removal is a continual, deliberate pursuit.

Part Six
Leading an Innovation Reformation

Innovation is regularly cited as a top three priority amongst leaders, yet the vast majority of their training and experience is in business-as-usual management. This section provides practical tools for leaders who need to lead their organisations to a new level of innovation performance.

42 The Innovation Leadership Mandate

The rough and the smooth of the leadership journey.

There's no denying that leading innovation is tough.

Intellectually, somewhat. Setting up a high-performing innovation ecosystem isn't a cakewalk, but it lends itself to existing programmatic, project-management–oriented skillsets. You can choose to build it and it'll happen in some shape or form.

Emotionally, though. That's the tough part. The not knowing. The ambiguity. The bets. The stakes of failure. The unknown outcomes. The dented egos. The anxiety. Who would *choose* these things?

I have good news and bad news. I'll start with the bad news.

The innovation leadership mandate isn't going away, in fact it's intensifying.

But the good news is that an effective innovation ecosystem overcomes many of the emotional chain-yankers that live on this side of the innovation journey.

What's more, innovation creates some of the most rewarding work people ever do in their careers. It connects people to purpose. It pursues better. It's a weird kind of soul food.

Based on my work with hundreds of leaders around the world, I've observed three factors that enable successful innovation leadership: Choose, Go, Grow. Let's take a look at each one.

43 Innovation Never 'Just Happens'

The deliberate leadership choice that kickstarts innovation performance.

It is not necessary to change. Survival is not mandatory.

W Edwards Deming

The most important differentiator between great innovators and 'normal' organisations seems too simple to be true: choosing.

Amazon, 3M, Tesla, Nike, Google, Gore, Netflix and Pixar aren't innovation giants by accident. They made a deliberate choice to pursue a particular performance state, created some values and metrics to cement that choice, and then went on the journey.

Most companies won't do that. Why not?

I was recently working with a group of senior leaders inside a global telecommunications company. During one of the conversations about leading innovation, a group member shouted out, 'Leading means knowing.' What he meant was 'always knowing the right answer'. Many nodded in agreement.

Innovation performance is often a function of a leader's need to know. We won't venture very far with disruptive ideas if the boundaries of our knowledge also mark the perimeter lines of our exploration.

© *Richard Johnston*

This is dangerous stuff. A leadership team's collective competence can inadvertently become a major constraint on future prosperity. If we're never prepared to explore unfamiliar territory, innovation will only ever be incremental. And whilst a level incremental innovation is necessary, in many industries it's woefully insufficient to keep track with the speed of change.

What's more, the competencies that built today's company are not the ones that will build tomorrow's. But when competence is king, the chances of choosing a state of higher innovation performance are slim.

Where in your organisation does innovation only happen on a 'need-to-know' basis?

Choosing to Choose

Max De Pree said that a leader's first responsibility is to define reality. In this context it means a leadership conversation about three things:

- Counting the cost of *not* making the innovation performance choice.
- Understanding the impact and influence of the senior team's collective competence on innovation performance.
- Initiating a journey that recalibrates the team's confidence around greater levels of exploration – which we'll cover in the next chapter.

Great, sustainable innovation always starts with a choice. When business magazines write about your company in years to come, initiating this conversation might be remembered as the most important thing that you ever did.

What is your organisation currently choosing?

44 Mapping the Leadership Territory

The key questions that leaders must confront in pursuit of better innovation.

If there's no map, there are few visitors.

It's one of the main reasons that incremental innovation marks the county line of ingenuity inside most organisations.

But my experience is that when executives see clear and proven innovation frameworks, their anxiety levels decrease and the choice to pursue bolder innovation becomes easier. Why? Because frameworks, systems and processes confer a measure of predictability and control. It becomes more like any other part of the business.

This whole book is designed to help you 'go' – to increase innovation performance quickly and practically using the *Turn It On* framework.

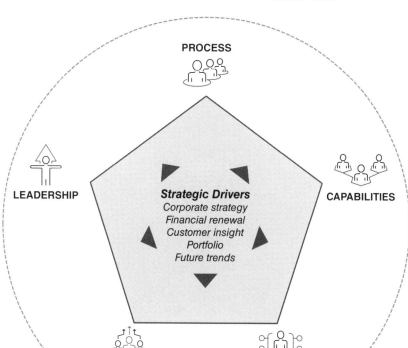

'TURN IT ON'
INNOVATION STRATEGY FRAMEWORK

PROCESS

LEADERSHIP

Strategic Drivers
Corporate strategy
Financial renewal
Customer insight
Portfolio
Future trends

CAPABILITIES

CULTURE

RESOURCING

Turn It On framework © *Elvin Turner*

This chapter aims to help you define reality around your current innovation performance and its drivers, and then to consider the journey that you'll need to lead.

I have developed an 'innovation health' survey that you can use with your teams for a deep-dive assessment. It can be found at www .belesszombie.com/turniton.

But in the meantime, here's a quick litmus test to help you get a sense of where you may need to go.

With the six areas of the *Turn It On* framework in mind, ask yourself:

'To what extent am I creating the conditions where bold ideas can emerge and develop?'

Flick back through the book (or use the questions at the end of this chapter) and give yourself an honest score of out 10 for each of the following areas.

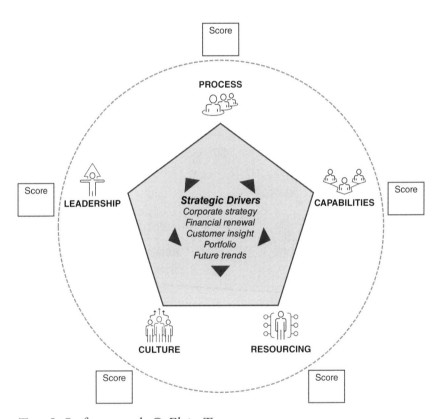

Turn It On framework © *Elvin Turner*

In which areas would a higher score have the greatest overall impact on your innovation performance?

Undoubtedly, you'll have a fairly strong instinctive sense about your performance in each of these areas. Yet we all have blind spots, so I always recommend opening up the conversation to your immediate team (and beyond). This helps you all to understand one another's experiences, perspectives and opinions on how to you can best move forward with innovation.

When leaders facilitate team sessions based around the innovation health survey questions, they often report that the ensuing conversations are amongst the most important that they have ever had.

When the team gets to discuss and plan the innovation performance journey from the start, confidence and engagement begin in a higher place and are more likely to endure.

Innovation Leadership Questions

What follows is a quick reference list of key leadership questions that keep innovation focused in the right direction, and the zombies at bay. If you'd find it useful to have a copy of them on your phone, I've created a downloadable list at: www.belesszombie.com/turniton.

You might consider scattering the questions across your calendar, one per week, so that the principles regularly pop up for your reflection and action.

Innovation Strategy

1. What clear lines have we drawn around who owns and funds innovation in our organisation?

2. The innovation strategy is fundamentally about progress. What important 'units of progress' are your customers trying to make? What important progress are your employees trying to make? How can we reduce friction and increase flow for both?

3. The department of the future asks, *What's happening, what does it mean, what should we do?*

4. Working back from a likely future scenario, what needs to be true for us to succeed? How do we need to organise?

5. Is our innovation strategy continually evolving or stuck in an annual process?

6. Is our innovation portfolio appropriately balanced to deliver our strategic goals?

7. Are we deliberately lowering the stakes, the risks, and the ambiguity of innovation?

Process

1. Do we have enough bold ideas coming down the pipeline?

2. What is the problem/opportunity? Who wins, how, and by how much?

3. Which 'needle' are we trying to move?

4. How well do we understand the problem/opportunity context?

5. Is this a feature, product or a business?

6. What catalytic question are we trying to answer?

7. Are people in the right state to generate great ideas?

8. How effective are our creative sessions at generating bold ideas?

9. Are we identifying the 'leap of faith assumptions' that our ideas hinge upon?

10. Do we 'spend a little, learn a lot' with our experiments?

11. Is our innovation investment 'pay-as-you-learn', i.e. learning unlocks investment?

12. What is the data telling us about the desirability, feasibility and viability of this idea?

13. Can our people tell compelling stories around opportunities, ideas, experiments and business cases?

14. How effective are we at designing business models that have built-in 'unfair advantages'?

Capabilities

1. Where might your personal innovation leadership capability be constraining your team's performance?

2. Is our innovation ambition supported with adequate training and development opportunities for employees?

3. Are our innovation outcomes, processes and capabilities aligned?

4. How capable are we at designing and sustaining innovation-friendly environments?

5. Is our dependency on internal resources constraining our ability to discover, develop and deliver truly differentiated ideas?

Culture

1. Are we calibrating culture to outcomes or hoping a one-size-fits-all culture will deliver incremental *and* disruptive innovation?

2. Are leaders and managers deliberate about creating 'rehearsal spaces' around innovation projects that don't neatly fit into existing lines of business?

3. Do our people have the 'kindred connections' with colleagues, their work and our purpose that are necessary to fuel bold innovation?

4. Do people feel safe enough to propose the ideas the future needs from them?

5. Are we continually tracking down and driving out sources of friction in our organisation?

Resourcing

1. Are we strategically funding our future or placing sporadic bets?

2. Are we thinking beyond money to resource innovation?

3. Do we have enough 'make-it-happen' people facilitating innovation around the organisation?

4. Does our planning process help or hinder innovation (speed, quantity, boldness)?

5. Are we relying on too few people to deliver too much of our innovation?

Leadership

1. Are we adequately stewarding the fortunes of the company with sufficient backing for innovation?

2. What is the maximum amount of time leaders should spend on running today's business vs pursuing strategy and innovation in a given month?

3. Are we being strategic enough about innovation or relying on ad hoc approaches?

4. Are we genuinely holding ourselves to account for the outcomes of our innovation strategy?

5. In what ways is the leadership team a constraint on our future prosperity?

6. Who will have to change, and how, if we pursue more innovation? What dynamics might we need to prepare for?

7. What profile of leaders does our future need, and how actively are we developing them?

Reality-defining questions like these should never be far from a leader's reach. They help disperse the fog of invisible corporate chloroform that can cause leaders to gradually nod off at the wheel.

Use this list as a starter-for-10, but even better, create your own. Design the questions that will keep *your* organisation awake amidst the hypnotic background hum of the status quo.

45 To Boldly Grow

Being honest about your innovation leadership capabilities and personal growth journey.

The choice to *'go' corporately* inevitably involves a requirement to *grow personally*. And this can be tough because many senior leaders believe they've done all of their personal development during the preceding 20–30 years.

Most leaders have trodden the traditional executive development path. Yet those programmes mostly focus on running 'today' better and offer little practical help on how to explore tomorrow meaningfully.

Be Less Beanbag

I once worked with the board of one of the world's largest newspapers. When I was briefed, I was warned, 'They've done the sitting-on-bean-bags-in-Silicon-Valley thing. But it didn't work.'

But even if programmes do dig deeper on leading innovation, because the organisation is calibrated around the status quo, on their return to the office business-as-usual trundles along uninterrupted.

Few leaders can honestly say that they've had the training and experience necessary to lead bolder levels of innovation sustainably. Whilst I'm a big believer in the right kind of leadership training (it probably accounts for 50% of what I do) I personally believe that much of the experience can only be acquired along the journey of doing it – starting with designing a strategy.

That said, there are some useful starting points to pursue. The next four chapters offer some suggestions on where to focus the personal growth.

46 It Takes a Leader

There are some innovation doors that only leaders can open. And you must.

S ome doors can only be opened by leaders. Strategic innovation is one of them. If leaders don't sponsor it, it simply doesn't happen.

I recently surveyed senior managers from around 25 corporations to ask them what single change would unlock greater innovation inside their organisations. Here is a verbatim snapshot of what some said:

- *Visible exec-level sponsorship.*
- *Allow time to explore new ideas.*
- *Collaboration with truly positive intent.*
- *Thinking differently and taking more risks.*
- *Give the innovation projects the time and budget to succeed.*
- *Acceptance of failure.*
- *Joined-up thinking and less risk-averse.*
- *Innovation as a KPI for every employee and the senior managers leading by example and celebrating stories for trying innovation.*
- *A clear innovation strategy.*
- *Quicker decisions.*
- *Acceptance and recognising failure.*
- *Empower innovative ideas at a team/individual level.*

- *Understanding that an innovation project that doesn't go anywhere isn't a failure.*
- *An innovation lead.*
- *Budgeted allowance for experimentation.*
- *Senior management change of style.*
- *Less silo working and hierarchy.*
- *Management Board Leadership on this issue.*
- *Increased involvement of different skills to achieve a broader aspect before ploughing in.*
- *Working at a faster pace.*

I daresay that it's a familiar list for most readers as the issues that provoke these kinds of suggestions are pervasive.

And most of them ultimately trail back to leadership's underlying preferences.

Holistic, strategic innovation that is bent on discovering a healthy and sustainable future can only happen when leaders intentionally step into it.

That's because only they can set strategy, command resources at scale, break through concrete silos, determine reward strategies, and shape the culture that's needed to orchestrate effective innovation at scale.

That doesn't mean that *no* innovation can happen unless leaders sign up. I know many plucky middle managers who can prove that point. But the height of the innovation ceiling is always relative to the extent of leadership buy-in.

And this is the first step into personal growth: Recognising that there isn't anyone else. That everyone is waiting for *you* to do something *different*. It's often a hard thing to do, but it's always the right thing to do.

King Solomon said, 'When the just are in authority, the people rejoice.' It may sound a little grand, but a choice toward strategic innovation is a 'just' choice for the future, for shareholders, for customers and for employees.

Where are you in this? Are you waiting for someone else to choose? Is your executive team looking at one another, or the CEO, to choose? Often, this choice falls between stalls because no individual executive owns the organisation's innovation performance journey. Maybe it has never even been a discussion. Either way, what best next step could you take to help your leadership team choose well?

47 You Are a User Experience

The cause and effect of you, and its impact on innovation.

'When he bangs his fist on the table it sends ripples right through the organisation. Really fast.'

This is how a top 30 leader inside one of Europe's biggest technology companies describes his CEO to me. 'He's a good guy though,' he quickly qualifies. 'So long as we're hitting the numbers.' He double-qualifies.

We can all create ripple effects, but some pebbles are bigger than others.

When an organisation is in pursuit of bolder ideas, a sense of safety amongst its employees is paramount. Low safety leads to low vulnerability. And low vulnerability leads to a harvest of low-hanging ideas.

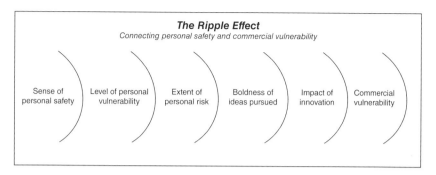

Diagram © Elvin Turner.

Leaders need to be acutely aware of how their words and actions can create ripple effects that compromise the sense of safety.

Not to put too finer point on it, the leadership's 'user experience' has a direct impact on the fortunes of the company.

So how do leaders upgrade their user experience and encourage bolder innovation around themselves? Alongside creating the broader environment that innovation needs to succeed, there is one question that I encourage leaders to continually reflect upon:

'To what extent am I a safe place to fail around?'

Based on my work with hundreds of teams, you likely won't be surprised that many leaders overestimate their Trustpilot score.

Bolder innovation deals in unknowns and testing assumptions. This means that in pursuit of 'new' there *will* be failures. You can design ways of working that limit the impact of failure (e.g. minimum viable experiments). But there will be failures nonetheless. And every other leader amongst your competitors faces the same challenge.

Creating an environment in which people feel safe to fail *well,* is an essential form of competitive advantage and a fundamental requirement for bold innovation.

Laying Safe Foundations

Shared values and decision-making principles create firm foundations for safety. When everyone knows 'how we do things around here', cause and effect is more predictable. When the opposite is true, people tiptoe on eggshells and bold ideas are scarcer than triple-yolkers.

When values shape behaviours that promote integrity, respect, excellence, learning, kindness and fun, we are more likely to create an environment of safety.

It has the potential to create a powerful paradox. Whilst chaos can be raging all around a team's perimeters, its well-rooted sense of safety creates a powerful resilience.

Here's a great team conversation to have. Work backwards from a future destination, understand the 'space' that the team will need to perform optimally on that journey, and then agree the values and behaviours that will be essential to your collective success. Create some sliders to help determine what you need more of and less of.

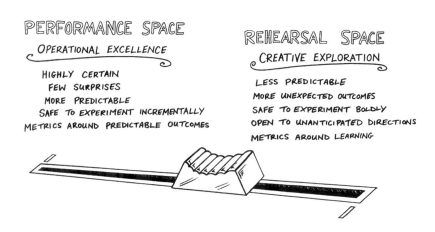

© *Richard Johnston.*

You'll likely need to identify some 'from–to' behaviour shifts, figure out how those shifts will happen, and how you'll hold one another to positive account along the way.

Going Deeper

Designing that shared space is a good general exercise to go through. But when it comes to creating a sense of safety around a particular project or idea, the focus can sharpen, and anxiety can suddenly increase. When this is the case it's time to go deeper.

First, it's important to acknowledge that the experience we create for others is contextual and based on multiple factors.

Self-awareness is crucial here. Knowing what you are thinking and feeling, and why. That's not always easy when we're navigating complex environments at speed.

If you've never invested in emotional intelligence profiling and coaching, I strongly recommend it as a step towards improving your ability to create a safer environment around yourself.

But it's also good to get some direct feedback from your team and other key stakeholders around the experience that you create, specifically related to safety. Although 360 profiling tools can help here, you may need to consider some bespoke elements. For example, are there any events that happened in the past that cause people to hesitate around you? You did *this*, therefore *that*.

Some things have an enduring impact and need to be fixed before people can move on. It's the leader's prerogative to continually pursue the strength of their connection with the people around them that their collective performance state needs. Swallow hard. It might mean apologising and asking for forgiveness for something long ago, two things that are proven to unblock underlying tensions and restore trust and performance. Modelling such choices is a sign of great leadership.

Often these are issues to which you can be oblivious, so creating an opportunity to discover them is important, brave and rare.

A User Guide to You

Yet this doesn't all have to be deadly serious. In fact, you may find that you make more progress when things are more light-hearted.

For example, consider commissioning your team to make a 'user guide to you' for new starters. It's deliberately light-hearted and yet creates a context for you to understand how people perceive you. If you're careful about the questions you ask you can uncover some very valuable insights. For example:

- How to communicate with you.
- What really annoys you and why.
- What kind of meetings you run (length, usefulness, etc.).
- What treat to buy you when they need something.
- How to sell you a big idea.
- What it's like to have a monthly review with you.
- What makes you angry.
- What makes your day.
- What biases you don't realise that you have.
- What time of day to avoid meetings with you.
- Etc. . . .

It's a good way to bring assumptions to the surface about how people perceive you and address any misconceptions in a non-threatening way. It also gives you data to help you adjust the way that you show up for people – increasing the feeling of safety as you go.

There's a nice side benefit to approaches like this, too. It subtly builds a level of confidence and respect around you for being open to doing something like this in the first place.

'Once you genuinely desire (and actively seek) direct and real-time feedback, you've reached the next level. It's a form of escape velocity in leadership,' says Scott Belsky, author of *The Messy Middle*.

Increasing How Safe *You* Feel

So far this has all been about increasing other people's sense of safety to encourage bigger ideas.

But when they actually do it, your own sense of safety can suddenly wobble. Look at the 'How the idea makes me feel' circle in the model below. Plenty of factors can cause you to cautiously call an idea 'interesting' when it secretly fills you with dread.

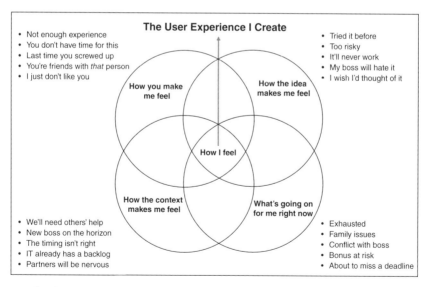

Leadership User Experience diagram © Elvin Turner.

There can be many valid reasons for having an allergic reaction to an idea, but often we can present reasons that are really covering up our loathing for ambiguity. When this happens, you need to co-develop a plan with the idea proposer.

You don't have to do this in the moment. Ask for some time to think about the idea and use that time to explore what's causing your anxiety (the user experience tool above can help here).

Ask yourself, 'What would need to be true for me to feel more confident about this idea?'

Some approaches that can help include:

- Agreeing a check-in communications schedule: when the idea owner will check in with you, what information you'll discuss, what progress is realistic to expect. This avoids long project silences where it's easy to assume the worst.

- Defining under what circumstances will you meet outside of that schedule (e.g. if an unexpected event arises).

- Agreeing the balance of autonomy and accountability: how much freedom does the idea owner have and which decisions will you want to be involved with?

- Lowering the stakes: always strive for maximum learning with minimum resources. This helps everyone sleep better because the pain of any failure is more tolerable.

- Agree success criteria at each stage of an experiment. This can stop wishful thinking from allowing ideas to run for too long. This needs care and flexibility, but agreeing some dependencies that need to be in place for a project to move to another level of funding is healthy.

Whatever the source of your concern, work together to find a solution. It's usually possible.

Also, get your people into the habit of doing some of this thinking before they share new ideas with you. Encourage them to consider how the idea is likely to make you feel and what they can do to limit your anxiety. Help them by sharing the different dynamics that you consider when assessing ideas. Encouraging them to step into your shoes is good leadership preparation for them. More human, less zombie.

Your 'user experience' is a huge issue. The ripple effects that you create have a direct impact on innovation performance (positive and negative). So in pursuit of bolder ideas, optimise the experience that you create for others and give them the sense of safety they'll need to release their latent ingenuity.

48 Confronting Personal Relevance

When leaders stop learning, everyone's future prosperity is threatened. Some rarely-asked questions can help.

'The people who need to lead the company in 10 years' time are not the people on that current career trajectory in most companies.' So says Rafael Orta, former eBay and Tesco executive, now chief product officer at moneysupermarket.com.

It's a threatening prospect for senior managers who are patiently waiting in line for one of the prized executive hot seats. It's also a source of unspoken anxiety amongst the executive team who are increasingly aware of their fading relevance.

The speed of change means that the half-life of skills and experience is shrinking. What created today is less likely to discover tomorrow. Most leaders need a mindset shift from confidence in know-how to the deliberate pursuit of 'new-how'.

When competency and comfort zones dictate the innovation agenda two subtle but powerful knock-on effects occur:

- Incrementalism, which is really an extension of our comfort zone.
- We give up too quickly on ideas that dig into areas that we don't understand.

'Building brands in the post-digital era is very different to building brands in the pre-digital era,' says Orta. 'It's no longer the case that you can poach executives from blue chip giants and relax. Their skillsets aren't necessarily the ones that your future needs.'

According to Orta, tomorrow's executives need to be much more adept in technology strategy and digital business modelling. 'The people with those skills today tend to lack the leadership skills needed to take the helm,' he says. 'That's the real leadership challenge that the boardroom needs to tackle.'

This is ultimately a talent strategy issue and one that should include some tough but ultimately healthy introspection and planning.

As part of that process, leaders who are serious about pursuing the company's future prosperity (and the requisite innovation) should consider the following questions:

- At what point would it be responsible for us to step down, or redesign our roles? When would we know that our individual and collective strengths have made us a source of strategic vulnerability?
- How aware are we of our resistance to change? How do we know when it's happening?
- Based on our industry's likely future trajectory, what do our leaders stand to lose personally and collectively in the next five years (e.g. eroding relevance of knowledge, perceived credibility, value

to the company, relationships, sense of identity)? What might be the implications?

- Are our leaders' personal motivations at odds with the company's success? For example, does the security that they draw from their position and package elicit decisions more likely to protect personal positions rather than the prosperity of the company? What 'safety valves' are in place to avoid this temptation?

- Roles vs relevance: does career progression overly emphasise attaining and holding a specific *role* (e.g. 'My goal is to be CTO') at the expense of developing skills and experience that produce future corporate *relevance*? Often the two aren't closely enough connected.

- What new skills and experience do leaders need in order to deliver maximum relevance and to sponsor the right levels of innovation? How would the company know that they have developed sufficient competency?

- What *aren't* leaders prepared to lose? Therefore, what do they try to control? How do those controlling behaviours manifest themselves? What are the implications?

- What is the ongoing learning strategy of the board? How do we prevent leaders from relegating their personal development to a level that guarantees their ultimate irrelevance, and threatens our collective prosperity?

These are not easy questions to confront, often because there is neither sufficient personal motivation nor a forum to risk being so vulnerable. What we divulge in *public* to colleagues, discuss in *private* with friends, and dread in *secret* alone, aren't always aligned the company's enduring fortunes. There is too much at stake. Too much to lose.

Yet ultimately, these reality-confronting questions are ones of integrity and responsible stewardship. When we protect ourselves ahead of our company, we have created a potentially fatal vulnerability in the system. And deep down, the inner conflict of avoiding right choices is a gnawing drain on our spirit.

If we have no mechanism to explore these questions in a healthy way, innovation and future relevance can hinge on personal motivation, which is often contingent upon circumstances, rather than strategy.

So what would need to be true for your leaders to regularly pursue questions such as these? In the end, they resolve down to a single, catch-all question that needs continual pursuit: 'Who does the future need us to become?'

49 Enduring the Bumps

How to lead people through innovation's tougher times.

For many people, a smaller but definite reward *today* is more alluring than a potential, bigger reward *tomorrow*. It's one of the underlying dynamics of failing to invest well in innovation.

It also points to one of the benefits of an innovation strategy with meaningful metrics – it forces us to do the things that we know are good for us but would easily exchange for a 'hit' of short-term certainty.

But forced compliance can also create an innovation prison camp mentality. If deep down we're just waiting for an opportunity to escape an innovation choice for a path of lesser resistance, it's more likely that at some stage we will.

'Unbegrudging' our mindset towards innovation is an important pursuit.

That can occur over time, as it becomes part of business-as-usual. But there's another useful technique that can help.

Change Your Time Zone

I once heard someone say, 'Live with a long narrative.' The context was dealing with short-term pain. When we increase the size of our perspective, the problems that we face today seem smaller and more endurable.

It's similar with innovation. Faced with choices to begin an unknown journey, or persist after a series of unexpected experiment failures, it can feel easier to bail out rather than press on.

But when we immerse ourselves on a regular basis in the future destination that we're pursuing, tougher short-term choices are easier.

This works on many levels: CEOs casting a compelling vision that helps pull corporate motivation forward, through to a team starting an ambiguous project journey with a picture of the potential it could deliver.

So cultivate the habit of visiting in the future regularly – individually and collectively. Be intentional at the start of every innovation project about provoking some 'strategic imagination' amongst your team. Create a shared picture of the future that you're pursuing and the benefits therein. Then continually remind people of two things:

1. How that picture of the future looks (the destination quickly fades when we're focusing hard on the step that's in front of us).

2. How far along the journey we are (a sense of progress is an essential motivator along uncertain trajectories).

A vivid picture of a long-term vision changes the way we frame and respond to short-term challenges.

Ultimately, you're helping people continually answer one of the biggest questions of innovation and change: 'Is it worth it?'

Part Seven
Turn It On,
Turn It Up

You've read the book and are ready to start. But where do you begin? What does 'Day One' look like? This section provides some pragmatic starting points to turn on and turn up your innovation performance.

50 Turning It On

'Day One' strategies for turning on innovation performance.

One of my favourite words is restitution. It means the restoration of something lost or stolen to its proper owner.

For many companies, that 'something' is their future prosperity, which suffers at the hands of today's choices.

My hope is that this book will help you become an agent of restitution inside your organisation. Turning on innovation in repeatable ways is one of the most important and valuable legacies that anyone can build inside a company.

But sometimes the hardest thing is knowing where to start. A senior vice president of an Australian bank once called me to talk about developing an innovation strategy. Towards the end of our call she said, 'This is all really helpful. But what do I *actually do* on day one?'

It's a great question and inevitably the answer will depend on how innovation currently shows up inside your organisation. But assuming that you're starting from somewhere near the ground floor, here are some Day One suggestions to consider:

1. Choose

If you're not intentional about turning on innovation, the status quo will almost always smother it. So the starting point is a deliberate choice to lean into innovation.

This starts with you making a choice for innovation, and then most likely, helping those around you, especially leaders, choose to turn it on. Where do you start?

First, help leaders see the costs and benefits of dialling up repeatable innovation. It's usually not difficult to create a compelling case for having your cake (innovation for the future) and eating it (operational excellence today).

Second, show a pathway that makes innovation feel doable. Often, it's all about the 'how' for senior management. If leaders don't have experience in managing innovation they usually can't see how the whole thing fits and moves together. If it's not clear, it's unlikely to be backed.

Three things can help here:

- The *Turn It On* innovation framework – how the big picture fits together and aligns with strategy.
- Showing them an innovation process – the stages of how ideas will emerge and develop (see the chapters on Process).
- Experimentation – when leaders see that the stakes of innovation can be significantly lowered, they generally become a lot more interested.

2. Count the Cost, Make It Matter

If no one cares, nothing happens. Turning on innovation is viewed as inconvenient in many contexts, a distraction from the important business of getting stuff out of the door.

So why *does* it matter? Why should we allow business-as-usual to share the stage with some other (equally important) priorities?

This is likely to be part of your own, personal 'choosing' process – helping you to become clear on why this matters so much.

It's also crucial for helping to influence others about the need for innovation.

Developing and articulating plausible scenarios of the future is a useful tool here. You could begin this in many different ways:

- Write an e-book with some colleagues about the future, its threats and opportunities, and circulate it internally.

- Find a cartoonist friend who can visualise scenes from the future to accompany a slide deck.

- Start a lunchtime group to talk about the future and its implications.

- Invite trends experts to come and give a talk.

- Send useful books and resources to leaders – anonymously if necessary. ('John, some important stuff in here, thought you'd like to see it,' signed with an unreadable signature.)

- Ask for a five-minute audience with the CEO, pitch your burning platform for innovation and ask for his/her thoughts on how you can help move the conversation forward. Leaders often love this kind of initiative when it's well-thought-through and visually communicated. Even more so if it points to real vulnerabilities in the areas of future growth and profitability.

These are just suggestions. You'll know what works best in your context. But the key is to start, curate and grow a conversation about the future and what it needs from your company today. Then help as many senior leaders as possible to see the need to act and how dependent the future is on their decisions today.

I'll be honest. This journey can be lonely and frustrating. So I recommend not doing this alone. Find some like-minded friends and form an off-the-radar team for mutual support and encouragement.

Co-design a 100-day engagement plan that works towards influencing at least one board member sponsoring a more strategic approach to innovation somewhere – even if it's in a small outpost (often the best place to start and learn). Who is the most likely executive candidate? What experiences would you need to create for her in order for her to back some pilot work? Be creative, be strategic, be dogged. It usually pays off eventually, even if you have to ultimately aim just below board level.

3. Work Back from the Future

Create a journey map showing how the organisation (or your part of it) would need transition to a higher innovation performance state.

What outcomes and impact will the strategy need to deliver in 3–5 years? If business-as-usual persists, will we realistically achieve those outcomes? If not, and based on emerging trends, what will need to be true in order for us to achieve those outcomes?

Work back in 6–12 month increments asking that question 'What would need to be true?' until you hit today. Where possible create clear and measurable outcomes and use the headings in the *Turn It On* framework to guide the conversations. Then translate your discussions into a prototype action plan.

Next, engage a wider group of employees to test the plan's key assumptions, flesh out the details and create a final plan that has metrics for which the board (or the most senior group you can muster) is accountable. Whoever they are, make sure that they are part of the conversation!

4. Make Time

The most common blocker to innovation inside large organisations is time. The status quo usually assumes rightful ownership of all resources, so we have to be deliberate about taking back what rightfully belongs to the future.

Ideally, as you design your innovation strategy, you'll be making some strategic choices about resourcing. But one of the fastest ways to free up time is to empower teams to stop or reduce low-value work. With your team's most valuable outcomes in mind, run a workshop in which people share how much of their working week or month is taken up with different categories of prioritised activity. Then ask, 'What should we stop or reduce so that we can free up time for more strategic value creation, including innovation?'

This exercise applies to leadership teams more than anybody.

This is also a good opportunity to make some commitments about how much we allow meetings and email to steal our time and energy. Look back to Part Four of this book on resourcing innovation.

The bottom line is that you need to take control of your time, or the status quo will do it for you.

5. Train People to Dream Big and Start Small

Give people the basic skills to design great questions, ideas and experiments. Whilst all are important, I would major on experiments as they have such a huge impact on creating executive confidence around innovation. For a starting point on training people with these skills, go to: www.belesszombie.com/turniton.

6. Do Something, Share Something

Once people know how to run experiments, get them started. Even if this is just in your team, choose to create a microculture of experimentation, learning (especially from unforeseen outcomes of experiments, otherwise known as failure), sharing learning with other stakeholders, and scaling projects as the data leads.

If your ambition is to help innovation become a strategic capability, it's especially important to share your work with leaders. When they see low-risk experiments producing data-driven business cases for important ideas, they tend to want more. And that means they are more likely to want to replicate your approaches outside of the tank, into the pond and ultimately, out in the ocean.

Often, this starts with you. What important progress does your team currently need to make? What ideas and experiments could you initiate now to take the first step forward?

Plan B – Start with experiments, not strategy   If those ideas feel like a good idea but are not immediate enough for you, I suggest just starting.

I've yet to work with a company where the power of experiments doesn't provoke a 'give me more' response amongst leaders. So if you're looking for a quick-and-dirty innovation activator, here's what I suggest:

Find a team: Track down a team (ideally yours) that needs more innovation and has a scattering of people who are motivated to try new things.

Equip the team: Buy copies of this book for each team member. This isn't a cynical sales ploy, it's simply one of the quickest and cheapest way to get the tools that they'll need into their hands. You could get them to read the whole thing in a week, but at this stage, the chapters on experimentation will probably be enough.

If you need more than a few copies, go to www .belesszombie.com/book to buy bulk orders. Discounts are available according to volume. Also, think about sending a few copies to some senior leaders whose help you may need at some point in the future.

Team practice: Gather the team to identify some experiments to run over the next 30 days. Start small. Stay under the radar at this stage and practice the principles of designing small experiments in pursuit of learning. Once everyone has run a couple of experiments, move on.

Activate a 'Team Lab': Identify some important areas of progress that your team or your customers need to make. Run some innovation experiments in those areas – knowing that only a few will succeed. For those that have proven themselves potentially valuable enough to graduate from 'tank' to 'pond' status, create a stakeholder plan. What experience do you need to create for different people to garner their support? What will that take?

A key here is telling stories about data-driven discovery: *We saw X opportunity, we had Y idea, we had Z assumptions, so we did ABC, DEF happened, we stepped out further, GHI happened – look. We think we're onto something, can you help us take a slightly bigger step forward? It would look like JKL and take MNO resources.*

Team influence: When your stakeholder plan is in place, turn it on and be ready to listen and learn. It's likely that your microscopic, low-risk, low-stakes approach will create some management buzz. In fact, it's likely that there will already be rumours that your team is doing something different. Not dangerous, just different.

What happens next can take several different directions:

- Management interest: Sure, happy to help. Now, where did you get this stuff from? What else are you working on? Hmmm … who else could benefit from working like this?
- Interest from other teams: Hey, I heard you did some cool stuff. Can you show us what you did and how you did it?
- Training programme: Hi, this is HR. We heard you did some cool stuff. Maybe we should have a training programme. Can we talk?

- CEO interest: This stuff is rocket fuel! The most important stuff I've seen in 30 years. Turn it on, lots of it! (This really happened at a global media company that I once worked with).

Either way, you're off and running. If you've activated some executive innovation taste buds along the way, consider showing them the innovation strategy sections of this book. It's more likely that they'll be open to a more strategic response once they seen that this innovation thing really can work without anyone getting killed.

I'd love to say that most organisations begin their innovation journey from a more strategic place. But the truth is that our instant-fix mindset sometimes needs something more immediate to get the executive attention required for a bigger conversation.

Experiments are often such a Trojan horse.

Be Less Zombie   Innovation is often an argument with the status quo, but it doesn't have to be. By applying some of the ideas in this book my hope is that innovation will begin to show up as an *inevitability* inside your organisation, not as an *anomaly*.

I'd love to know how you get on and also how you've found this book. So please drop me a line at: elvin.turner@belesszombie.com.

And keep being less zombie.

INDEX